Borders and Immigration

Borders and Immigration

The Geo-Politics of Marketplace Demands and Ethnic Relations

Laurence Armand French
and Magdaleno Manzanárez

LEXINGTON BOOKS
Lanham • Boulder • New York • London

Published by Lexington Books
An imprint of The Rowman & Littlefield Publishing Group, Inc.
4501 Forbes Boulevard, Suite 200, Lanham, Maryland 20706
www.rowman.com

6 Tinworth Street, London SE11 5AL

British Library Cataloguing in Publication Information Available

Library of Congress Control Number: 2019950360
ISBN 978-1-4985-8404-3 (cloth)
ISBN 978-1-4985-8406-7 (pbk)
ISBN 978-1-4985-8405-0 (electronic)

Contents

Introduction

Boundaries help define our sense of *self,* who we are, which group or cohort we belong to, or wish to belong to. The ideal of boundaries transcends landmarks, fences, borders, and nations. At its basic level, it defines which tribe we belong with. Boundaries have both sociological and social psychological ramifications defining the dynamics of inclusion and exclusion, those who are "insiders" and those who are seen as "outsiders." Self-identity is contingent upon not only inherited (genetic. familial, clan, tribe) identity—that is, our ascribed status, but also on which group we identify with—our reference group. Phenotype, language, accent, caste/class, geographical residence, ethnic/race, sex/gender, and sectarian/ideological differences all play a role in defining individual and group boundaries. Group boundaries, in turn, define our in-group identity and membership as well as discerning those considered to be our adversaries, the out-groups. Marketplace demands also play a critical role in inter-group relations. Herein also lies the basic tenets of group dynamics and processes that can fuel inter-group cooperation or hostilities. European twentieth-century sociologists Emile Durkheim and Georg Simmel articulated the phenomenon of intergroup dynamics. Both addressed the potential transitory nature of group dynamics addressing the often fluid interplay within, and between, groups and how this process helps maintain both individual and group psychological boundaries.

Durkheim noted that shared psychological boundaries are needed for the group's members to know, at any given time, what behaviors are acceptable, what Plato finally noted in the last entry in his Socratic dialogue, *Laws.* Here Plato reluctantly admitted that human benevolence is not sufficient to regulate a society of men (humans), concluding that rules, like laws, are necessary in order to effectively determine the acceptable norms for behavior at any given time.[1] Durkheim alluded to the fact that social change is inevitable even in seemingly stable, homogeneous cultures and that there needs to be an instrument for denoting the boundaries of acceptable behaviors. In this sense, violators of social norms are identified (scapegoats) and punished in a public fashion so as to get the message to all members of the group.

> Imagine a society of saints, a perfect cloister of exemplary individuals. Crime, properly so-called, will there be unknown; but faults which appear venial to the layman will create there the same scandal that the ordinary offense does in ordinary consciousnesses. If, then, this society

> has the power to judge and punish, it will define these acts as criminal and will treat them as such. . . . Crime is, then, necessary; it is bound up with the fundamental conditions of all social life and by that very fact it is useful, because these conditions of which it is a part are themselves indispensable to the normal evolution of morality and law.[2]

The marketplace, that is, the exchange of goods and services, is an integral component of all societies. This exchange process can be the cause of tension within any group at any given time. Francis Bacon, the seventeenth-century British philosopher and Lord Chancellor under Charles I, noted that short of universal norms and standards for behavior, the society dictates these norms at any given time with variations in expectations depending on the group's circumstances. He describes these expectations as *idols.* The *idols of the tribe* describe basic human nature inherent in all people, our neuropsychological processing mechanism, in today's terminology. It describes our capacity to figure things out from the perspective of our socialization, that is, the social distortions of reality inherent in our enculturation. According to Bacon, our capacity to interpret reality, what Plato describes in the *allegory of the cave,* is what he termed the *idol of the den.* The *idols of the marketplace,* on the other hand, describe the social expectations placed upon us in inter-personal interactions, the prescribed norms for social interactions. This includes language, rites, and customs. Lastly, the *idols of the theatre* alludes to the philosophy from what we derive our thoughts and beliefs, those overall values that drive the other idols.[3]

A more contemporary version of Bacon's thesis was put forth by Erich Goode in 1969:

> All civilizations set rules concerning what is real and what is not, what is true and what is false. All societies select out of the data before them a world. One world, the world taken granted, and declared that to be the real world. Each one of these artificially constructed worlds is to some degree idiosyncratic, unique in itself. No individual views reality directly, in the raw, so to speak. Our perceptions are narrowly channeled through concepts and interpretations. What is commonly thought of as reality, that which exists, or simply is, is a set of suppositions, rationalizations, justifications, defenses, all generally collectively agreed upon, which guides and channels each individual's perception in a specific and distinct direction. The specific rules governing the perceptions of the universe which man inhabits are more or less arbitrary, a matter of convention. Every society establishes a kind of epistemological methodology.[4]

Georg Simmel took this argument a step further explaining the relationship between in- and out-group members either within a society or between societies:

> A certain amount of discord, inner divergence and outer controversy, is organically tied up with the very elements that ultimately hold the group together . . . the positive and integrating role of antagonism is shown in structures which stand out by the sharpness and carefully preserved purity of their social divisions and gradations. . . . Hostilities not only prevent boundaries within the group from gradually disappearing . . . often they provide classes and individuals with reciprocal positions which they would not find . . . if the causes of hostility were not accompanied by the feeling and expression of hostility.[5]

Lewis Coser interpreted Simmel's concepts as such:

- Conflict serves to establish and maintain the identity and boundary lines of societies and groups;
- Conflict with other groups contributes to the establishment and reaffirmation of the identity of the group and maintains its boundaries against the surrounding world;
- Patterned enmities and reciprocal antagonisms conserve social divisions and systems of stratification. Such patterned antagonisms prevent the gradual disappearance of boundaries between the subsystems of a social system;
- Hostile feelings of the lower strata frequently take the form of *ressentiment* in which hostility is mingled with attraction.
- Distinction has to be made between conflict and hostility or antagonistic attitudes. Social conflict always denotes social interaction whereas attitudes, or sentiments, are predispositions to engage in action. But such predispositions do not necessarily eventuate in conflict; the degree and kind of legitimating of power and status systems are crucial intervening variables affecting the occurrence of conflict;
- Conflict with Out-Groups Increases Internal Cohesion;
- Conflict acts as a stimulus for establishing new rules, norms, and institutions, (e.g., Department of Homeland Security), thus serving as an agent of socialization for both contending parties;
- Two types of conflict: *Realistic Conflict*—goal-oriented conflict (e.g., resource wars; border enforcement); and *Non-Realistic Conflict*—spontaneous conflict that is not goal oriented but for tension release (riots . . .).[6]

The process of demonizing out-groups is a form of realistic conflict in that it is often for the purpose of increasing in-group cohesion. This is a significant process during times of societal insecurity (anomie) used to draw attention from real causal factors while directing blame to that of out-group members.

Following this framework on group dynamics, human behavior is such that we tend to perceive the actions of in-group members differently than those of out-group members, a process known as the *attribution bias*—skewed collective perception of social situations. Essentially, the dynamics of inclusion/exclusion are that those in control tend to make rules that benefit their group while creating rules that exclude members of the out-group. This perversion of distributive justice then fosters a *self-fulfilling prophecy* that systematically places the out-group members at a disadvantage while exacerbating negative attributes of the group per se. Major social institutions such as education, religion, and public service are often the instruments of this process. The general attribution bias is rooted in inter-group dynamics whereby a social-cultural distance occurs between the in-group versus out-group(s). Often hostile actions directed against the perceived out-group are rooted in a moral imperative. The intended goal is to increase the moral/sectarian/ethnic position of one group at the expense of the other.

To illustrate the psychological mechanisms of collective attribution biases, that is, the group's rationalization of individual/group superiority vis-à-vis that of out-groups nemesis, if someone within our group (in-group) succeeds at a task, we tend to attribute their success to inherent factors; while, on the other hand, if someone in the out-group succeeds along similar lines, we tend to attribute this to external factors including luck or unfair advantages. Likewise, if someone in the in-group fails, or is caught doing something bad or criminal, we tend to look for external factors and influences contributing to this situation. However, if someone in the out-group fails, members of the in-group commonly attribute this behavior exclusively to the individual excluding any mitigating circumstances. Similarly, *risky-shift behavior* is a form of Gestalt group-think that facilitates risky actions including impulsive aggression directed against the out-group factions. These are collective actions that defy otherwise logical solutions to the situation and are often flooded by emotions. Simmel noted that the process of demonizing out-groups is often for the purpose of increasing in-group cohesion. This is a significant process during times of societal insecurity (anomie) used to draw attention from real causal factors while directing blame to that of out-group members.[7]

Sociologist Howard Becker stated that out-group members, those excluded from the acceptable realm of society, are seen as being *outsiders* and are labeled as such, often using derogatory terms that have racial/ethnic, sectarian connotations. A similar process occurs when defining undesirable people outside the society. The labels reflect extreme negativity when associated with inter-group conflicts like wars, hence the labels of Asians by American forces during the Second World War, Korea, and Vietnam: Japs, Chinks, Slopes, Slant Eyes, Yellow Peril, Gooks. . . . Ironically, intra-group labeling of *outsiders* often is associated with foreign workers enticed to a country in order to perform labor otherwise seen as undesirable by local workers. Others were brought in as slaves. This input of alien immigrants, those of a difference race, ethnic, or religious background, who speak a different language and practice different customs, are often the same ones that the larger society denigrate and segregate from the acceptable society. Within North America, the United States is the major magnet for migrant workers, licit or illicit. Clearly, economics, the exchange of goods and services, has long involved transactions that transcend borders and boundaries being internal between states, regions, provinces, or across international boundaries. The interaction between different cultures within a society leads to those not yet deemed suitable for assimilation or accommodation being labeled as being *outsiders*. During times of uncertainty, it is the outsiders who are targeted by the insiders both physically and verbally with reciprocal animosities reaching the level of hate speech and hate crimes as well as discriminatory laws and practices. The dilemma is that economic and market conditions often drive both the need for migrants, and the furor against them.

Marketplace transactions, whether they are at the local or international level, involves some degree of interpersonal interactions. Colonialism dictated much of this process up to the Second World War and extended to Cold War conflicts such as Korea and Vietnam. The neo-colonial era fueled numerous conflicts within the Americas (notably Central America and the Caribbean), Africa, and Asia where battles waged over the respective resources and economies of these emerging nations. The establishment of a neutral arbitrator emerged with the advent of the United Nations. Shortly following the establishment of the United Nations (UN), the General Agreement on Tariffs and Trade (GATT) was established in Geneva in 1947. It provided the foundation for the World Trade Organization (WTO) that replaced it in 1995. GATT was an international organization designed to reduce trade barriers through multilateral negations. Out of GATT came the *most-favored nation* principle requiring a nation that grants a trade privilege to one country needs to grant the same privilege to all GATT (now WTO) members. Another major trade principle associated with GATT/WTO is that of *national treatment,* requiring a nation to provide equal treatment to foreign import of goods and services as it does to its domestic goods and services. The WTO grew out of GATT when the U.S. Congress approved the former in 1994, the same year it approved the North American Free Trade Agreement (NAFTA). Today, the WTO is the most powerful economic entity in the world superseding even the authority of the World Bank, International Monetary Fund, and the International Finance Corporation. The reemergence of trade wars, initiated by President Donald Trump, and the vast international illicit drug and human trafficking trades, complicate the scene as events transpire in the early twenty-first century. Our book addresses these issues.

NOTES

1. A. E. Taylor. Laws, *The Collected Dialogues of Plato* (E. Hamilton & H. Cairns, editors). New York, NY: Bollingen Series LXXI; Pantheon Books, 1966, pp. 1225–1512.

2. F. Bacon, *Novum Organum* (1620), (Idols of Perception), *The World of Psychology: the Worlds of Perception—Man and His Emotions* (G.B. Levitas, ed.). New York, NY: George Braziller/ Toronto, Canada: Ambassador Books, 1963, pp. 161–168.

3. E. Goode. Marijuana and politics of reality. *Journal of Health and Social Behavior,* Vol. 10, 1969, pp. 83–94.

4. G. Simmel. *Conflict* (K.H. Wolff, trans.). Glencoe, IL: The Free Press, 1955, p. 107.

5. L. Coser. *The Functions of Social Conflict.* New York, NY: The Free Press, 1956, pp. 38, 87, 128, 156.

6. Ibid.

7. H.S. Becker. *Outsiders: Studies in the sociology of deviance.* New York, NY: The Free Press, 1963.

ONE

Genesis of the North American Trade Market

Aboriginal Trade Routes and Boundaries Before and During European Contact

Pre-Columbian North American Indian cultures extended beyond the current boundaries of Mexico in the south to Alaska and Canada in the north. In the former, Mayan culture extended into Central America and the Caribbean while Inuit cultures extended into Greenland and Siberia. At the time of White contact in the 1500s, North America was well populated with a variety of linguistic groups and extensive trade routes. Accurate portrayals of traditional pre-Columbian life are scarce due to the lack of significant documentation, at least any that has been accurately transcribed into the major European languages. The scarcity of any records, other than oral histories, also leaves a tremendous void relevant to the social-psychological dynamics of indigenous life, notably its stratification defining how these peoples defined themselves both within their own societies and in interactions with others. Hence, the picture that emerges is mainly one of speculating on the meaning of surviving artifacts as the interpretation of Euro-Americans who initially interacted with these tribes and, later, the concerted efforts of ethnologists and anthropologists to glean elements of these rich oral histories from tribal leaders, commonly termed American Indian myths and legends. Even then, it is doubtful that these disclosures were totally accurate and without distortions.

Kopper noted that linguists believe at least 200 languages were spoken in North America at the time of European contact. The difficulty in understanding this variety of languages was the fact that all but Mayan was unwritten.[1] Regarding the Mayan language, Josephy and Branson noted that despite their cultural riches, we know very little about them, making them the most profound enigma in American history, especially considering that their empire was built without metal tools or draft animals, other than dogs, or the use of the wheel:

> The Mayas attained the highest civilization known in ancient America, and one of the highest known anywhere in the early world. They developed a genuine written language, or a near thing to it—hieroglyphic ideographs. . . . And the people remain, two to three million who speak the various related Mayan dialects, and, in many cases are so similar in appearance to the muscular, ugly, delicately posed little men on the temple walls that they could be the stuccoed frescoes come to life. . . . Their "cities," for want of a better term to describe their ceremonial centers, numbered at least 116 great and small, for that many are already known as archaeological sites, and more, perhaps remain to be discovered. Besides the great temple-topped pyramids, various of the centers contained bridges, aqueducts, "palaces," reviewing stands, vapor baths, monumental stairways, ceremonial plazas, covering many acres or even extending for miles.[2]

What is not known is the pre-Columbian population of the Americas, including North America. Carl Waldman, in his *Atlas of the North American Indian,* notes that population estimates are speculative given that early estimates were made after Europeans spawned disease and warfare that greatly decimated the indigenous populations during the years of early contact. These estimates ranged from 15 million to 60 million. Even then, the greatest density of Indians was in the Andes region of South America with a lesser density for Indian groups north of Mexico (United States and Canada) with estimates ranging from a few million to ten to twelve million inhabitants. Nonetheless, Waldman noted that rapid change occurred with initial White contact and settlements:

> After European contact, the patterns of Indian population density began to change. Many Indians along the East Coast were displaced early because of extensive British settlement. With the introduction of the horse into North America, many tribes migrated onto the Great Plains. Many other tribes were forcibly moved to the Indian Territory which eventually became the state of Oklahoma. And with outbreaks of disease and warfare, indigenous populations everywhere began to decline. It was not until the twentieth century that the Native population began to grow again.[3]

PRE-COLUMBIAN TRADE AND INTERACTION

Pre-Columbian intertribal trade extended from South American tribes up through what is now Canada. The only known exception to this enterprise were the northernmost Inuit people who appear to have maintained their isolated self-sufficiency until exposed by White explorers. These historic trade routes allowed for the sharing of agricultural and other resources including copper, tobacco, corn, turquoise, cotton, shells, canoes, pottery, and the like:

> A number of rules governed intertribal commerce, with traders guaranteed safe passage. Special trade languages were developed, with words from different dialects—Chinook Jargon of Northwest Coast Indians and the Mobilian (or Chickasaw) Trade Language of Southeast Indians, as well as the sign language of Plains Indians. Certain trade items came to represent fixed values, becoming a kind of money: wampum in the Northeast; dentalium along the Northwest Coast; beaver furs in the Subartic; and chocolate (cacao) beans in Mesoamerica. The Aztec and Maya both had a professional class of traders, who had their own laws and even gods. Trade routes included well-beaten paths, rivers, and lakes. People traveled on foot, single file, or by canoe with portages. Coastal peoples traveled by boat along shorelines to neighboring villages.[4]

Slavery was also a component of the pre-Columbian Indian trade albeit never matching that of the Black African slaves brought to North America by the Europeans. Aboriginal tribes kept captured enemies as individual slaves prior to European contact, but this paled in comparison with the enslavement of the Tlaxcalan Indians by the Aztec empire of central Mexico who were used to build the Great Pyramid of Cholula—the largest ancient structure in the New World, covering 25 square acres and rising to 180 feet. Hence, while Indian slavery already existed in the Americas prior to European conquests and the arrival of African slaves, the colonial powers expanded this practice considerably among the tribes north of central Mexico. Indian and Black slavery played a significant role in both the colonial trade and the extermination of most of the southeastern tribes.

The combination of disease, physical genocide, and slavery reduced the numerous southeastern tribes to five durable groups that collectively became known as the Five Civilized Tribes: the Cherokee, Choctaw, Chickasaw, Creek, and Seminole. Indian slavery emerged as a deliberate process of exploitation used mostly by the British as a lever for generating inter-tribal hostilities and alliances. Enslaved Indians were often forced to fight against other European colonial powers, notably the French and Spanish. Gary Nash, in his book *Red, White, and Black,* noted that the Indian slave trade was a feature of all British colonies and was especially crucial to the development of Charleston, South Carolina. He cites the 1708 Charleston census that listed its population as consisting of 5,300 Whites and 4,300 slaves, of whom 1,400 were Indian slaves and the others Black slaves.[5]

The Indian slave trade involved all the horrors, both physical and psychological, associated with the worst images of this institution, including beatings, killings, and tribal and family separation. The British were not alone in this practice. The Spanish held Indians as slaves for the duration of their colonial era which ended in 1821 in Mexico. Indeed, Indian slaves were used to build the Catholic missions that dot the California coast. Hence, Indian and African Black slavery were integral components of the colonial economy in the New World. The practice of enslaving Indians resulted in the emergence of *Black Indians,* the outgrowth of the mixing of these two slave populations. Many of these mixed-slaves escaped to the Florida Everglades comprising a significant proportion of the Seminole Indian tribe, later designated one of the Five Civilized Tribes of the Southeast. William Katz, in his book *Black Indians,* posits that a new race of mixed Indians and Blacks emerged during the colonial era emerging from the miscegenation of these two racial groups. He noted that this came about due to the shared slave economy from which they escaped.[6]

ABORIGINAL SUBSTANCE USE PRACTICES

Another element of inter-tribal pre-Columbian trade was that of mind-altering agents—the forerunner of the drug trade that dominates border tensions today. This element of aboriginal traditional life challenges the long-held perception that Europeans introduced alcohol to indigenous tribes of North America. Low-grade alcohol had a long tradition among many tribes prior to White contact and it was the introduction of distilled spirits that were new to the New World peoples. Alcohol and other psychoactive agents had played a role among American Indians since aboriginal times but under controlled circumstances with use highly restricted by ceremonial customs and rituals. The New World had a number of indigenous psychoactive plants, in addition to the native corn (later a major ingredient for distilled spirits by Whites). For the most part the use of these psychoactive agents was linked to socially prescribed customs and rites.

Fermented corn beer was perhaps the most common aboriginal substance used during the pre-Columbian era among American Indians. It was an integral component of Incan rites, including human sacrifices. Spanning the current U.S./Mexico border in southern Arizona, the Tohono O'odham (aka Papago) traditionally made fermented wine by boiling the fruit of the saguaro cactus. This drinking ritual was most prominent during their fall festival, *Wihgita,* which occurred during August. Behavior license was allowed during the celebration, much like it is with the Catholic celebration of Lent. It is very likely that the combination of a highly restricted substance use coupled with allowable drunkenness during special celebrations led to the current social drinking habit among many Indians today known as bout drinking, known in contemporary Indian Country as *forty-niners*.[7]

Tobacco was another psychoactive agent long associated with aboriginal customs and rituals. With its use dictated by custom, tobacco abuse was not widespread during pre-Columbian times. Indeed, lung disease at that time was not from smoking but from prolonged exposure to unvented or poorly vented pit fires used for cooking and heat. Tobacco during aboriginal times, according to the traditional ways of the three largest tribes today (Athapaskan, Sioux, and Cherokee), was used sparingly due to its spiritual significance linking man with Father Sky. James Mooney, a nineteenth-century ethnographer, was one of the first Whites to describe the ritual use of another New World substance, tobacco:

> Tobacco was used as a sacred incense or as the guarantee of a solemn oath in nearly every important function—in binding the warrior to take up the hatchet against the enemy, in ratifying the treaty of peace, in confirming sales or other engagements, in seeking omens for the hunter, in driving away witches or evil spirits, and in regular medical practice. It was either smoked in the pipe or sprinkled upon the fire, never rolled into cigarettes, as among the tribes of the Southwest, neither was it ever smoked for the mere pleasure of the sensation. Of late years white neighbors have taught the Indians to chew it, but the habit is not aboriginal. It is called *tsalu,* a name which has lost its meaning in the Cherokee language, but is explained from the cognate Tuscarora, in which *charhu,* "tobacco," can still be analyzed as "fire to hold in the mouth," showing that the use is as old as the knowledge of the plant. The tobacco originally in use among the Cherokee, Iroquois, and the eastern tribes was not the common tobacco of commerce (*Nicotiana tabacum),* which has been introduced from the West Indies, but the *Nicotiana rustica,* or wild tobacco, now distinguished by the Cherokee as *tsal-agayun'li,* "old tobacco," and by the Iroquois as "real tobacco."[8]

The sacred use of tobacco is best illustrated by the Plains Indians, notably the Sioux. According to aboriginal Siouan tradition, the sacred tobacco ritual centers around the sacred pipe. The sacred pipe with a bowl of pipestone, a stem of wood, and adornments of twelve eagle feathers, shell fragments, and colored beads sewed into a buckskin wrap is symbolic of the universe (Mother Earth and Father Sky). The bowl represents both Manka (Mother Earth) and man's blood, while the red beads represent the west, the blue beads, the north, the green beads, the east, and the yellow beads, the south. The sacred pipe rite was/is the most significant and common of the Sioux's seven sacred rituals.

Tobacco and pipestone were two important trade items in pre-Columbian trade. Tobacco from the eastern tribes was traded across the country for pipestone in the western quarries. According to Wilbert, shamans of the Warao Indians of Venezuela used tobacco as their primary mode for communication with their gods: "Tobacco may be one of several vehicles for ecstasy; it may be taken in combination with other plants, as we have seen, to induce narcotic trance states; or it may represent the sole psychoactive agent employed by shamans to transport themselves into the realm of the supernatural, as is the case among the Warao of the Orinoco Delta in Venezuela."[9] Like their counterparts in North America, the Warao believed that the smoke from their cigars allowed communication with the supernatural, providing a celestial bridge with the Great Spirit. Smoke communication with the spirits was used for both good and evil purposes. Accordingly, tobacco use among the traditional Warao was restricted to certain rituals and used only by the priest-shaman.[10]

Peyote, like fermented alcohol (corn or cacti-based) and tobacco, played a special and sacred role within aboriginal societies. Peyote is a small, spineless round cactus with psychedelic properties containing more than fifty alkaloids, most notably mescaline. It grows naturally in the deserts of the southwestern United States and northwestern Mexico. It was termed peyote by the Aztecs as it is today. This cactaceae plant species was first documented by Europeans in 1651 by Hernandez who called it *Peyote zacatecensis.* Francisco Hernandez noted that it appeared to have a sweetish and hot taste and that when ground up it was used to alleviate joint pain. He also noted its hallucinogenic properties and its use in sacred rituals by medicine men. It was also used by warriors, providing them with courage in battle and the ability to withstand thirst, hunger, and fear. Its aboriginal use among American Indians extends from the Yanomamma Indians of Venezuela to the Plains Indians of the United States and Canada.

The use of peyote among the Huichol Indians of Mexico illustrates a ritual similar to the Siouan Sun Dance, the ultimate "making of man" ritual of adult male warriors. Within Siouan culture, men who have completed four Sun Dances are considered to have successfully "counted coup," that is, taking the challenges of life in the raw, having obtained the critical element of wisdom needed to join the rank and status of "respected elders" (tribal grandfathers). The Huichol Indian rite-of-passage for its respected elders, *Peyoteros,* is the peyote quest, or pilgrimage. Furst describes the significance of this ritual: "The pilgrimage helps one attain whatever one desires—health, children, rain, protection from lightning and sorcerers, or divine intervention against the ever-troublesome vecinos ('neighbors') who encroach illegally on the Huichol lands with their lands. . . . Above all, one goes to attain visions of great beauty, to hear the voices of the spirits, the diving ancestors, and to receive their guidance."[11]

Other psychoactive agents were used during aboriginal times including the Cherokee's *black drink.* Mooney noted that the concoction drunk by all adults at the New Year purification fire was a root the Cherokee called *unsdte' tstiyu,* also known as the Virginia or black snakeroot (*Aristolochia serpentaria).* It produces hallucinations while inducing vomiting and sweating, the basic elements required for traditional individual cleansing much like the purification sweats and vision quests of the Plains Indians or the role of tobacco or peyote.[12] Schultes also noted that the snake plant, a member of the morning glory family, was used for its hallucinogenic properties among Mexican Indian tribes. The Aztecs used hallucinogenic mushrooms, known as *teonanacat*—god's flesh—in their sacred rituals as did the aboriginal tribes of western Mexico. Mexican Indians used the seeds of the *sophora secundiflora* shrub for thousands of years prior to European contact. These tribes participated in what is known as the mescal, or Red Bean, cult. Archeological evidence also indicated pre-Columbian use of the morning glory, whose seeds have a hallucinogenic property. Indeed, dozens of plants, mushrooms, and tree barks were used for their psychoactive and medicinal properties by aboriginal groups in the Americas, mainly in conjunction with sacred rituals. There is little evidence that these agents were used for recreational use. They were, however, valuable trade items between the tribes residing in pre-Columbian America.[13]

Although tribal identity was maintained within regional boundaries, intra- and inter-tribal trade existed allowing for the free movement across territories accommodating a free trade agreement even among traditional enemies. Most tribes divided their year into planting and harvest times and war and hunting times. Trade seems to have occurred during certain times of the year when a general truce prevailed. Two major trade routes were established, one that extended from South America to Canada with Taos Pueblo in New Mexico the central trading market for South/North; and East/West routes. Another trade route existed along the Northwest Coast where Indians and Inuit/Aleuts traded among themselves as well as with Siberians and other northeast Asians. Here the sea played a significant role in their existence, culture, and trade.[14]

Geo-political divisions in North America came with European colonialism. Surveyed partials of territory and the defense of such "property" is basically a European concept. While territorial claims existed during aboriginal times, tribal boundaries were usually defined by rivers, bodies of water, mountains, and other natural phenomenon, as well as by villages and camps; hard and set boundaries, such as maps and legally defined borders per se, did not exist. Contested areas usually were in relation to fishing and hunting claims. Conflicts over traditional territories increased dramatically with the advent of Whites as tribes were pushed first from the East Coast and later pressured from all sides following the Louisiana Purchase (1803) and the Mexican War (1846–1848) and the Gadsden Purchase (1853). By the time of the Alaska Purchase (1867) both the Canada/U.S. and Mexico/U.S. borders were finalized, often cutting off certain tribes as well as traditional trade routes. It was with the establishment of these "legal" boundaries that restricted mobility of peoples and goods occurred. The European colonial powers defined their boundaries enshrining them into written laws that defined not only the dimension of the territory they claimed but also acceptable membership of the colony, later state or province.

These same laws also labeled those considered to be unacceptable for legal residency, often including the indigenous peoples that originally occupied the land. Laws were established regulating the influx of outsiders and conditions for their eventual membership. Those peoples who were not considered "desirable" members of society were deemed "outsiders" often labeled as "illegal immigrants," or in the case of indigenous peoples and Black slaves, as non-persons excluded from any protection the society provided for its "legal" members. Laws were also established determining acceptable trade between colonies/nations with restrictions placed on undesirable items deemed contraband. These laws and international interactions underwent considerable changes from colonial times to the present in North America with the United States playing a major role in the changing dynamics of boundaries, both geographic and human.

NOTES

1. P. Kopper. *The Smithsonian Book of North American Indians Before the Coming of the Europeans.* Washington, DC: Smithsonian Books, 1986.
2. A.M. Josephy, Jr., & W. Brandon. *The American Heritage Book of Indians.* New York, NY: American Heritage Publishing Company, 1982, pp. 19, 20, 21.
3. C. Waldman. *Atlas of the North American Indian* (3rd edition). New York, NY: Checkmark Books, 2009, p. 41.
4. Ibid., p. 81.
5. G. Nash. *Red, White, and Black: The Peoples of Early America.* Englewood Cliffs, NJ: Prentice-Hall, 1974.
6. W.L. Katz. *Black Indians.* New York, NY: Atheneum Books, 1986.
7. P.C. Rivers. *Alcohol and Human Behavior: Theory, Research, and Practice.* Englewood Cliffs, NJ: Prentice-Hall, 1994.
8. J. Mooney. "The Sacred Formulas of the Cherokees," *Seventh Annual Report of the Bureau of Ethnology to the Secretary of the Smithsonian Institute 188–86.* (J. W. Powell, dir.). Washington, DC: Government Printing Office, 1891, p. 423.
9. J. Wilbert. "Tobacco and Shamanistic Ecstasy among the Warao Indians of Venezuela," *Flesh of the Gods: The Ritual Use of Hallucinogens* (P.T. Furst, ed.). New York, NY: Praeger, 1972, p. 57.
10. Ibid.
11. P.T. Furst. "To Find Our Life: Peyote among the Huichol Indians of Mexico," *Flesh of the Gods,* op. cit. #9, p. 151.
12. J. Mooney, op. cit. #8.
13. R.E. Schultes. "An Overview of Hallucinogens in the Western Hemisphere," *Flesh of the Gods,* op. cit. #9, pp. 31–32.
14. Op. cit. #1, "The Northwest Coast," pp. 201–217.

TWO

Colonial Antecedent to White Supremacy and Ethnic Cleansing

COLONIAL CAPITALISM

The Americas were seen as an untapped resource for raw goods to be exploited by European colonists. The major problem was the indigenous peoples that already occupied these lands and acted as guardians over the abundant natural resources. In this scenario the American Indians were the "inhabitants" while the European colonists and their African slaves were the uninvited immigrants, that is, illegal immigrants. Nonetheless, the first European settlements in North America were established as capitalist enterprises with the specific purpose of exploiting the rich resources long preserved by the original inhabitants. Ironically, the initial colonies existed due to the hospitality of the indigenous groups they encountered. Jamestown settlement illustrated this phenomenon. Jamestown, in what is now the state of Virginia, began as an English joint-stock company whose initial survival was dependent upon the indigenous Algonquian tribe providing them with food and shelter. This dependency on the Powhatan continued for 15 years (1607–1622) until the colonists felt sufficiently strong enough to turn on their host and begin encroaching on desired tribal lands, taking over Indian cornfields accounting for thousands of acres. Hence a pattern developed where coveted land and resources led to White encroachment into traditional Indian Country resulting in conflict. Moreover, Indians were soon forced to take sides in inter-European conflicts over indigenous lands, further complicating the dimensions of these conflicts. One result was the intensity of traditional inter-tribal conflicts that existed prior to White contact.

Regarding the Virginia colony, a leader of the Powhatan Confederacy, Opechancanough, led an attack on White settlers on March 22, 1622, ending the era of harmonious relations with the European intruders. The death of 347 settlers shocked the London capitalist sponsoring the colony resulting in the establishment of a foundation for British North American Indian policy, one that encouraged violent retaliation to any tribal interference in their capitalist endeavors including forced removal of Indians to designated regions, enslaving them, or hunting them down with horses and hounds. Being of Christian denominations, Protestants or Catholics, the European colonists needed a moral justification for such harsh treatment of American Indians. They found this justification by labeling the Indians as uncivilized barbarians who were a rude, savage, naked Godless people who deserved to be hunted down and torn apart by hounds for sport just like other game animals. The Virginia policy was so successful that by the time of American Independence the Powhatan Confederacy numbered fewer than a thousand members.[1]

The 13 original British settlements, some which were called plantations, originally occupied the east coast of what is now the United States. The 13 colonies were further divided into three geographic sections—New England, the Middle Colonies, and the Southern Colonies. While initially predominately Anglo-Saxon, other White European emigrants began to emerge in the late 1600s, including the Scots-Irish, Germans, Huguenots, and Swiss, challenging the extension of the Puritan theocracy beyond the New England colonies. In the New England colonies three religious groups represented British Protestants in the New World. There were those who subscribed to the Church of England (Anglicans); the Puritan Presbyterians (Scots, Scot-Irish); and the most conservative Puritan sect, the Congregationalists. French (Calvinist Puritan) Huguenots were also members of the colonial Congregationalists. Notably, among the conservative British colonies is Massachusetts, which was envisioned as a continuation of Oliver Cromwell's failed Commonwealth in the British Isles. Hence, the name of the Puritans' land grant—the Commonwealth of Massachusetts. Even then, these colonies operated on a Crown charter that dictated the boundaries of their land holdings as well as the terms and conditions for their civil government with corporate officers serving as magistrates and with stockholders' meetings serving as legislative bodies known as General Courts. Within this Calvinistic capitalist system, the corporate chairman, the holder of the Crown's grant, John Winthrop, became the de facto *Governor of the Commonwealth.* Winthrop's original charter was good for sixty years. Henceforth Provincial governors were appointed directly by the English Crown with the authority to approve land grants to settlers. Provinces later became states following the American Revolution.

Religious conflicts played an important role in the ensuing conflicts over ownership of North America. The conservative Puritans were adamantly anti-Catholic and even wanted to formally separate themselves from the Church of England. Membership in the Puritan sect was greatly restricted, allowing only White males who were deemed *visible saints,* thus establishing the moral foundations for *White Supremacy*—the doctrine that dominated *ethnic cleansing* in North America. Indeed, Puritan asceticism fueled not only ethnocentric elitism, but a ferocious hatred of anything they saw as being based in superstition, such as aboriginal beliefs, countering alternative beliefs, and behaviors with harsh punishments including the death penalty. The Puritans executed women within their own communities labeling them demonized witches. Between 1648 and 1692 twenty-five women were executed—twenty-two hanged, one pressed to death by boulders, while two died awaiting trial. The Puritans also executed outsiders from different Protestant denominations such as the Quakers. During the colonial era, offenses warranting the death penalty within the Puritan theocracy included blasphemy, "idollitry," treason, witchcraft, and insubordination by children. The asceticism of the Puritans, notably the Congregationalists, fueled not only ethnocentric elitism but a ferocious hatred of anything that they saw that challenged their concept of *Divine Providence.*

The major Catholic colonial powers in North America were France and Spain. The Spanish occupied Florida and Mexico during the seventeenth century and until the establishment of the United States republic. Spain, like England, enslaved American Indians, using them to build the Catholic missions along the California coast. This factor contributed to the high percentage of mixed Anglo/Indian peasants known as Mestizos. The exploitation of the poor, Mestizos, Blacks, and Indians under the pretense of religious conversion led both to the abolishment of slavery at the time of Mexican independence in 1821 and, later, the exclusion of the Catholic Church in Mexican governance. The Spanish had other problems in what is now the western United States when the Pueblo Indians rebelled in 1680, driving the priests out and destroying their hated missions and churches. A confederacy of Pueblo tribes successfully drove the Spanish out of what is now New Mexico, Arizona, and west Texas in 1680 making it one of the most successful Indian campaigns against colonial powers. While the war waged on, the superior Spanish forces eventually got the Pueblo tribes to sign an agreement whereby the Missions could be reestablished in return for protected Pueblo land grants where their aboriginal cultural ways would be respected. Spanish General de Vargas' four-month expedition in 1692 eventually restored Spanish colonial rule to 23 Pueblos, entering the territorial capital Santa Fe on December 20, 1692. The Pueblo tribes accepted their Spanish land grants with 19 Pueblos located in New Mexico, most along the Rio Grande, and the Hopi in their traditional mesas in Arizona.[2]

Colonial Wars

In the British and French North American colonies, the European wars of the seventeenth and eighteenth centuries carried over into the New World, notably New England, New France, and Spanish Florida. American Indian tribes were caught up in these disputes. The Indians of New England attempted to regain their lands, engaging in battles with the intolerant Puritans in what became known as "King Philip's War" in 1675–1676. King Philip was the title taken by Metacom, a Wampanoag chief who led an alliance of tribes in fighting the Puritans of the Plymouth colony. This intense, but short-lived uprising ended with Metacom's death in 1676 resulting in the movement to purge all Indian tribes from New England, marking the beginning of *ethnic cleansing* as a British-American policy. The year 1676 saw the beginning of the eradication policy within the New England colonies with the tribes either exterminated or driven north into French Canada. Most tribes were targeted except those in Maine whose border with New Brunswick was not settled until 1842, hence the cross-border tribes that still exist today. The trickery that prevailed among Whites toward Indians was illustrated in Dover, New Hampshire in 1677 when Major Waldron, the local militia leader and a wealthy shipbuilder, invited local tribes to a friendly sporting event. The Indians were then surrounded and captured by the armed militia. The chiefs were taken to Boston and summarily hanged while hundreds of others were sold as slaves.[3]

The French and Indian Wars (1689–1763) illustrate the involvement of American Indians in these European conflicts. Here each side recruited local tribes as allies, expanding pre-Columbian conflicts to a more deadly level. The War of the Grand Alliance (aka War of the League of Augsburg) was commonly known in North America as "King William's War" (1689–1697). The French in Quebec had the Algonquin tribes constituting the Wabanaki Confederacy as their allies while the British colonies recruited the Iroquois Confederation to join their side. Both sides used their Indian confederates on raids on enemy settlements as the major European colonial powers fought to carve out their New World boundaries, ironically, often at the expense of their unsuspecting indigenous allies. Indeed, the constant fear within the White settlements of Indian raids led to the establishment of militia units in both the French and British settlements. The Treaty of Ryswick settled the King William conflict in 1697 with little gained by either side, although the French were successful in signing a peace accord with the Iroquois which only lasted five years before the next round of inter-colonial conflicts. The Treaty of Utrecht of 1713 resulted in Great Britain gaining control over Acadia, renamed Nova Scotia, along with sovereignty over Newfoundland and the Caribbean island of St. Kitts. France continued to hold on to Cape Breton Island as well as other islands within the Gulf of St. Lawrence in addition to fishing rights in Newfoundland. While the 1713 Treaty of Utrecht ended this portion of the French and Indian Wars, it also fostered discontent among the British colonies in New England when part of the treaty allowed the French Canadians, now under British authority, to continue to maintain their traditional feudal community system of seigneurs and habitants run by the Catholic Church as long as they signed an *oath of allegiance* to Britain.[4]

Conflict intensified in 1745 when French and Indian forces destroyed Saratoga in New York colony. At the same time, British colonial forces captured the French fortress, Louisburg. This was a joint Canadian British and New England militia endeavor supported by the governors of Nova Scotia and Massachusetts designed to take over the rich fishing and farming lands of the Acadian French, many of which were of mixed Indian/French heritage, *Métis*. Wealthy Puritan capitalists funded the substantial mercenary New England militia, known as *Blue Coats* distinguishing them from the British regular Army Red Coats. The merchant's crusade of some 4,000 blue coats took a heavy toll in taking Louisburg only to have it returned to France in exchange for the city of Madras in India as stipulated in the Treaty of Aix-la-Chapelle. This further angered the New England Puritan leaders fostering the unilateral actions of colonial governors William Shirley of Massachusetts and Charles Lawrence of the Canadian Maritimes. Indeed, this was a home-grown conspiracy to take actions outside of the greater European theatre. The *Acadia Expulsion* was a de facto rebellion from British home rule setting the stage not only for the American Revolutionary War, but the War of 1812 as well.

ACADIAN EXPULSION—AMERICA'S ETHNIC CLEANSING DEBACLE

The roots of Manifest Destiny, based on the Puritan concept of moral superiority among humans, were used to justify the extermination of Indian groups and justify slavery. The principle of *predestination,* and its inherent concepts of discrimination and genocide, was implemented in Nova Scotia during the forced acquisition of indigenous lands and the expulsion of the Acadian French in the mid-eighteenth century. The Acadian French differed from most other White settlers in that they integrated into the Mi'kmaq (Micmac) culture forging a harmonious community of mixed Indians and Whites, hence attracting the wrath of Puritan New Englanders. The fact that Britain allowed French self-governance in Quebec by treaty further angered the Yankee Puritans, increasing their angst toward both French Catholics and the British homeland. The expulsion scheme was devised by governors Shirley and Lawrence over the objections of the British military commander. John Mack Faragher cited a September 4, 1755 article in the *Pennsylvania Gazette* that justified the expulsion order:

> We are now upon a great and noble Scheme of sending the neutral French out of this Province [Nova Scotia], who have always been secret enemies, and have encouraged our Savages to cut our Throats. If we effect their Expulsion, it will be one of the greatest Things that ever the English in America; for by all Accounts, that Part of the Country they possess, is as good Land as any in the World: in case therefore we could get some of good English farmers in their Room, this Province would abound with all Kinds of Provisions.[5]

Acadia was the name the French gave to the region comprising what is now Nova Scotia, New Brunswick, Prince Edward Island, Quebec's Gaspe Peninsula, and portions of northern Maine bordering on the Gaspe and New Brunswick. This entire geographical area, except Prince Edward Island and Cape Breton, was claimed by Great Britain following the Treaty of Utrecht in 1713. The expulsion plan orchestrated by William Shirley and Charles Lawrence ignored the pleas of Major General Paul Mascarene (of French Huguenot decent), the British military commander of the maritime region of British North America. Mascarene noted that the Acadian French, Métis, and Mi'kmaq did not pose a threat and were not involved in any of the French and Indian raids on British colonies in America. The expulsion went on despite General Mascarne's objections. During the expulsion, Acadian families were rounded up and placed in stockades, their communities burned, animals slaughtered, and food supplies destroyed. Harry Bruce, in his history of Nova Scotia, noted:

> The troops compelled to do the dirty work during "le grand derangement" were mostly blue-coated American soldiers like (John) Winslow. . . . This was the expulsion: they forced everyone at bayonet point to embark on boats in the midst of confusion, without any concern as to whether they put on the same boat members of the same family. . . . The Acadian people were effectively scattered. They were set ashore in the English colonies, along two thousand miles of the American coast. Hundreds were taken to France, many by way of prisons in England. The West Indies received large numbers, and others ended their wandering in Quebec and in the French possessions along the Mississippi. The sea took heavy toll of them, through sickness and shipwreck. Along the trails and in the fastnesses of the forest many perished of hunger and exposure. . . . The expulsion did more than drive a people from its land. It disrupted the Acadian community with its traditions and distinctive ways of life, and left it scattered and stranded amidst alien and unsympathetic peoples.[6]

Some 7,000 French Acadians were forcefully removed from the rich lands and waterways along the shores of the Bay of Fundy so that English colonists could steal their land and displace and disperse the Mi'kmaq Indians. Clearly, the purpose of the Acadian expulsion was to rid the region of what the Puritans labeled the "Indian-loving Catholic Frenchmen" and to provide this fertile land to Protestant Yankee families from Massachusetts (which included Maine and parts of New Hampshire at the time), Rhode Island, and Connecticut. Thousands of New Englanders migrated to Nova Scotia during the resettlement period of 1760 to 1765 taking over the fishing and agricultural communities that make up present-day Nova Scotia.

At the same time, the Seven Years' War waged among the European powers, playing out as the latest French and Indian War (1756–1763). This conflict inadvertently provided the future rebels with the training and resources necessary for their successful rebellion against the homeland, allowing them to lay claim to the rich resources of the 13 colonies without sharing these spoils with Britain or the Loyalists. The stage for this actually began in 1754 during the Acadian Expulsion, predating the Diplomatic Revolution in Europe (Seven Years' War) that began two years later. Among the Yankee militia leaders who distinguished themselves in this phase of the French and Indian Wars was George Washington, an officer with the Virginia militia. In 1753, at age 21, George Washington held the rank of major and was placed in charge of a militia force fighting the French over western territory that both France and Britain claimed. Virginia Governor Robert Dinwiddie and Washington's family were shareholders in a company that would greatly benefit from British colonial expansion into the Ohio Valley long claimed by New France. The following year, Washington rose to the rank of colonel in the Virginia militia leading a force against the French at Fort Duquesne, now Pittsburgh, Pennsylvania. This success gave him considerable recognition in both England and British North America resulting in his being placed in charge of the Virginia militia at 23. Nonetheless, Washington became disenchanted with the military given that he was denied a full commission within the British military. This disappointment led to his resigning from the militia and returning to Virginia to serve in the Virginia House of Burgesses.[7]

Prelude to the American Revolution

This last phase of the French and Indian Wars ended in 1760 while the conflict raged on in the European theatre with all hostilities ending in early 1763. The Treaty of Paris ended the North American component with its signing on February 10, 1763. This was followed by the signing of the Treaty of Hubertusburg five days later, ending the conflict in Europe. It was the conditions of the Treaty of Paris that fueled the fires of revolution in America. The Treaty of Paris gave Britain control of all New France claims in North America which included some 80,000 French Catholics. France, on the other hand, gave Spain Louisiana as compensation for its support in the conflict, which was later traded back to France and subsequently sold to the United States in 1803, igniting yet another quest for expansionism and boundary challenges. The residents of the former New France, notably Quebec (Lower Canada), were given the same conditions that were provided to their Acadian cousins in the 1713 Treaty of Utrecht that ceded Nova Scotia to the British and fueled the Acadian Expulsion some forty years later. It was, however, the Royal Proclamation of 1763 that irked the Yankees most. The Royal Proclamation was first and foremost a reprimand for the unilateral actions of the Royal governors of Massachusetts and the Maritimes for the Acadian Expulsion, an action that greatly embarrassed Great Britain. Indeed, it is apparent that the Royal Proclamation was a contributing factor in the American Revolution, especially among the land speculators who gained considerable wealth in taking Indian lands.

Many of the American-grown aristocracy, including George Washington, were land speculators and the Royal Proclamation put an end to their continuing exploitation of Indian tribes, the major premise for the French and Indian Wars. The Royal Proclamation replaced the much abused *Doctrine of Discovery* that previously provided justification for colonial sovereignty and claims over territories and over indigenous peoples providing that the European colonists respected tribal territory as long as the tribes subscribed to the Christian faith. The Puritans of New England had a long history of provoking "praying Indians" into fights by stealing their crops and lands, making a mockery of this doctrine. The Royal Proclamation that grew out of the 1763 Treaty of Paris gave protection to Indigenous peoples on their traditional lands, making the Crown the sole authority in tribal intercourse. It was one of the first actions taken to define Indian Territory, essentially protecting indigenous peoples from being driven off their traditional lands. While the American Revolution ended this protection in the United States, the Royal Proclamation laid the foundation for land claims by the indigenous peoples of Canada—First Nations, Inuit, and Métis. Indeed, the Royal Proclamation of 1763 is the first legal recognition of aboriginal rights by the British Crown.[8]

One could look at the American Revolution as a resource war with the rebellious Yankees warring with both the Motherland, England, and with their fellow colonial citizens who wished to remain part of Great Britain. Indeed, the American Revolution could best be described as a "civil war" and not a true revolutionary war. Charles Tilly, an authority on European Revolutions from 1492 to 1992, lists the "War of American Independence" as a relatively minor incident in the chronology of colonial conflicts.[9] Similarly, Clifton Kroeber noted that few so-called revolutions signify marked social change. Those that did were the French Revolution of 1789; the transformation of China from a dynasty in 1911 and, later, to a communist state in 1949; and the Russian revolution of 1917.[10] The American Revolution was instead a slow-brewing conflict over which colonial elite was going to dominate the vast unspoiled wealth awaiting the victor.

Accordingly, the American Revolution waxed and waned from the Declaration of Independence on July 4, 1776 until the signing of the Treaty of Paris ending the war on September 4, 1783 with its outcome not decided by either the Yankee rebels or the British, but rather by the French, the traditional enemy in the New World since the first settlements in North America. While seemingly ironic, the shifting of alliances during the colonial wars came into play in the American Revolution as well. Essentially, the American Revolution became yet another proxy war with Louis XVI funding the rebels, providing the equivalent of 100 million dollars for the Continental Army and the defeat of General Cornwallis and his army at Yorktown in October 1781 for which the mastermind was French Admiral DeGrasse and not General George Washington. Indeed, the 17,000 Rebel forces at Yorktown included some 5,000 French troops. Even then, the Revolutionary War did not account for a substantial combat death total—the official list for Americans Killed-in-Action (KIA) was 6,824. This was for the period of active fighting of eight years, two months, and 17 days (1775–1783). Numerous single-day battles during the United States' second civil war (1861–1865) exceeded this total.[11]

The Revolutionary War provided yet another chance for expulsion, this time of the Loyalists, those American-born colonists who did not want to separate from England. Many Loyalists (Tories), estimated to comprise up to 20 percent of the 13 British colonies, did not take sides during the Revolutionary War. Those who migrated to Canada prior to the Declaration of Independence became known as the *United Empire Loyalists*. Discrimination against Loyalists increased following the Declaration of Independence when all Loyalists were ordered expelled. About 20 percent of that population (some 62,000) fled to other parts of the British Empire, many to Canada. It is estimated that 46,000 went to Canada with the majority (34,000) residing in Nova Scotia—the land earlier stolen from the Acadian French and Micmac Indians. Those Loyalists that refused to leave despite discrimination from the so-called Patriots settled in the Middle Colonies and the South. These groups comprised different ethnic groups including the Dutch in New Jersey, Germans in Pennsylvania, and Quakers and Highland Scots in the Carolinas. Thus, while most Loyalists were Anglican, others were Amish, Quakers, and some Presbyterians.[12]

An unintended consequence of the Loyalist expulsion, notably into Canada, was the significant infusion of Protestants into heavily French-Catholic Canada. The United Empire Loyalists settled in areas that were predominately French Catholic causing a seismic change in Canadian culture resulting in the spin-off of a new province, New Brunswick, and the division between Upper (Ontario) and Lower (Quebec) Canada. Land grants were provided the migrant Loyalists of around 200 acres (81 hectares) as an initial enticement for migration during the early years of the Revolution which included many whose families extended to the founding fathers of America. These prominent families now provided the foundation for British Canada resulting in the split between Upper and Lower Canada at the war's end in 1783. This led to a compromise in British North America, e.g., Canada, notably Quebec province. In addition to language and religion, French Quebec was allowed to retain the French legal system, which differed from the British Common Law system that was used by both the English Canadians and the newly minted United States of America. A downside to the refugee migrant Loyalists from the 13 colonies was slavery. The refugee migrant Loyalists brought some 17,000 Black slaves with them into Canada. On the other hand, Black slaves who joined the Loyalist side in the Revolutionary War were provided freedom and citizenship in Canada accounting for about 8,000 freed *Black Loyalists.*[13]

The influx of refugee Loyalists caused further disruption in Canada resulting in more traditional tribal lands being absorbed by Whites forcing both the Maliseet and remaining Mi'kmaq onto smaller reserves while, at the same time, causing friction between the former Yankees who participated in the Acadian Expulsion of the 1750s and acquired (stole) the lands occupied by the Mi'kmaq and Acadian French. The earlier Yankee settlers mostly sided with the Rebels hoping to include the Maritime Islands as part of the new U.S.A. republic. This rift resulted in the division of Nova Scotia (formerly Acadia) into two provinces, Nova Scotia to the south and New Brunswick to the north. G.G. Campbell, in his history of Nova Scotia, noted that the new immigrants were victims of persecution at the hands of the Rebels who stole their lands and property while some were tarred and feathered and others summarily executed. Hence, the greatest number of Loyalist refugees came from New York, New Jersey, Pennsylvania, and the Carolinas. Most were English in origin with Scot and Scot-Irish as well as Dutch and German descent. Thus, in 1783, the Loyalist refugees more than doubled the population of Nova Scotia. The newly arrived gave the derogatory label *bluenose* to their less than hospitable former blue-coat Yankees. This social division became less significant as more immigrants arrived from Scotland and Ireland (during the Great Famine) forging a more unified society in the Maritime Provinces.[14]

The atrocities perpetrated upon the Loyalists within the rebellious 13 colonies is illustrated in the treatment of a popular, native-born colonial governor, John Wentworth of New Hampshire. The provincial police constituted the militia and its Committee of Safety, virtual vigilante committees, who carried out the dictates of martial law enforced by the Yankee rebels. Eva Spear noted that every town in New Hampshire had its Committee of Safety which could confine any Loyalist, without due process for an indefinite term, who they felt was problematic. Following the

Declaration of Independence of New Hampshire in December 1775, the Committee of Safety of the Provincial Congress established a law stating that Loyalists had three months to sell their property and leave the colony. In April 1776, the New Hampshire Committee of Safety required each town to poll its citizens requiring them to sign a statement of support for the Revolution. Those who refused to sign were labeled Loyalists. In 1778, a law was enacted stipulating that the property of Loyalists, including some of the wealthiest families, be confiscated and sold to increase the treasury of the Patriot rebels. Moreover, refugees were forbidden to return to New Hampshire under the threat of death, including the former colonial governor. Indeed, the exiled governor, John Wentworth, went on to become governor of Nova Scotia, residing there until 1820. While he was banned from ever visiting his native home, his wife and son were eventually allowed to visit relatives in Portsmouth.[15]

Once the United States established its position as a force to contend with within the Americas, especially following the acquisition of the Louisiana Purchase from France, designs for an expanded United States took hold. A convenient target was to capture and control the rest of British North America, Canada. *War Hawks* like John C. Calhoun of South Carolina and Henry Clay of Kentucky entertained the notion of declaring war on Great Britain under the guise of retaliation for impressing U.S. seamen, with the real purpose of conquering Canada. Hence, on June 18, 1812, a divided Congress barely supported a declaration of war against Great Britain. President James Madison signed the war measure making this the first time the United States declared war on another nation, setting the stage for its policy of war making under the shroud of *Manifest Destiny*. Hopes of annexing Canada were quickly dashed when the majority of Canadians declared their support for Great Britain. The War of 1812 ended in a stalemate with the Treaty of Ghent in 1815, also ending the direct use of military force in order to expand northward into Canada. Border disputes continued until the 1870s but without another declaration of war. Yet, the War of 1812 had the unintended consequence of providing Canadians with their unique identity. The war brought Canadians together to fight a common enemy, helping forge their national identity as being uniquely Canadian. With the United States as the aggressor, both Upper Canada (English Canada) and Lower Canada (French Canada) united in repulsing the U.S. forces with Canada providing the bulk of British forces deployed in the war. Indeed, many of the English Canadians fighting the United States' aggression were U.S.-born Loyalists who fled or were expulsed during the American Revolution. The War of 1812 ended future U.S. efforts to take Canada by force, instead sowing the seeds for the eventual process of Canadian Confederation in 1867.[16]

NOTES

1. "A Declaration of the State of the Colony and Affairs in Virginia," *Chronicles of American Indian Protest*. Greenwich, CT: A Fawcett Premier Book, 1971, pp. 1–6.

2. F. Folsom, *Indian Uprising on the Rio Grande: The Pueblo Revolt of 1680*. Albuquerque, NM: University of New Mexico Press, 1973.

3. E. Speare. "King Philip's War." *Stories of New Hampshire: A Living History of the Granite State*. Chelsea, MI: Sheridan Books, 2000.

4. F. Anderson. *The War that Made America: A Short History of the French and Indian War*. New York, NY: Viking, 2005; & F. Jennings. *Empire of Fortune: Crowns, Colonies, and Tribes in the Seven Years War in America*. New York, NY: Norton, 1990.

5. J.M. Faragher. "Preface," *A Great and Nobel Scheme: The Tragic Story of the Expulsion of the French Acadians from their American Homeland*. New York, NY: W.W. Norton, 2005, p. vi.

6. H. Bruce. *An Illustrated History of Nova Scotia*. Nova Scotia, Canada: Nimbus Publishing Limited & Province of Nova Scotia, 1997, p. 113.

7. M. Beschloss. *The Presidents: Every Leader from Washington to Bush*. New York, NY: American Heritage/Simon & Schuster, Inc., 2003.

8. C. Calloway. *The Scratch of a Pen: 1763 and the Transformation of North America*. New York, NY: Oxford University Press, 2006.

9. C. Tilly. *European Revolutions, 1492–1992*. Hoboken, NJ: Blackwell Publishing, 1995.

10. C.B. Kroeber. "Theory and history of revolution," *Journal of World History*, vol. 7: 1996, pp. 21–40.

11. M.M. Boatner, III. *Encyclopedia of the American Revolution*. Mechanicsburg, PA: Stackpole Books, 1994.

12. J.B. Brebner. *The Neutral Yankees of Nova Scotia: A Marginal Colony during the Revolutionary Years*. New York, NY: Columbia University Press, 1937.

13. J.M.S. Careless. *Colonists and Canadians, 1760–1867*. Toronto, Canada: Macmillan of Canada, 1971; & A.S. Everest. *Moses Hazen and the Canadian Refugees in the American Revolution*. Syracuse, NY: Syracuse University Press, 1976.

14. G.G. Campbell. *A History of Nova Scotia*. Toronto, Canada: The Ryerson Press, 1948; & J. Reid, et al. *The Conquest of Acadia, 1710: Imperial, Colonial, and Aboriginal Constructions*. Toronto, Canada: University of Toronto Press, 2004.

15. E. Spear, op. cit. #3.

16. Ibid.

THREE

Manifest Destiny and U.S. Expansionism during the Nineteenth Century

Finalizing Its Borders

AMERICA DEFINES ITS BORDERS AND PEOPLES

Following the absorption of Loyalist lands, the 13 original states began their expansionistic plans to extend their internal boundaries by redefining Indian Country as well as by external expansion by either purchase or war. Indeed, nineteenth-century America was defined by its pursuit of expanding its boundaries within North America and the Caribbean as well as internationally in the Pacific Rim. These exploits required an infusion of immigrants to settle these lands and to build the infrastructure needed to connect the East to the West. This process led to a rash of policies designed to define the emerging social strata based on ethnicity, race, and sectarianism. The Puritan Yankees' experimentation with Indian removal and extermination in New England under the guise of Divine Providence fostered the United States' mantra of *Manifest Destiny.*

One of the first actions of the United States was to define what constitutes a full-fledged citizen. In its first census (1790), devised for the purpose of proportionate representation in the United States Congress (House of Representatives) only White Protestant males age 21 or older were eligible to vote. The states were provided Congressional representation according to their population demographics with Whites having a full count, and Black slaves constituting 3/5 of a person (although not enfranchised), while American Indians did not count at all. These demographics were then used to allocate Congressional districts where only enfranchised White males were eligible to run for office. Hence, the slave population became a significant political factor in the composition of the United States Congress up until the mid-nineteenth century. The legal definition of Blacks and American Indians as "lesser humans" within American society laid the foundation for subsequent laws that often discriminated against minorities, raising the issue of the systemic socialization of prescribed inferiority and the numerous psychological problems inherent in such a system.

The racist element of White Supremacy was illustrated at the highest levels of American society where 15 of the 18 U.S. presidents, from George Washington to U.S. Grant, were slaveholders. The exceptions were the second and sixth presidents, John Adams and John Quincy Adams, and the sixteenth president, Abraham Lincoln. Even then, the Adamses were fervent Puritans who believed in Divine Providence and Manifest Destiny while Lincoln's White House continued to be staffed by Black slaves until emancipation. The Adamses' sentiment was articulated by President John Quincy Adams in a letter to his father, John Adams, the second U.S. president:

> The whole continent of North America appears to be destined by Divine Providence to be peopled by one nation, speaking one language, professing one general system of religion and political principles, and accustomed to one general tenor of social usages and customs.[1]

John Quincy Adams linked the destiny of the United States to the Old Testament's divine providence. From this perspective, providence had provided the North American continent for the United States to conquer, occupy, and convert. Here, the "finger of God" directed the Puritans to America for its domination. White supremacy under the dictates of Manifest Destiny coupled with the newly purchased Louisiana Purchase emboldened states, notably those in the South, to forcefully remove the indigenous populations west of the Mississippi River into an area designated *Indian Territory.* Here, Napoleon's need for money to establish his new French Republic was seen by America's leaders as God's gift to the emerging United States.

Jefferson's Indian policy was articulated prior to the Louisiana Purchase where it offered a false hope to Indian tribes residing east of the Mississippi River. The Jefferson policy was that tribes could remain on their traditional tribal lands if they changed their cultural ways to conform to the dictates of the White society. The tribes that followed the Jefferson dictate were known as *civilized tribes* much like their colonial counterparts who were deemed *praying Indians.* However, the Louisiana Purchase changed things with a new solution that created new tribal lands west of the Mississippi River, sowing the seeds for the United States' policy of Indian expulsion, a form of ethnic cleansing, known officially as the "Removal Policy." The Louisiana Purchase doubled the size of the United States with lands extending west of the Mississippi River north to British North America (Canada) and east of the Missouri River, whetting America's appetite for even further expansion into Canada, hence setting the stage for the War of 1812 as well as the War with Mexico (1846–1848).[2]

INDIAN REMOVAL: EXPULSION AS A MEANS FOR EXPANDING INTERNAL BOUNDARIES

Indian sovereignty, as established by Britain during the colonial era, posed a major obstacle to evicting Indians from their traditional lands leading to a host of legal judgments designed to codify Manifest Destiny. The first of a series of judicial reviews was *Johnson v. McIntosh* decided in 1823. In this decision, the newly minted U.S. Supreme Court reinstated the primary authority of the federal government as the major arbitrator with Indian tribes, ending the private purchase, often by deceit, of tribal lands by White individuals and corporations. *Johnson v. McIntosh* laid the foundation for the Trade and Intercourse Acts beginning with the first edition established on July 22, 1790—the same year that the U.S. Marshals service was established as the law enforcement agency for the federal judiciary. In this decision, Supreme Court Chief Justice John Marshall cited the European colonial tenet guaranteeing Indian tribes collective occupancy of their traditional lands thus establishing the implied legality of Indian tribes to continue to occupy their traditional lands under the European colonial concept of "aboriginal title," or "Indian title." This ruling by the High Court provided protection for Indian lands from being taken by individuals, corporations, or political entities (e.g., "states") other than the U.S. government and then only through purchase or conquest.

U.S./Indian relations changed dramatically during the reign of President Andrew Jackson (1829–1837). Jackson's anti-Indian sentiments were widely known, dividing the country while fostering strong support for the forceful removal of the remaining major tribes within the country, notably those in the conservative South. Jackson, the Trump of the nineteenth century, emboldened the Southern slave states with his blistering racist rhetoric leading to passage of the Indian Removal Act in 1830 by a bitterly divided U.S. Congress, and in defiance of the U.S. Supreme Court:

> Indian Removal Act of 1830
> An Act to provide for an exchange of lands with the Indians residing in any of the states or territories, and for their removal west of the Mississippi.
> Be it enacted. . . . That it shall and may be lawful for the President of the United States to cause so much of any territory belonging to the United

> States, west of the river Mississippi . . . to be divided into a suitable number of districts, for the reception of such tribes or nations of Indians. . . .[3]

Passage of the Removal Act was an impetus for the state of Georgia to lay claim to parts of the Cherokee Nation, one of the Five Civilized Tribes that subscribed to a Euro-American social system prescribed by former President Jefferson. Now Georgia wanted that portion of the Cherokee Nation lying within its claimed boundaries. By doing so, Georgia challenged the federal exclusive jurisdiction over Indian Country fostering two subsequent U.S. Supreme Court challenges. During the Jackson administration, Georgia attempted to extinguish Indian title within its state boundaries invalidating the laws of the Cherokee Nation. A catalyst for this was the discovery of gold by White prospectors illegally snooping on Cherokee lands. Georgia's challenge to the government's authority led to an 1831 U.S. Supreme Court case *Cherokee Nation v. the State of Georgia*:

> This bill is brought by the Cherokee nation, praying an injunction to restrain the state of Georgia from the execution of certain laws of that state, which, as is alleged, go directly to annihilate the Cherokees as a political society, and to seize, for the use of Georgia, the lands of the nation which have been assured to them by the United States in solemn treaties repeatedly made and still in force. . . . Though the Indians are acknowledged to have an unquestionable and, heretofore, unquestioned right to the lands they occupy, until that right shall be extinguished by a voluntary cession to our government; yet it may well be doubted whether those tribes which reside within the acknowledged boundaries of the United States can, with strict accuracy, be denominated foreign nations. They may, more correctly be denominated *domestic dependent nations.* They occupy a territory which we assert a title independent of their will, which must take effect in point of possession when their right of possession ceases. Meanwhile, they are in a state of pupilage. Their relation to the United States resembles that of a ward to his guardian. . . . The Court has bestowed its best attention on this question, and, after mature deliberation, the majority is of opinion that an Indian tribe or nation within the United States is not a foreign state in the sense of the Constitution, and cannot maintain an action in the Courts of the United States. . . . The Motion for an injunction is denied.[4]

The Cherokee Nation decision was significant in that it ended any pretense that Indian tribes were autonomous nations while, at the same time, establishing their "dependent" status denying them the right of original jurisdiction relevant to U.S. laws. Moreover, the dependent status placed the tribes and Indian Country under the "protection" of the U.S. Congress. This status led to numerous Indian policies designed to redefine U.S. Indian relations oscillating from extermination to self-determination. There is little question that Indians became "dependent wards" of the United States from 1830 to the present. Any pretense of tribal total autonomy is unfounded in the realities of their "dependent nations" status. The bottom line is that the U.S. government has the ultimate say in Indian Country.

Another U.S. Supreme Court case the following year challenged Georgia's attempt to regulate state/tribe laws when Georgia arrested a White missionary, Samuel A. Worcester, for residing with the Cherokees without first swearing an oath of allegiance to the state of Georgia and obtaining an official permit. This case represents one of the first cases involving border control further fueling the divide between White liberals and conservatives:

> The plaintiff is a citizen of the state of Vermont, condemned to hard labor for four years in the penitentiary of Georgia; under colour of an act which he alleges to be repugnant to the Constitution and laws of the United States, the rights, if they have any, the political existence of a once numerous and powerful people, the personal liberty of a citizen, are all involved in the subject now to be considered. . . . The Cherokee Nation, then, is a distinct community occupying its own territory, with boundaries accurately described, in which the laws of Georgia can have no force, and which the citizens of Georgia have no right to enter, but with the assent of the Cherokees themselves, or in conformity with treaties, and with the acts of Congress. The whole intercourse between the United States and this nation, is, by our Constitution and laws, vested in the government of the United States. . . . It is the opinion of this Court that the judgment of the Superior Court for the county of Gwinnett, in the state of Georgia, condemning Samuel A. Worcester to hard labor in the penitentiary of the state of Georgia, for four years, was pronounced by that Court under colour of a law which is void, as being repugnant to the Constitution, treaties, and laws of the United States, and ought, therefore, be reversed and annulled.[5]

These early U.S. Supreme Court decisions set the parameters of what constituted Indian Country and its federal regulation. The 1832 Worcester case further articulated what constitutes Indian Country by noting that tribes were distinct political entities with territorial boundaries established solely by the federal government. The Worcester decision consolidated the federal government's authority over Indian tribes, superseding that of states with the exception of those states that had prior recognition and protection treaties with tribes residing within their boundaries (all of which were eventually transferred to federal protection status during the twentieth century).

Regarding intra-tribal affairs, tribes were allowed to administer their own affairs so long as they conformed to the moral standards set forth by White missionaries and White Indian agents, that is, as long as they subscribed to the dictates of the Protestant Ethic like that expected of the "praying tribes" of the colonial era. Tribal laws and customs did not, however, deter forced removal often at the end of an Army bayonet.

Although these harsh policies were long administered, albeit in a de facto fashion, they became official policy under President Andrew Jackson's administration. Indeed, Gloria Jahoda traced the de facto removal era back to 1813 and, then, General Andrew Jackson's illicit war with Spain and the subsequent Indian removal from Florida.[6]

Andrew Jackson, an unabashed White supremacist, subscribed to George Washington's *trickery by treaty* philosophy where tribes were duped or coerced into signing treaties resulting in their removal to Indian Territory. Indian removal clearly sent a message to American Indians that the United States had no intention of accepting non-Whites into the larger American society, while, at the same time, soliciting European immigrants to populate the lands vacated by the tribes. Hence, American Indians became unaccepted immigrants in their own country. The 1830 Indian Removal Act compelled all southeastern tribes to relocate to Indian Territory west of the Mississippi River. The state of Georgia used this Act as a pretext for its intrusion into the Cherokee Nation, confiscating national property, including schools, council houses, printing presses, and other community facilities and, at the same time, condoning raids into Cherokee villages and plantations by White vigilantes known as "pony clubs," a forerunner of the Ku Klux Klan which emerged during the Reconstruction era following the U.S. Civil War (1861–1865). No federal relief was afforded the Cherokees despite treaties and supposed *parens partriae* protections guaranteed under Supreme Court rulings. Indian Territory soon became a dumping ground for tribes removed from the expanding western United States following the annexation of Texas in 1845 and the Treaty of Guadalupe Hidalgo ending the War with Mexico in 1848 as well as the forceful acquisition of more Mexican territory with the 1853 Gadsden Purchase. Indeed, Indian Country saw its boundaries diminish considerably following the westward expansion and Indian Wars (1862–1892) and the punitive sanctions following the U.S. Civil War. The nineteenth century witnessed a considerable influx of European White immigrants coupled with the massive reduction of Indian Country in order to provide land for these newcomers. The combination of these two events added to the already racial polarization between the privileged Whites vis-à-vis non-Whites, notably American Indians, Blacks, Hispanics, and Asians.

REVOLUTIONARY WAR—PART TWO

Although much attention is paid to U.S. southern expansionism, the first major plan for international exploits involved British North America, first in the Maritimes and later along the West Coast. Many "War Hawks" in Congress thought that this would merely be an extension of the Revolutionary War. The desirability of expansion north was considerable given that this population, with the exception of Lower Canada's French population, was the same as that which comprised the United States, White Protestants. Moreover, given the success of the Acadian Expulsion, many War Hawks felt that the targeted Canadians would willingly join the United States without a fight. This rationale was the prelude to the War of 1812.

The War Hawk leaders, John C. Calhoun of South Carolina and Henry Clay of Kentucky, wanted to declare war on Great Britain under the pretext of retaliation for impressing U.S. seamen. On June 18, 1812, a divided U.S. Congress narrowly supported the declaration of war against Great Britain. President James Madison (1809–1817) signed the war measure marking the first time the United States declared war on another nation. The delusion of a quick and successful completion of this endeavor was quickly dashed when Canadians mustered overwhelming support for Great Britain. While the War of 1812 ended in a stalemate three years later with the Treaty of Ghent in 1815, it essentially ended official armed conflict in order to expand northward to Canada; it did not end other less aggressive efforts at expanding the U.S./Canada border characteristics.[7]

An unintended consequent of the War of 1812 was the unification of Canadians into a sense of a shared union. It helped forge a sense of nationalism unifying an otherwise divided colony. There was little question that the United States was the aggressor, clearly exposing America's ruthless expansionistic ideals. What stopped America's aggression was the unification of Canadians from both Upper Canada (English Canada) and Lower Canada (French Canada), including the U.S.-born loyalists who fled or were driven out during the Revolutionary War. Indeed, Britain's ability to thwart the Americans was its heavy reliance on Canadian militias, the same type of units that were established in the 13 colonies prior to the U.S. revolution. Ironically, U.S. wars provided the catalyst for forging Canadians into a unified nation. Both the War of 1812 and the U.S. Civil War sent shockwaves into Canada leading to its eventual Confederation in 1867. The War of 1812 also provided an opportunity for American Blacks, including escaped slaves, to migrate to Canada.

Until unification in 1867, Canada was what remained of British North America. America's behavior prompted a closer union between Upper and Lower Canada, the Maritimes, and the western territories. Internal battles also provided challenges to the integrity of British North America. In 1837, a series of revolts by the French population occurred coupled with border disputes between New Brunswick province and the U.S. state of Maine. The Maine/New Brunswick border conflict was termed the *Aroostook War.* Here, the United States was attempting to annex the rich forestland along the questionable international border, notably that section below the St. Lawrence River separating Quebec province and New Brunswick and the U.S. state of Maine. This conflict was also known as the "Pork and Beans War." Again, Canadians saw this as yet another attempt by the U.S. to take advantage of internal discord within British North America, this time the uprisings in Quebec by the French Canadians. Instead of spreading internal conflict, the United States' intervention helped forge the creation of the Canadian Union in 1840, a crucial step toward Confederation twenty-seven years later. Interestingly, the international border dispute was represented by Daniel Webster, the U.S. Secretary of State in President Van Buren's (1837–1841) administration. While the Webster-Ashburton Treaty of 1842 favored the United States more than Canada, its unintended consequence was to further strengthen Canada's national identity. Unfortunately, it also divided the Algonquin tribes (Maliseet and Mi'kmaq) that had long resided between the Maritime Provinces of Canada and the U.S. state of Maine. The splitting of traditional tribal lands in 1842 placed more relevance on the *Adams-Onis Treaty of* 1819—and its provision for the free movement of Indians across the international borders with the United States.

In 1840, the Union Bill established the Province of Canada along with a cabinet-type executive accountable to the elective legislature. It was approved in 1848. However, the Union Bill did not address the issues pertaining to the Maritime Provinces. Toward this end, an alternative Union was being proposed, one with the United States and with support from elements of both the Anglo and French Canadians, each with their own interests in mind. French Canadian radicals supported the ideological concept of *ultramontanism*—the concept that the Catholic Church held supremacy over the government. That papal authority superseded that of any representative body. This ideal gained support from members of Canada's Irish and French Catholics, but the Irish raids from the United States as well as continued harassment of Acadian Catholics in northern New England quickly dissolved any hopes of a Canada-U.S. union.

Irish rebels, known as *Fenians,* played an important role in helping forge Confederation unifying all of Canada, except Newfoundland. The Fenian Brotherhood was one of many revolutionary groups supporting an independent Irish Republic following the devastating potato famine of the 1840s. Following the ill-fated 1848 insurrection by the Irish Republican Brotherhood, one of the leaders, John O'Mahony, fled to the United States where he began organizing Irish immigrants into his brand of the of the Irish Brotherhood, calling it the Fenian Brotherhood named after the legendary Irish warriors called Fianna. O'Mahony's organization gained traction following the U.S. Civil War, drawing on the substantial group of unemployed Irish men who served in the war. The Fenian plan was to attack and capture the British North American colonies (Canada) and exchange them to England for an independent Irish Republic. The Fenians had among its militia leaders, U.S. Civil War Brigadier General "Fighting Tom" Sweeny who planned raids into New Brunswick whose border with the United States was articulated in 1840. These raids forced the Maritime Provinces as well as the rest of Canada to reassess its home guard militias. Using the same tactic initiated during the War of 1812, the Fenian raids failed to muster the substantial Irish population of New Brunswick and Ontario to join their forces in overthrowing their government.

The Fenian raids ended only when the United States enforced the laws of neutrality that they had with Britain, ending the cross-border raids. Even then, the initial tacit approval of the Fenian raids from the United States reflected the de facto policy of Manifest Destiny endorsed by President Franklin Pierce through his administration's encouragement of *American Filibusters,* armed private armies, to instigate insurrections in Mexico and Central America. General Sweeny, the Fenian Secretary of War who led raids into Ontario, was not reprimanded for his illegal activity; instead he was able to receive his full retirement from the U.S. Army in 1870. An unintended consequence of the Fenian raids was the unification of Canada leading to Confederation in 1867. The British North American Act (Constitution Act) expanded the Canadian Union of 1840, creating the *Dominion of Canada* comprised of the provinces of Quebec, Ontario, Nova Scotia, and New Brunswick. Confederation overcame long-seething conflicts between French and English Canadians due mainly to threats from United States vigilante and militia groups. Confederation came about due to the cooperation of John A. Macdonald and Georges Cartier with Macdonald becoming Canada's first Prime Minister (1867–1873).[8]

UNITED STATES LOOKS SOUTH FOR EXPANSION

Spain watched with trepidation as the United States attempted to expand into Canada in 1812, knowing that it would only be a matter of time before its plans for expansionism would look south to its territories. The War of 1812 brought U.S. forces into Spanish territory in Florida and its former colony of New Orleans. Stung by France's sale of its former buffer territory—the Louisiana Purchase—Spain now felt compelled to populate its northeastern border as a protection against the potential encroachment from the United States. The Adams-Onis Treaty of 1819, also known as the Transcontinental Treaty of 1819, articulated settlement limits between the United States of America and His Catholic Majesty of Spain. Specifically, the 1819 treaty ended the Seminole Wars ceding Florida to the United States as well as establishing the Mexico–United States border along the Sabine River. The treaty also ended Spain's opposition to France's right to sell the Louisiana Territory.[9]

The Adams-Onis Treaty ended U.S. claims that the Louisiana Purchase included Spanish-held territory up to the Rio Grande and the Rocky Mountains. On the other hand, by agreeing to the U.S. purchase of

Florida for five million dollars, Spain also forfeited its claims to the Oregon Territory in the Northwest leaving this contested area up to the United States and Canada (Great Britain) to settle later. By the time of its ratification two years later (February 22, 1821), Mexico was seven months away from declaring its independence from Spain (September 21, 1821) setting the stage for the U.S. to attempt to negate the Treaty's territorial conditions. Clearly, this was yet another example of America's "trickery by treaty" method of international relations. By the time of Mexico's independence, Spain had already set the stage enticing migrants to populate its northern frontier bordering on the United States.

Spain, and later Mexico, used the *empresario land grants* as the vehicle for bringing migrants to its northern territory as a means of checking American territorial aggression and expansionism. Little did the Spanish colonial government know that they were populating the northern territory with Americans with their own designs on carving out their own country, one with values quite dissimilar from that of Mexico and its antislavery stance. Spain granted its first empresario permit on January 17, 1821 to Moses Austin allowing him to settle 300 families in what is now the state of Texas. Two events in America precipitated these migrants to move to the Spanish colony: one was the economic panic of 1819 and the other was the high cost of public lands. The cost of public land in the United States was set by Congress at two dollars per acre while in Spain, later Mexico, the cost was 12.5 cents per acre with six years to pay. Mexico's independence from Spain did not immediately alter these arrangements. An empresario could accommodate up to 800 families with six years to fill its proposed allotment of families. Another condition was that the immigrants convert to Catholicism if not already of the Roman Catholic faith. Another major departure was that Mexico outlawed slavery and continued the Iberian legal tradition of recognizing women's property rights—conditions that would not occur in the United States for decades.[10]

Although the Anglo-American immigration into Texas/Coahuila began with the Austin empresario during Spanish colonial rule, the vast majority of expatriate Americans came under the Mexican Republic laws. A month following passage of the state colonization law of March 24, 1825, the governor of the combined state of Coahuila and Texas contracted for 2,400 American emigrant families. The flood of Anglo-American emigrants continued until 1832. Clearly, the Austin contracts were the most successful empresarios. Also successful were the empresarios of de Witt and de Leon. At any rate, the predominant Anglo-American empresarios totaled some 30,000 at the time of the Texas revolution in 1836.[11]

A precursor to the Texas rebellion was Mexican President Guerrero's 1829 decree abolishing slavery throughout the Republic of Mexico sending a shock wave throughout the Anglo settlements in Texas. President

Bustamante later reinforced the anti-slavery mandate as well as curbing further Anglo-American immigration into northeastern Mexico. Slavery and Catholicism were the two main objections of Anglo-American settlers in Texas. Seeds were now sown for Texas' independence. Anglo-American colonists saw their opportunity for rebellion following protests by Mexicans against the rule of President Santa Anna. Both Tejanos (Mexican Texans) and Anglo Texans joined in this protest. On March 2, 1836 a provincial assembly signed a Declaration of Independence. President Santa Anna reacted by sending his poorly equipped Mexican army north to quell the rebellion.[12]

Santa Anna's forces retook the Alamo in San Antonio and later lost to the stronger rebel force, under the command of General San Houston at San Jacinto. Three weeks later, the Treaty of Velasco was negotiated with President Santa Anna conceding Texas independence. However, this treaty was never ratified by the Mexican Congress providing Texas with de facto independent status given that the Mexican military was too weak to retake its wayward province. Interestingly, the constitution of the Republic of Texas was based on that of the United States with a strong Southern U.S. influence reflecting its anti-Catholicism and pro-slavery stance:

> Constitution of the Republic of Texas
> Article I: Section 7. The senators shall be chosen by districts, as equal in free population (free negroes and Indians excepted), as practicable; and the number of senators shall never be less than one third nor more than one half the number of representatives, and each district shall be entitled to one member and no more.
> Article V. Section 1. Ministers of the gospel being, by their profession, dedicated to God and the care of souls, ought not to be diverted from the great duties of their profession; therefore, no minister of the gospel, or any priest of any denomination whatever, shall be eligible to the office of the executive of the Republic, nor to a seat in either branch of the Congress of the same.
> General Provisions: Section 6. All free white persons who shall emigrate to this Republic, and who shall, after a residence of six months, make oath before some competent authority that he intends to reside permanently in the same, and shall swear to support this Constitution, and that he will bear true allegiance to the Republic of Texas, shall be entitled to all the privileges of citizenship.
> Section 9. All persons of color who were slaves for life previous to their emigration to Texas, and who are now held in bondage, shall remain in the liked state of servitude; provided, the said slave shall be the bona fide property of the person so holding said slave as aforesaid. Congress shall pass no laws to prohibit emigrants from bringing their slaves into the Republic with them, and holding them by the same tenure by which such slaves were held in the United States; nor shall Congress have the power to emancipate slaves; nor shall any slave holder be

> allowed to emancipate his or her slave or slaves without the consent of Congress, unless he or she shall send his or her slave or slaves without the limits of the Republic. No free person of African descent, either in whole or in part, shall be permitted to reside permanently in the republic, without the consent of Congress; and the importation or admission of Africans or Negros into this Republic, excepting from the United States of America is forever prohibited, and declared to be piracy.
> Section 10: All persons (Africans, the descendants of Africans, and Indians excepted) who were residing in Texas on the day of the Declaration of Independence, shall be considered citizens of the Republic, and entitled to all the privileges of such. . . . [13]

The pro–United States, anti-Spanish/Mexican, pro-White sentiments are clearly articulated in the Republic of Texas Constitution with little doubt as to its racist intent. And while most of the Tejanos absorbed into the new Texas Republic remained neutral during the rebellion, they too would suffer considerable injustices at the hand of the Anglos whose status was deemed superior to Hispanics, White or Mestizo.

The Texas rebellion, while celebrated widely in the U.S. South, was not universality applauded. Former U.S. president John Quincy Adams (1825–1829), coauthor of the Adams-Onis Treaty of 1819, saw the Texas revolt as a blatant act of self-interest for slave owners and land speculators. These divided sentiments in the United States caused considerable unrest that would eventually lead to the annexation of Texas, the ensuing War with Mexico, and the U.S. Civil War. Texas annexation was seen as inevitable given that it lacked international legitimacy due to Mexico's refusal to recognize the Treaty of Velasco and the fact that it was designed as a slave haven. Annexation was seen as the only route open to preserve the Texas slave state. Annexation was initially rejected by the U.S. Senate but became a major part of president-elect Polk's political platform. With James K. Polk's inauguration, the U.S. Congress passed the annexation resolution on February 28, 1845, with the Texas Republic agreeing to become part of the United States in October the same year.

Clearly, annexation of Texas sowed the seeds of war with Mexico. Following annexation, President Polk then pushed his war with Mexico agenda under the pretense that it was over a dispute over the U.S./Mexico border. While this was presented as the main reason for the conflict, it soon became clear that the latent reason was shrouded in Manifest Destiny and the massive land-grab extending the United States to the Pacific coast. A weak Mexico became the target of U.S. expansionism following America's failure to expand its northern border to the 49th parallel of the Alaskan border under the Buchanan-Pakenham Treaty of 1846 that awarded Great Britain all of Vancouver and the United States the Puget Sound, concessions that avoided yet another war with England. Ostensibly, Polk's administration (1845–1849) calculated that it was far easier to fight a struggling, impoverished country like Mexico instead of one with a colonial superpower.[14]

Again the United States was divided over the blatant act of American imperialism under the guise of Manifest Destiny. It became obvious to the international community that the United States was willing to forcefully take what it could not obtain through negotiations. The War with Mexico (aka Mexican-American War) of 1846–1848 led to the signing of the Guadalupe Hidalgo Treaty on February 2, 1848 which established the Rio Grande as the official southern border of the United States along the new state of Texas. The War with Mexico provided the United States with a fresh corps of military leaders replenishing the Indian fighters of the past: Ulysses S. Grant, Ambrose Burnside, Stonewall Jackson, George Meade, and Robert E. Lee. It also established a generation of U.S. presidents and presidential candidates including Zachary Taylor (1849–1850), Franklin Pierce (1853–1857), Winfield Scott, U.S. Grant (1849–1877), and Jefferson Davis (1861–1865 Confederate). The United States political leadership during the nineteenth century had a strong military component, a factor relevant to the country's aggressive expansionism and intervention under the guise of *Manifest Destiny.*

A major outcome of the War with Mexico, beyond territorial gain, was its fueling of the unresolved slavery issue in the United States ultimately leading to the U.S. Civil War (aka War Between the States). Despite stated conditions, the Treaty of Guadalupe Hidalgo did little to provide protection to the peoples occupying this newly acquired territory, notably Mexican residents and American Indians. Mexicans were relegated to second-class status while some of the most intense Indian Wars and ethnic cleansing occurred in the former Mexican Territory under U.S. possession. New Mexico Territory (the states of New Mexico and Arizona) was especially problematic in that it was the exception to the overall plan of expunging the land of its Mexican and Indian occupants. This was not a problem with Texas and California where Anglo-Americans soon outnumbered their Mexican and Indian counterparts.

Complicating the newly acquired populations of New Mexico Territory was the 1853 Gadsden Purchase which further expanded the territorial borders. Little attention was given to the captured population given that New Mexico Territory was seen by Anglos mainly as a transited passage route to the riches of California. The obstacle was that it had an established Spanish/Catholic population consisting of some 40,000 White (Spanish) Hispanics and 60,000 Mestizo and 15,000 Pueblo Indians as well as numerous, uncounted and unrecognized, tribes collectively labeled as "savages"—Apache, Arapaho, Cayuga, Cheyenne, Comanche, Navajo, and Ute. Under the conditions of the Treaty of Guadalupe Hidalgo the White colonial residents of the former Mexican territory were to become U.S. citizens. However, the U.S. was reluctant to offer full citizenship to the "mixed" (Mestizos) bloods regardless of their Mexican citizenship at the time of the Treaty. The U.S. offered the Mestizos the choice of relocating south to Mexico or they could maintain dual citizenship with their U.S. status being federal and not necessarily territorial or state citizenship. This stipulation allowed the Anglo-Americans greater political power despite their fewer numbers while allowing the Mestizo elite to control its population.[15]

While the use of Indian slaves was a long tradition during Spanish colonial rule and continued beyond the War with Mexico, the prohibition of Black slaves in New Mexico Territory and California strained the delicate balance established by the 1820 Missouri Compromise. Added to this turmoil was Texas' claim to a substantial portion of New Mexico. As a solution to this chaos, Congressional leaders Henry Clay, Daniel Webster, John C. Calhoun, and Stephen Douglas forged the "Compromise of 1850" that got Texas to fall back to its original treaty boundaries, while New Mexico, Arizona, and Utah agreed to suspend the slave issue until statehood. According to the Compromise, California would remain slave-free while the slave trade was abolished in the District of Columbia while preserving its slaveholding status. In an attempt to appease Southern slaveholders, the Compromise contained the Fugitive Slave Act in an attempt to address the Underground Railroad for slaves attempting to escape to non-slave states. Under this law, all U.S. citizens were compelled to assist in the recovery of fugitive slaves. Unfortunately, without adequate judicial oversight free Blacks were captured and sent south to be enslaved, a situation further widening the gap between slaveholders and abolitionists.[16]

During this time, the 1850s, the United States embarked on international efforts to expand American trade using force in what became known as "gunboat diplomacy." President Millard Fillmore (1850–1853) used the U.S. Navy to force Japan to open its ports to American and European trade resulting in the U.S./Japan Treaty of Kanagawa of 1854 during Franklin Pierce's presidency (1853–1857), unwittingly sowing the seeds for U.S. involvement in World War II. In addition to the expansion of U.S. territory with the Gadsden Purchase, obtained under the threat of war with Mexico, Pierce's administration also witnessed and sanctioned intervention into Central America, notably Nicaragua, under the dictates of the *Monroe Doctrine*—the hemisphere application of *Manifest Destiny*. The Gadsden Purchase provided the U.S. an opportunity to renege on conditions stipulated in the 1848 Treaty, notably the provision protecting Mexican residents from attacks by Indian tribes. The Purchase also allowed the United States to build and run a railroad across the Isthmus of Tehuantepec allowing U.S. business interests access to Mexican natural resources. The expansion of White exploitation into the newly acquired lands from Mexico in 1848 and 1853 was articulated by John O'Sullivan in an article published in August 1845: "It is our manifest destiny to overspread the continent allotted by Providence for the free development of our yearly multiplying millions." James S. Calhoun, first Indian agent, and later governor, of New Mexico Territory set the stage for extinguishing the Navajo Indians by allowing slave raids among the Navajo by both New Mexicans and other Indian tribes, a practice that continued until the end of the Long Walk in the mid-1860s.[17]

The Monroe Doctrine did not deter outside interference in the Americas when in 1861 the Tripartite Convention of London authorized the armed intervention in Mexico with forces from Britain, France, and Spain in order to recover Mexico's 82-million-peso debt. The United States could do little at this time given that it was consumed with its own civil war. The European challenge to the Monroe Doctrine was short-lived when in 1866 Napoleon III pulled his support of Maximilian, the European-appointed Emperor of Mexico, resulting in Maximilian's defeat and execution in 1867, freeing Mexico again for U.S. exploitation. The end of the U.S. Civil War (1861–1865) was followed by increased military operations during the 30-year Indian Wars (1862–1892) raging mostly in the territory acquired earlier from Mexico. Another casualty of the U.S. Civil War was the end of Reconstruction, the ambitious plan for the enfranchisement of freedmen. The withdrawal of U.S. occupation forces from the vanquished South led to the failure of the Freedmen's Bureau setting the stage for extralegal actions by southern Whites directed against the newly freed Blacks resulting in America's version of apartheid where the resulting enforced caste system led to the emergence of Jim Crow laws separating White and Black facilities, including churches and schools. Jim Crow laws also bred vigilante-type racist justice known as lynching administered by ruling Whites and their de facto police—the Ku Klux Klan (KKK). Here, Blacks were adjudicated without trials or due process often mutilated, burned, and/or hanged by White mobs. This process went on unabated for 100 years until passage of the U.S. Civil Rights Acts of the mid-1960s.[18]

The last half of the nineteenth century also witnessed Indian Country's boundaries greatly diminish through war and legislation. Indeed, the instruments of Manifest Destiny nearly completely destroyed the aboriginal indigenous cultures in the United States during this era. Following the U.S. Civil War, Congress ended treaty-making via the Indian Appropriations Act of 1871 setting the stage for the acquisition of tribal lands by force instead of through negations. President U.S. Grant (1869–1877) called this process his *peace policy.* At the same time, the U.S. House of Representatives expanded its authority over Indian policy by eliminating the role of the U.S. Senate from its traditional role of ratifying Indian treaties by virtue of ending the treaty era. Now agreements with tribes required ratification of both houses of Congress. Executive orders and Congressionally-approved federal statutes now dominated U.S./Indian policy virtually eliminating Indians from the process.

The goal for this radical change in U.S. Indian policy was to end the long-held colonial tenet of *aboriginal right of occupancy.* Now the federal government could by fiat, without tribal input or consent, classify so-called "uncooperative" tribes and individual Indians as outlaws, renegades, and/or savages (enemy combatants), hence authorizing those so-labeled to be hunted down and destroyed by the military, militias, and vigilantes. Despite its name, President Grant's Peace Policy, full-assimilation for American Indians was never a serious consideration. Even an Indian version of *Jim Crow* accommodation, like that that emerged from the failure of Reconstruction, was not part of this policy. The main purpose of this policy was the acquisition of more Indian treaty lands for White settlers. President Grant was in an excellent position to initiate and enforce his policy given his success during the U.S. Civil War and his subsequent role as the first four-star general in charge of the U.S. military. With the assistance of his two leading Civil War associates, William T. Sherman and Philip H. Sheridan, President Grant was instrumental in using the U.S. Army to accelerate the already simmering Indian Wars (1862–1892).

Although Indian wars existed throughout the colonial and early republic era, they were usually associated with larger conflicts like the French and Indian War, the Revolutionary War, the War of 1812, or the pre–Civil War removal policies. The Indian War of 1862–1892 was the longest official American war, with its own campaign medal awarded for services in its innumerable campaigns. The Indian Campaign Medal was issued only once regardless of how many battles or campaigns a soldier was involved in. However, a silver citation star was awarded for meritorious or heroic conduct making it the predecessor of the Silver Star, the third-highest military award for combat heroism.[19]

During and immediately following the U.S. Civil War the western portion of the United States was divided into combat regions: the Department of Dakota; Department of the Platte, Department of the Missouri; Department of Texas, Department of Arizona; Department of California, and the Department of the Columbia (Northwest). The major Army officers during the Indian Wars were Generals U.S. Grant, William T. Sherman, Philip H. Sheridan; Lieutenant General John McAllister Schofield; five major generals and 16 brigadier generals and numerous colonels and lieutenant colonels. Among this group were Colonel John (Black Jack) Pershing and Lieutenant Colonel George Armstrong Custer. A major component of the enlisted personnel was the *Buffalo Soldiers,* liberated freedmen. The name Buffalo Soldier was conferred on Black soldiers by the Indians. The Black soldiers were led by White officers including Colonel Pershing who gained his nickname, Black Jack, from heading a Buffalo component. Rebel prisoners-of-war were also recruited to fight in the Indian Wars in the early campaigns (1862–1865). They were known as *Galvanized Yankees* and had to swear allegiance to the Union with the promise of full pardons in exchange for their successful service in the Indian Wars.

The Indian Wars provided the military enforcement of the government's planned provocation of Indians so that the Army could intervene. The government would then use this confrontation as justification for obviating previous treaty conditions resulting in the massive reduction of tribal lands. This deceit was a prominent element of President Grant's "Peace Policy." The Indian Wars included the largest mass public execution when President Lincoln authorized the hanging of 38 Santee Sioux warriors in Mankato, Minnesota on December 26, 1862. A year later, Colonel Kit Carson led a scorched-earth punitive expedition against the Navajo Nation resulting in the tribe being force marched from their traditional lands to an Army garrison in New Mexico. The Indian Wars also resulted in Lieutenant Colonel George A. Custer's defeat at the Little Bighorn on June 25, 1776 and the subsequent assassination of the Sioux leaders involved, killing Crazy Horse in 1877 and Sitting Bull in 1890 while both were in federal custody. In 1886, with the capture of Geronimo, the federal government classified all members of the Chiricahua Apache as "enemy combatants," including decorated U.S. Army scouts, incarcerating the entire tribe as prisoners of war (POW) at a squalid military prison in Florida. The last memorable event in the Indian Wars was the Wounded Knee Massacre of December 28, 1890 when the U.S. Army confronted Sioux Chief Big Foot at Wounded Knee Creek on the Pine Ridge Reservation in South Dakota, killing 148 of the 370 hungry and mostly unarmed old men, women, and children. Many were killed by the Army's Hotchkiss machine gun.[20]

On the civilian side, the U.S. Congress extended U.S. jurisdiction in Indian Country by passing the Major Crimes Act of 1885 making major felony crimes (Seven Index Crimes) committed by Indians federal offenses: murder, manslaughter, rape, assault with intent to kill (aggravated assault), arson, burglary, and larceny. These offenses were now to be adjudicated within the federal District Court system instead of being left to tribal customs. Initially the U.S. Marshals, in their capacity as officers of the federal judiciary, served as the major White police authority in Indian Country. Later in the early twentieth century this service was shared, and often superseded, by the authority of the Federal Bureau of Investigation (FBI). This policy established the superior weight of the United States and White interest in Indian Country given that Indians were not citizens or otherwise enfranchised. This played a significant role in the great land grab created by the Allotment policy that soon followed.[21]

Allotment was designed to break up collectively-held tribal lands into individual allotments with "excess," or "surplus" lands opened up to White settlers.[22] Land deeded to individual Indians under Allotment was to be federally protected from exploitation by non-Indians. The protective trust aspect was never a serious consideration of the Allotment policy with numerous allotted plots taken by unscrupulous Whites in collusion with the White-run courts resulting in a substantial number of non-Indians residing within the tribal boundaries. In 1898, at the time of the Curtis Act, U.S. federal courts held exclusive jurisdiction over all civil and criminal cases in Indian Territory (Oklahoma). In 1901, the U.S. Congress granted federal citizenship to Indian allottees but this did little to protect Indian landowners since this did not provide them equal protection before White courts. Indeed, from the time of the Curtis Act in 1898 and Oklahoma statehood in 1907, many Indian Allotments were stolen from Indian landholders through a widespread conspiracy of unsavory "boomers" (White settlers) and discriminatory courts. In all, more than 60 percent of Indian Country, some 86 million acres, was taken during the Allotment era, 1886–1934.[23]

NOTES

1. M. Beschloss, *The Presidents: Every Leader from Washington to Bush.* New York, NY: American Heritage/Simon & Schuster, 2003, p. 50.
2. B. Sheehan. *Seeds of Extinction.* New York, NY: Norton, 1974; & A. Stephanson. *Manifest Destiny: American Expansion and the Empire of Right.* New York, NY: Hill & Wang, 1995.
3. *Indian Removal Act,* U.S. Statutes at Large, 4: 411–12, May 28, 1830.
4. *Cherokee Nation v. Georgia,* 5 Peters, 15–20, 1831.
5. *Worcester v. Georgia,* 6 Peters, 534–36, 558–63, 1832.
6. G. Jahoda. *The Trails of Tears: The Story of the American Indian Removals, 1813–1855.* New York, NY: Wing Books, 1975.
7. H.L. Coles. *The War of 1812.* Chicago, IL: University of Chicago Press, 1966; & J.K. Mahon. *The War of 1812.* Gainesville, FL: University of Florida Press, 1972.
8. S. B. Ryerson. *Unequal Union: Confederation and the Roots of Conflict in the Canadas, 1815–1873.* New York, NY: International Publishers, 1968; & S. Kaufman. *The Pig War: The United States, Britain, and the Balance of Power in the Pacific Northwest, 1846–1872.* Lanham, MD: Lexington Books, 2004.
9. S.B. Ryerson, ibid.
10. Ibid.
11. M.V. Henderson. "Minor Empresario Contracts for the Colonization of Texas, 1825–1834," *Southwest Historical Quarterly,* vol. 31 (4), 1928, pp. 295–324.
12. Ibid.
13. F. Merk, *Slavery and the Annexation of Texas.* New York, NY: Knopf, 1972.
14. R.B. Campbell. *An Empire for Slavery: The Peculiar Institution in Texas, 1821–1865.* Baton Rouge, LA: Louisiana University Press, 1989.
15. J.H. Schroeder. *Mr. Polk's War: American Opposition and Dissent, 1846–1848.* Madison, WI: University of Wisconsin Press, 1973.
16. L.E. Gomez. "Off-White in an Age of White Supremacy: Mexican Elites and Rights of Indians and Blacks in Nineteenth-Century New Mexico." *Chicano-Latino Law Review,* vol. 25 (Spring), 2005, pp. 9–59.
17. E.C. Rozwenc (ed.). *The Compromise of 1850: Problems in American Civilization.* Boston, MA: Heath and Company, 1957; R.F. Locke. "The Navajos and the American Conquest," *The Book of the Navajo.* Los Angeles, CA: Mankind Publishing Company, 1992, pp. 266–302.

18. *Gadsden Purchase Treaty,* December 30, 1853, Articles 1–9. New Haven, CT: The Avalon Project at Yale Law School.
19. M. Beschloss. "Abraham Lincoln: The Great Emancipator," *The Presidents: Every Leader from Washington to Bush,* op. cit. #1, pp. 189–208; & R. Ginsburg. *100 Years of Lynching.* New York, NY: Lancer Books, 1962.
20. J.D. McDermott. *A Guide to the Indian Wars of the West.* Lincoln, NE: University of Nebraska Press, 1998.
21. R.W. Stewart. *Winning the West: The Army in the Indian Wars, 1865–1890.* Vol. 1. Washington, DC: U.S. Printing Office (Army Historical Series), 2001; D. Brown. *The Galvanized Yankees.* Lincoln, NE: University of Nebraska Press, 1963; & F.N. Schubert. *Black Valor: Buffalo Soldiers and Medals of Honor, 1870–1898.* Wilmington, DE: Scholarly Resources, 1997.
22. *Major Crimes Act,* U.S. Statutes at Large, 23: 385, March 3, 1885.
23. *General Allotment Act (Dawes Act).* U.S. Statutes at Large, 24: 388–91, February 8, 1887; & *Curtis Act,* U.S. Statutes at Large, 30: 497–98, 502–5, June 28, 1898.

FOUR

Labor Exploitation and Emerging Immigration Policies

Together the Louisiana Purchase (1813), the War with Mexico (1846–1848) and the Gadsden Purchase (1853) not only tripled the size of the country, these added territories provided the United States with a wealth of raw materials and natural resources requiring a sufficient labor source to exploit and develop these riches. With the end of slavery, new human resources were needed for common labor positions in dirty, often dangerous, jobs that White Americans felt were below their social station. Toward this end, Chinese laborers were brought to work in mines and build the railroads needed to exploit these resources as well as transport settlers to this new land. At the same time, French-Canadians and Irish workers were sought to work in the mills and factories in the Northeast, while freedmen and their families were held in virtue perpetual servitude on the plantations in post-Reconstruction Southern states. Mexicans provided another affordable source for Anglo ranchers and farmers with Filipinos joining them following the Spanish-American War (1898). Unfortunately, when these ethnically and racially different peoples' service was no longer needed, America attempted to expel them or shut the door to further migration. This process of providing foreign, notably non-white, laborers set the stage for America's immigration policies. Exploitation of these newly acquired territories and resources required humans to extract these riches, including clearing the land of Indian tribes and bringing in migrant laborers for the difficult and dangerous jobs needed to connect the United States from the Atlantic to the Pacific oceans.

BOUNDARIES AND MIGRATION UP TO THE U.S. CIVIL WAR (1813–1861)

The early events leading to the current geographical boundaries of the United States have been detailed in previous chapters, including Indian Removal and the influx of other non-Protestant ethnic whites like the French Canadians and Irish. Our discussion now focuses on marketplace demands and racial exploitation. Clearly, the Louisiana Purchase in 1803 whet the appetite of American imperialism, with plans made to expand the United States from coast to coast setting the stage for a major American policy on human rights, that of *ethnic cleansing* of an entire indigenous population. The original plan was to transfer non-"civilized" tribes west of the Mississippi to Indian Territory but Southern states had a different plan—that of removing even the "Civilized Tribes" (Cherokee, Choctaw, Chickasaw, Creek, and Seminole) so that Whites could take over their villages, farms, and forests. Thus, it could be argued that the United States' first formal immigration legislation was the 1830 Indian Removal Act, an act initiated by the U.S. Congress and fiercely enforced by President Andrew Jackson. The Removal Act set the stage for the state of Georgia to lay claim to parts of the vast Cherokee Nation lying within its boundaries.[1]

In geopolitical terms, Removal was enforced by the U.S. Army, a process that continued throughout the nineteenth century. While Indian removal is officially traced to the 1830 act, General, and later President, Andrew Jackson initiated the de facto removal of the Creek Indians in 1813, again using the Army as the agent of enforcement. While the most notable removal to Indian Territory was that of the Cherokees in 1838, known as the *Trail of Tears,* numerous other tribes were forcefully removed during the 40 years following Congressional authorization of Indian forced migration. Many of these tribes experienced hardships equal to or greater than those suffered by the Cherokee Nation in 1838. In all, 63 tribes were removed to Indian Territory with 39 federally-recognized tribes now residing within the state of Oklahoma.[2]

INDUSTRIALIZATION AND THE INFLUX OF WHITE ETHNIC CATHOLICS

The demands for cheap labor coincided with the rapid development of industrialization in New England, a process that also facilitated the slave-driven cotton plantations of the Southern states. As noted earlier, French-Canadian Catholics have a 400-year presence in North America first settling in Acadia (Nova Scotia) and along the St. Lawrence River, establishing their headquarters at Quebec City. French explorers and trappers established forts and trading posts in Indian Country at places that now are major U.S. cities—Detroit, Dubuque, and St. Louis and New Orleans—places later acquired by the United States. Huguenots (Protestant French) also trace their heritage in America to the colonial era with such prominent figures as Paul Revere. This population became divided during the American Revolution with many fleeing to Canada as "Loyalists," a factor that quelled America's ambitions to capture the Canadian Maritimes during the War of 1812. While the French-Canadian presence has been here as long as the White Protestants, their numbers surged during the 1840s following a number of situations in British North America (Canada).[3]

Economic conditions on either side of the U.S./Canadian border set this migration in process. New England was rapidly being transformed by textile mills along its numerous rivers soon matching that of England, a phenomenon crying for a readily available work source. At the same time, agricultural woes were plaguing Lower Canada (Quebec) and its rapidly growing French Canadian populace. Not enough farm jobs were available for the rapidly growing working-class French Canadian workers who often had to split their time between working in the woods and in agriculture. Plus, Canadian industrialization did not match the rapid growth that was occurring to its south. Canada was experiencing its own mini–Civil War between predominately English Upper Canada (Ontario) and French Lower Canada (Quebec) in the mid-1830s with a number of French Canadians fleeing south to the United States—this plus continued conflicts with the United States over its eastern border between Maine and New Brunswick. Fearing continued intrusions into the Maritimes by Americans resulted in the border being finalized in 1840 and Canada forging itself into an autonomous Union in 1848, providing the Province of Canada with a singular form of government. The Canadian Union was seen as providing greater protection from American border aggression. Another salient factor was the rapid advancement made by the railroad in order to facilitate the cotton and woolen textile industry. When the local Protestant Yankee female population began to complain about the working conditions and asked for higher wages, they were no longer deemed an adequate workforce for the textile mills, and other sources were to be considered.[4] Initially, the newly arrived influx of Irish fleeing the famine in their homeland provided an alternative to the local Protestant female workforce.

The Irish, notably Protestant Scot-Irish, had a long tenure in America dating back to colonial British North America. They worked with French Canadians in the lucrative fur trapping era throughout Canada and were used as frontiersmen in the 13 colonies, forging into Indian Territory in upper Massachusetts (Maine and New Hampshire). The Scot-Irish, however, were tolerated because they were Protestants, namely the Presbyterian branch of the Puritans. The Great Famine caused by the potato blight brought an influx of two million Irish Catholics to the east coast of North

America in the 1840s, settling in both New England and Canada. The Irish refugees worked at menial jobs with low pay building the massive railroad network, digging canals, as well as replacing the unsatisfied Yankee girls in the textile mills. The Irish Catholics were not well received by the local Protestant Yankees resulting in a backlash by the anti-Catholic Puritanical Yankees known as "No-Nothings," a sentiment that was quickly transferred to the French Canadians who came to replace the Irish as strike breakers.

The mill barons needed a replacement for the troublesome Irish Catholic and Yankee girls, a replacement that did not involve a tremendous transportation and settlement cost. The French Canadians' collective persona proved to be more docile than either the Yankees or Irish workers making them the "ideal" replacement. Moreover, unlike the Irish refugees who had no intention or means for getting back home to Ireland, the French Canadians saw themselves as transitory workers who maintained their family and community ties in Canada and planned to return when the homeland economy improved. While many did return, as many did not, creating "Little Canada" ghettos in the major mill enclaves in New England. The influx of workers was facilitated by Yankee "agents" who recruited the French Canadians from the local Canadian parishes. French Canadians were also seen as more manageable in that their parish priests from Quebec often accompanied them to their New England ghettoes. In all, some 900,000 French Canadians migrated to New England to work in the textile industry between 1840 and 1930 when the border was sealed due to the Great Depression. Both the Irish and French Canadians immigrated to the United States before any immigration laws were enacted. While they represented the largest Catholic ethnic class prior to the mass migration of the post–Civil War/pre–World War I era, the Irish soon came to dominate the Catholic Church in America. Indeed, Franklin Pierce (1853–1857) credited Catholics with his narrow win over popular Army General Winfield Scott, legitimizing Catholics by being the first U.S. president to appoint James Campbell, a second-generation Irish-American, as Postmaster General. Conservative Yankees' fear of Catholics dominating America soon played out in the twentieth century when Catholics emerged as the single largest sectarian faith in America. But these fears were unfounded in that Catholics, in general, proved to be as conservative as their most ardent Protestant counterparts.[5]

U.S. Secretary of State Daniel Webster, under President Martin Van Buren (1837–1841), was instrumental in resolving the U.S./Canada border dispute in 1842, ending a low-level altercation between Maine and New Brunswick known as the Aroostook War or the "Pork and Beans War" with the signing of the Webster-Ashburton Treaty. During this same era the United States settled its western border with Great Britain (Canada) in 1846 with the Oregon Treaty demarking the international border along the 49th parallel. While smaller scrimmages would continue throughout the nineteenth century, any major conflict with Canada was for the most part diminished forcing the United States to look south to Mexico for its expansionistic appetite, beginning with the bizarre case of U.S. emigrants settling in what was the northern Spanish territory known as Texas/Coahuila. Spain welcomed settlers to better protect its northern border from United States excursions. Ironically, the settlers were expatriate Anglo-Americans seeking land during economic difficulties in the United States.

The annexation of Texas in 1845 and the ensuing War with Mexico (1846–1848) and the 1853 Gadsden Purchase of 45,000 square miles in what is now southern New Mexico and Arizona, followed by the devastating U.S. Civil War (1861–1865) and acquisition of Alaska in 1867, greatly expanded the United States. Moreover, the 30-year Indian Wars (1862–1892) helped cleanse the new territory in the West for White settlers. Coincidently, it was at the end of the Indian Wars when tribes were concentrated on heavily guarded reservations with their former lands opened for settlement that the United States opened its doors to more European immigrants, among them a considerable number of ethnic Catholics and Jews, adding to the already substantial Irish population (both Catholic and Protestant Scot-Irish), truly making America a "melting pot." This era of unfettered European immigration was not so much a humanitarian effort as it was the need to populate this vast territory extending from the Mississippi River to the Pacific.

TURBULENCE ALONG THE U.S./MEXICO BORDER

There has always been a marked contrast between the northern and southern borders of the United States. The U.S./Canada border has been, for the most part, an "open" border up until its closure at the onset of the Great Depression in 1930. Initially this was to seal off the cross-border flow of French Canadians between Quebec and New England. Border security then intensified during Prohibition when Canada became a major supplier of illicit liquor. Following Repeal, the northern border was again "open" making it one of the longest minimally secured borders in the world. This was not the case with the U.S./Mexico border. When Texas joined the Union in 1845, it was a major slave state and its concern with the border was not so much keeping Mexicans out as much as it was to keep its slaves from escaping to slave-free Mexico. This was one of the major functions of the Texas Rangers. Border security with Mexico intensified across its entire length with passage of the Fugitive Slave Act of 1850 which was vigorously enforced during the Pierce administration (1853–1857). With the Gadsden Purchase, and the Indian Wars following the U.S. Civil War, the border was freely crossed by the Apache when avoiding pursuits by either the Mexican or U.S. army, a situation that forged a compromise allowing the U.S. Army to pursue Indians into

Mexico. Both the pursuit of fleeing Black slaves and Apache warriors provided the incentive for vigilante groups who hunted their prey for rewards and bounties. These groups are the forerunner of the current border vigilantes camping out along the United States' southern border often with the tacit support of local White ranchers, those who acquired the lands stolen from the very same group they now pejoratively reject as undesirable intruders.[6]

Even then, a substantial region transcending the U.S./Mexico border had a vitality of its own creating a de facto *Borderland* with its own flourishing economy and sub-culture. It was a symbolic economic and cultural landscape different from either country's interior, a situation fostered by the close relationship between the United States and Mexican autocrat Porfirio Diaz, who ruled from 1877 until 1911, an era known as the *Porfiriato.* Diaz's regime was strongly supported by the United States for a number of reasons including his ability to reduce border tensions while at the same time opening up Mexico's resources and markets for U.S. capital endeavors. The Porfiriato era brought prosperity to the Mexican upper classes as well but at the expense of the poor lower class, Mestizos and indigenous Indians, who continued to live in dire poverty.

Clearly, Diaz provided an environment ripe for both U.S. and European capitalists opening up Mexico's resources for their exploitation and profit, an environment that provided cheap labor, significant tax breaks, and favorable judicial rulings for foreign interests as well as those of the elite *cientificos.* U.S. capitalists like William Randolph Hearst invested heavily in Mexican mines, petroleum, and textiles while amassing large land holdings along with the elite *cientificos.* These business endeavors were facilitated by the establishment of a massive rail system connecting southern Mexico to the United States. This same rail system provided a means of transportation for cheap Mexican laborers. In the name of international capitalism peasant lands and Indian communal lands were expropriated by the Mexican government to appease foreign interests. Toward this end, Diaz abrogated Spanish laws protecting Indian lands and peasant collective farms forcing the Indians and peons to continue to live on their former lands as cheap labor for their new landlords. This bondage of the impoverished peasants was further welded by forcing the peons and Indians to purchase all essentials from the hacienda store thereby forcing them into debt that was then transferred from one generation to another, making these workers virtual slaves much like the sharecropper system in existence in the post–Civil War Jim Crow U.S. south. Taking another chapter from the U.S. Jim Crow model, education for the Indians and peons was substandard at best, and often denied these de jure Mexican slaves.

However, the level of international investment within Mexico at this time allowed for greater mobility for the *Criollos* (Mexicans of Spanish heritage aka White Mexicans), opening up positions as clerks, teachers, small businessmen, and legal and clinical practitioners. This new social class wedged between the elite *cientificos* and the larger peon/peasant class helped fuel the Mexican Revolution by joining the lower-class Mexicans in what initially became a protest over social injustices and Mexican exploitation by outsiders, factors explored in chapter 6, and border events during the twentieth century.[7]

THE ASIAN IMMIGRANT

At the same time, the United States was flexing its military might throughout the Americas under the guise of the Monroe Doctrine with the manifest role of protecting U.S. business interests in Mexico, Central and South America, and the Caribbean. In Asia, U.S. intervention extended to the 1850s and America's "gunboat" diplomacy forced Japan and China to open their doors to international trade. The 1842 Treaty of Nanking forced China to cede Hong Kong to Britain during the *opium war* that compelled China to open its doors to the lucrative opium trade. The United States soon joined the British in gaining trade facilities in China by participating in the Treaty of Wanghai in 1844. France and Russia then joined in this effort, participating in the 1858 Treaty of Tientsin resulting in Kowloon being ceded to Britain and portions of Manchuria to Russia. These forced intrusions into non-White cultures were mainly for the benefit of European and American business enterprises. A downside to these strong-arm arrangements was the influx of not only trade, but people of color, a factor fueling America's latent racism beyond its traditional scapegoats, African Americans and American Indians.

Chinese males, barred from applying for U.S. citizenship, immigrated to the United States in the mid-nineteenth century as a source of cheap manual labor in the expanding western states and territories. They first arrived in substantial numbers following the conclusion of the Mexican War in 1848 and the opening up of California's gold fields. Once the dangerous work like the transcontinental railroad was completed, they migrated to urban ghettos known as *China Towns* where they took on low-wage jobs working in restaurants and laundries. White neighbors clamored for their deportation leading up to the United States' first immigration laws that were specifically designed to target a particular racial group. With the post–Civil War economic woes, Chinese workers became scapegoats for depressed wages leading California to write into its constitution a provision allowing the government to determine which peoples were allowed to reside in the state, a factor leading to passage of the Chinese Exclusion Act by the U.S. Congress in 1882.

Restrictions already existed under the Page Act of 1875, a law restricting federal immigration of Asians who were deemed "undesirable." Indeed, the Page Act established the federal government as having sole jurisdiction over immigration ending the various state immigration mandates. The Page Act, also known as the Asian Exclusion Act, was designed to curtail the onslaught of Chinese laborers who were seen as undermining White laborers in the depressed workforce as well as denying the entry of Chinese women under the pretense of restricting prostitution when the real reason was to prevent the Chinese from establishing families in America. The act also prohibited entrance to any Asian convicted of a crime in their home country. It was designed to curb the pool of Chinese cheap laborers collectively known as *coolies*. The discrimination against Asian (mainly Chinese) women was obvious given that prostitution was quite prevalent throughout the western United States at the time. While prohibiting prostitution was the manifested purpose of the Page Act, its latent function was clearly to restrict Asian families from setting roots in America. Prominent American institutions like the American Medical Association fueled the demonization of Asians in general and Chinese in particular by stating that they carried germs to which they were immune but were deadly to others.[8]

The next major federal immigration act also targeted Chinese immigrants. The Chinese Exclusion Act, signed by President Chester A. Arthur in May 1882, prohibited all Chinese laborers from entering the United States. Chinese, like the French Canadians, were a unique workforce in that they resided within their own cultural enclaves without relying on the use of public institutions including schools, hospitals, and the like. But the racial factor came into play when a scapegoat was needed to direct public angst during economic hard times. Federal legislation was also needed to enforce the earlier Page Act authorizing only the federal government to make immigration laws. The Naturalization Act of 1790, and its prohibition of the naturalization of non-Whites, a provision that qualified the U.S. Constitution providing the foundation for American citizenship and hence its census, provided a precedent for the Chinese Exclusion Act. The 1891 Immigration Act created the Office of the Superintendent of Immigration within the Treasury Department whose duties were to inspect and document the arrival of immigrants at ports of entry into the United States: a duty formerly carried out by the customs officials since 1820. In 1893, the Treasury Department Superintendent of Immigration's office was charged with providing Boards of Special Inquiry to review exclusion cases. In March 1895 the Office of Immigration was named the Bureau of Immigration.

While the Chinese Exclusion Act did not exclude all Chinese from entering the United States, it required certification from the Chinese government verifying that applicants met the stringent qualifications required for emigration. The class of acceptable applicants was limited mainly to diplomats and businessmen and their house servants. It was a sunset act intended for a ten-year duration although it was renewed in 1892 and 1902. This action did not curtail the demands for cheap Chinese laborers in that illegal coolies entered the United States via the loosely guarded U.S./Canadian border. The Canadian Agreement of 1894 was designed as an international effort to curb illegal Chinese migrants by attempts to stop them from entering Canada via its ports.

Racial prejudices and economic conditions of the time lent strong support from the public and labor unions. California Congressman Thomas J. Geary proposed extending the Exclusion Act for ten-year intervals plus requiring Chinese residing in the United States to carry official documentation of residency, obtained from the Internal Revenue Service (IRS). The Geary Act of 1892 also imposed a one-year sentence of imprisonment of hard labor followed by deportation for anyone found without these certificates on their person. The Geary Act was upheld by the U.S. Supreme Court in its 1893 decision, *Fong Yue Ting v. United States.* In another case, *United States v. Wong Kim Ark,* the U.S. Supreme Court in 1898 ruled favorably for Chinese born in the United States even if their parents were from China either documented or undocumented. This case had larger ramifications in that it defined the "Citizen" clause in the Fourteenth Amendment to the U.S. Constitution that stated: "All persons born or naturalized in the United States, and subject to the jurisdiction thereof, are citizens of the United States and of the State wherein they reside. No State shall make or enforce any law which shall abridge the privileges or immunities of citizens of the United States; nor shall any State deprive any person of life, liberty, or property, without due process of law; nor deny to any person within its jurisdiction the equal protection of the laws."

The exceptions to the Amendment passed in 1866 were American Indians. The 1892 decision was intended to hold children born in the United States by foreign parents to the laws of the U.S. and not to a foreign nation (*jus soli).* This inherent right of citizenship for those born in the United States has met with challenges during the twentieth and twenty-first centuries, especially regarding the inherited citizenship by birth (*jus sanguinis)* of those labeled as "illegal aliens"—a legal concept not yet coined at the time of the Wong Kim Ark decision. This decision followed the 1896 *Plessy v. Ferguson* decision that upheld the dire caste system instituted in the South following the end of the Reconstruction Era allowing for a complex social boundary system that greatly restricted and stigmatized an entire race of "citizens" and their rights ostensibly granted under the 14th Amendment.[9] At the same time, American Indians who had not yet received federal citizenship were being held to federal jurisdiction in Indian Country (America's Indian reservations) under the 1885 Major Crimes Act.[10]

The nineteenth century ended with the United States exerting its colonial interest beyond the Americas with the concocted war with Spain leading to the short-lived 100-day Spanish-American War of 1898. The pretense for the Spanish-American War was the mysterious sinking of the gunboat *USS Maine* in Havana harbor on February 15, 1898, setting the stage for U.S. military intervention against the remaining Spanish holdings in the Americas and beyond. These acquisitions included Cuba and Puerto Rico as well as Spanish colonial holdings in the Pacific—the Philippines and the Caroline, Marshall, and Mariana Islands including Guam. The Spanish-American War made President William McKinley (1897–1904) and his Assistant Secretary of the Navy, Theodore Roosevelt, instant American heroes. Theodore Roosevelt (1901–1909) succeeded McKinley following his assassination in September 1901. Despite America's desires for Cuba, the Teller Amendment that provided Congressional approval for the Spanish-American War precluded the United States or any foreign nation from colonizing Cuba with the exception of that section captured by the United States Marine Corps known as Guantanamo Bay (aka GITMO) where the U.S. has held a perpetual, irrevocable lease of this section of Cuba since 1903. The Paris Treaty provided for U.S. spoils to include Puerto Rico, Guam, and the rest of the Mariana, Caroline, and Marshall Islands while Spain was forced to relinquish the Philippine Islands for 20 million dollars—a tactic similar to U.S. extortion of Mexico for the Gadsden Purchase less than fifty years earlier. In Hawaii the native monarchy was overthrown by American filibusters supported by the sugar industry in 1893 and annexed by the United States in 1895. The Anglo-run sugar industry brought in Japanese, Korean, Chinese, Filipino, and Portuguese laborers to work on the pineapple and coffee plantations adding to the complex ethnic mix of the Islands.[11]

Thus, the nineteenth century saw the United States greatly expanded both on the continent and overseas making it not only the most powerful force in the Americas but a colonial power in the Pacific. At the same time, it had to develop policies designed to control its own growing population including laws regulating both internal and external migrations. The twentieth century reflected the success and failures of these efforts while challenging the domain of the White elite that had ruled America from its inception.

NOTES

1. *Indian Removal Act*, U.S. Statutes at Large, 4:411–12, May 28, 1830.
2. G. Jahoda. *The Trail of Tears: The Story of the American Indian Removal, 1813–1855*. New York, NY: Wing Books, 1975; & R. Costo, & J. Henry-Costo. *Indian Treaties: Two Centuries of Dishonor*. San Francisco, CA: Indian Historian Press, 1977.
3. P. Berton. *Flames across the Border, 1813–1814*. Markham, Ontario, Canada: Penguin Books, 1988; & H.L. Cole. *The War of 1812*. Chicago, IL: University of Chicago Press, 1966.
4. L.A. French. *Frog Town: Portrait of a French Canadian Parish in New England*. Lanham, MD: University Press of America, 2014.
5. Ibid.
6. L.A. French. *Running the Border Gauntlet: The Mexican Migrant Controversy*. Santa Barbara, CA: Praeger Press, 2010.

7. Ibid.
8. *Chinese Exclusion Act of 1882,* U.S. Statutes at Large, 22 Stat. 58, May 5, 1882; Public Law 47-126.
9. M. Meijer (ed.). *Dealing with Human Rights: Asian and Western Views on the Values of Human Rights.* Oxford, England: World View Publishing, 2001; & S. Barbour (ed.). *Immigration Policy.* San Diego, CA: Greenhaven Press, 1995.
10. *Major Crimes Act.* U.S. Statutes at Large, 28: 385, March 3, 1885.
11. G.A. Cosmas. *An Army for Empire: The United States Army in the Spanish-American War.* Columbia, MO: University of Missouri Press, 1971; & T. Roosevelt. *The Rough Riders.* New York, NY: Charles Scribner's Sons, 1899.

FIVE

Geo-Political Foundations of Contemporary Border Trade and Security

What accounts for one neighbor being viewed perennially as dangerous and the other as not? Is it sheer geopolitics? The answers are complex at some level, but at/on another level, they are simple. The challenge resides in the acceptability of circumstances and a realization that both neighbors are not going anywhere. This fact poses a fundamental question, what is best for the future of the three nations? That is, for Canada, Mexico, and the United States. Nothing could be more shortsighted than the overall dynamics of the United States' foreign policy regarding both its southern and northern allies. Current enunciations by President Donald Trump about the dangers that both Canada and Mexico present are misguided. Canada, in the current U.S. administration's assessment, represents an economic danger seen from the perspective of trade imbalances. For Mexico though the picture is far murkier for it presents, according to President Trump, a danger based on the illegal entry of Mexican nationals into the U.S., the illegal drug traffic, the potential for terrorists entering through the U.S. border, the failure to be an effective buffer zone to contain migration from Central America principally, and of course the economic danger based on trade imbalances.

UNITED STATES AND MEXICO BORDERLANDS

While the analysis of these issues is far from simple, they do follow a pattern, at least as it concerns U.S.-Mexico relations. Animosity and mistrust between the United States and Mexico erupted several times during the twentieth century and it had direct consequences for life in the borderlands. The outbreak of the Mexican Revolution in 1910 and the ensuing decade of violence, which pitted Mexican against Mexican, also involved the United States in direct ways. The gestation of this armed conflict had its roots in the obscene inequalities pervading Mexico, where the great majority of the population lived in horrid conditions.[1] The political stability which supporters of dictator Porfirio Díaz were proud of was accomplished by a regime of fear. As is the norm in totalitarian political systems, the Mexican political configuration rested on the premises (and promises) that social order was essential for political and economic stability and that once these goals are accomplished everyone would benefit. However, after three decades of strong rule there was no indication that the continued stability had brought any obvious benefits to the great majority of Mexicans.

In fact, education levels for the masses were dismal and most of the rural population, which comprised the majority of the 15 million people in the country, lived in extreme poverty. A small elite, both national and foreign, benefited from the political stability and macro-economic growth of the nation. Mexico was able to pay its external debt during the years of the *Porfiriato,* the era so-named after the dictator's name. This accomplishment was lauded as a sign of Mexico coming into modernity. The nineteenth century was plagued by revolts and counter-revolts dating to 1810 when the country began its war for independence. The myriad coups d'état and the contracting of a foreign debt since 1824 coupled with foreign interventions by Spaniards, French, and Americans had left the country in a very precarious situation. In the process, Mexico lost more than half of its current territory to the United States in the U.S.-Mexico war of 1846–1848. It is not surprising that a long period of stability was a welcomed development for all Mexicans. Nonetheless, that period of peace preceding the Mexican Revolution of 1910 was achieved at great cost to the bulk of the country's population.[2]

The outbreak of the armed rebellion caused alarm among the population, primarily among the elites. In relative quick succession Porfirio Díaz was deposed when Francisco Villa defeated the government troops in Ciudad Juárez, across from El Paso, Texas. The impact of the Mexican upheaval, the largest of its kind in the world at the start of the twentieth century, was witnessed in more ways than one by the people from the U.S.-Mexico borderlands. In the battle of Ciudad Juárez, El Paso inhabitants set watching chairs from the hills of the American city to have a view of the carnage taking place just across the Río Grande. The first stage of the rebellion came to its end in May 1911, after a few months of armed confrontations between the revolutionaries and the federal troops. The deposed dictator took a transatlantic ship to France where he ended his days, while Francisco I. Madero ascended to the Mexican presidency through a democratic process.

As the months went by President Madero found it difficult to break the grip of the bureaucracy and the military establishments left behind by Porfirio Díaz. Although elected for a period of five years by a wide margin in October of 1911, Madero did not finish his term as constitutional president (Siempre 2011). Former allies and other groups led by followers of the deposed dictator rebelled against the new president. The rebellions came mostly from regions in the central and northern parts of the country, with the exception of the revolutionary troops commanded by Emiliano Zapata south of Mexico City. The internal turmoil gave way to plots and counterplots for the overthrow of President Madero. Throughout the whole decade of the revolutionary war external powers meddled directly and indirectly in Mexico. Great Britain, Germany, and the United States attempted to influence the direction of the revolution for geopolitical and economic reasons, particularly as the advent of World War I became obvious.[3]

One such plot involved the United States. U.S. ambassador to Mexico Henry Lane Wilson's assessment of President Francisco Madero was negative. It did not help much that aside from support of the old regime, Madero's allies during the confrontation with Porfirio Diaz, such as Pascual Orozco and Emiliano Zapata, turned against him. It was in this context that foreign investors in Mexico, in Ambassador Wilson's view, would be hurt economically. The Taft administration made clear to Madero that it would not sit idly by and watch Mexico jeopardize foreign investment, a threat it backed up by ordering warships to Mexican waters and stationing more troops along the border.[4] Ambassador Wilson had also other choice words to describe Madero. The representative of President Taft in Mexico referred to Madero as a "lunatic" and considered the Mexican government to be "apathetic, inefficient, cynically indifferent or stupidly optimistic."[5]

It was in this context of political instability and barely 15 months after Madero's election that Ambassador Wilson along with General Victoriano Huerta and Felix Diaz signed what became known as the Pact of the Embassy.[6] Huerta had been a general in the *Porfirista* army as well as political appointee of Porfirio Diaz in several civil posts in the country. After retiring for a few years before the revolution erupted, Huerta applied for a position in the Madero administration. He was given the same rank as before and joined the newly formed government as a general in the armed forces. Felix Diaz by virtue of being Porfirio Diaz's nephew and because he headed a revolt from the state of Veracruz against Madero became a player in the plot to overthrow President Madero. The pact signed in the American Embassy in Mexico City under the sponsorship of Ambassador Henry Lane Wilson sealed the fate of President Madero. On February 19, 1913, at the end of the *Decena Trágica*, the Ten Tragic Days, when Mexico City was rattled by military confrontations between counterrevolutionary forces and the troops loyal to President Madero, the signatures of the plotters were affixed to the document. Francisco I. Madero was apprehended along with his vice president. On February 22, while being transported ostensibly from the National Palace, where they had been detained, to the penitentiary the president and the vice president were executed. In a matter of hours after the assassination of Francisco I. Madero and José María Pino Suárez, General Victoriano Huerta ascended to the presidency.[7]

THE MEXICAN REVOLUTION AND THE BORDERLANDS

The coup d'état aided by the American government unleashed the second stage of the Mexican Revolution, the most deadly and chaotic period of the revolt. The hands of the United States as well as other world powers were all over the place during this conflict. As documented by Katz, Great Britain and Germany were also jockeying for influence in the zigzagging pattern of revolutionary leaders who seemed to be in control of the movement at a rapid pace but only for short spans of time.[8] From the onset of the revolutionary period the United States/Mexico border was affected by the developments in Mexico. Nearly 20,000 American troops were deployed along the border by 1911. The Maneuver Division of Buffalo Soldiers (African American troops) was stationed in San Antonio standing ready to repel any cross-border intrusion as byproduct of the violence that was erupting on the Mexican side.

In a span of less than ten years the United States violated Mexican sovereignty three times. A relatively minor incident in April 1914 led the American navy to raise the United States flag in the port of Tampico located to the south of Texas. It involved eight sailors from the *USS Dolphin* who went ashore to get fuel that had been previously bought from a German merchant. However, they wandered off beyond the zone established by the warring factions, who at the time pitted the federal forces of dictator Victoriano Huerta against the Constitutionalists led by the revolutionary Venustiano Carranza, and they were arrested. The American officials asked for the release of the sailors which once the Mexican higher officials learned of the apprehension of these marines were promptly released. The American officials had also asked for Mexicans to raise the United States flag and a 21-gun salute. The Mexicans sent an official apology, but refused to acquiesce to the flag raising and gun salute petition.[9]

President Wilson considered this a major affront and proceeded to ask the U.S. Congress for authorization to invade Mexico. Congress granted such request, but two days earlier, on April 21, 1914, American marines landed in the port of Veracruz. At the end of the bombing of Veracruz on April 22, there were 126 Mexican and 19 American deaths. By the end of the seven-month occupation several hundred casualties were registered.[10] Both the Tampico incident and the Veracruz landing by the U.S. Marines were driven by a twin set of reasoning by the American government under Presidents William Taft, 1909–1913, and Woodrow Wilson, 1913–1921. One was to control the direction of the Mexican Revolution in order to install a regime that was, if not pro–United States, at least favorable to American interests. Secondly, as the events leading to the First World War developed, keeping Germany out of Mexico was also relevant. President Taft's *Dollar Diplomacy* relied partially on American investments in foreign countries to create economic dependency that would affect these nations vis-à-vis the United States. President Wilson's *Moral Diplomacy* was couched in ideas that essentially only democratic countries were to be beneficiaries of American assistance.

Wilson's foreign policy was tested by events in Mexico, but only in terms of execution. The overall approach to the Latin American nations had been framed for almost a century in the Monroe Doctrine, which unilaterally elevated the United States to the status of "protector" of the Western Hemisphere. Under this doctrine, the American government would oppose any European intervention in Latin America, thus giving itself carte blanche to intervene at will in hemispheric affairs. The interventionist approach was broadened and deepened by the *Roosevelt Corollary* of 1904, an addition to the Monroe Doctrine. Under President Theodore Roosevelt, 1901–1909, the notion of European powers exercising control over Latin America was considered a threat to American national security. As an emerging world power at the dawn of the twentieth century, the United States began to implement its "Big Stick" policy, which called for a threat of force in international negotiations. President Roosevelt's big stick policy was framed in his Corollary which allowed for direct United States intervention when American interests where threatened by internal struggles or domestic policies of the countries where American investments were located.[11]

Taft's Dollar Diplomacy and Wilson's Moral Diplomacy were nothing more than further variations to the implementation of the Monroe Doctrine/Roosevelt Corollary. In Mexico of the early twentieth century the Monroe Doctrine, the Roosevelt Corollary, and the diplomatic approaches used by Presidents Taft and Wilson converged. The Tampico incident and the bombing of Veracruz were only the latest instances of the United States' interventions in Mexican internal affairs. The uneasy relations between both countries date back to the 1820s when American attempts to buy Mexican territory fell on deaf ears. The Mexican Congress refused such overtures. However, in the United States' expressed desire to expand west Mexico represented an obstacle. Guided by notions of racial superiority, framed in part in the Manifest Destiny ideology, and initially a weak implementation of the Monroe Doctrine, American advance to the western territories led to military confrontations with Mexico. Eventually, at the end of the Mexican-American war of 1846–1848,

Mexico would lose over half its territory to the United States. For nearly half a century following the end of the war frequent incidents of violence occurred along the newly created political border. Some semblance of peace was introduced during the nearly three decades of ruthless rule exercised by Porfirio Diaz, a regime that collapsed in 1910 when the Mexican Revolution exploded. By the time Roosevelt's, Taft's, and Wilson's approaches to international relations were implemented for Mexico they represented a continuation of a century-long American approach to dealing with Latin America and the world.

Although the U.S. government under President Taft, and more precisely with Ambassador Wilson's tacit support, sided with the anti-democratic forces vying for power after the fall of the dictator Porfirio Díaz, when President Woodrow Wilson came into office the American government threw its support behind the revolutionaries. It is not surprising then to figure out why the American quick decision to bomb Veracruz a few days before the U.S. Congress actually approved such action. By the spring of 1914 the United States was decidedly supporting the Constitutionalist faction led by Venustiano Carranza. In April a shipment of German weapons for the new dictator Victoriano Huerta was scheduled to be unloaded in the port of Veracruz. From the American perspective, it is conceivable to speculate, that German intrusion into the Mexican domestic affairs represented a challenge to American interest. Not only were weapons bought by a regime that by now the United States opposed, but under Wilson's moral diplomacy the very government that Germany was supporting by selling arms was anti-democratic and therefore repugnant to President Wilson's stated foreign policy. Even though World War I began in July 1914, the Wilson administration was already preparing to enter such conflict. Never mind that Wilson was elected by promising to keep American troops out of the war. Thus, from the American point of view U.S. troop intervention in Mexico was justified on many grounds. The German presence in Mexico, even though it was relatively small, was taken seriously. Since the events leading to World War I were rapidly developing, and what the United States did not need was a Mexican government sympathetic to or at least involved in trade relations with Germany.[12]

Secondly, the level of American investment in Mexico was of such proportions that an unstable Mexico was not in the U.S.'s best interests. At the very least continued violence in Mexico could distract President Wilson from concentrating on the major developments taking place in Europe. German overtures to General Victoriano Huerta in the form of weapons sales and at least three other events that took place in the following three years further exacerbated friction in the borderlands. The San Diego Plan incidents, General Francisco "Pancho" Villa's attack on Columbus, New Mexico, and the Zimmermann Telegram all contributed to create a context for further militarization of the U.S.-Mexico border.

In early 1915 a draft of the Plan of San Diego, in southern Texas, called for a rebellion against white Americans. It called for the killing of all white males over the age of 16 and forming a Chicano nation in the southwestern United States comprised of Texas, New Mexico, Colorado, Arizona, and California. The leader was a man by the name Basilio Ramos. However, neither Mexicans nor Mexican-Americans lent credibility to this plan, which called for an uprising February 10. Nothing happened on that date. But the level of hostility against Latinos in southern Texas increased as consequence of the Plan of San Diego. As Acuña points out, the discovery of this plan reached hysteric proportions in the region. With the escalation of violence against non-white border inhabitants, resistance from some Mexican-Americans and Mexicans contributed to an upsurge of border raids; for a couple of days starting on July 15 the rebels supporting both Victoriano Huerta and Venustiano Carranza with a force of 50 men made about 30 raids into Texas.

> The Euroamericans' angst over what they perceived as revolutionary incitement led to the killing of hundreds of Mexicans. In the end, the U.S. authorities admitted shooting, hanging, or beating to death 300 "suspected" Mexicans, while the rebels killed 21 Euroamericans during this period.[13]

Although racial tensions were present in the borderlands ever since the political border was drawn, the fact that Mexico was engulfed in a civil war and world powers such as Germany loomed on the horizon as a potentially additional destabilizing force in the whole conflict, episodes such as the Plan of San Diego intensified distrust among the people living along the border. Germany had supported Victoriano Huerta but as time went by it gradually shifted its support for Venustiano Carranza. In its efforts to influence the course of the armed conflict in Mexico, the U.S. government also had given tacit support, for a brief period, to General Francisco Villa. The Germans were also seeking to support Villa by selling arms to him. While the machinations of the United States and Germany played out on the world stage, their less-known role in the Mexican revolution continued to affect the U.S.-Mexico border zone. General Villa's attack on the town of Columbus, New Mexico exacerbated the already negative view that Americans, near and far from the border, held of Mexicans and of Mexico.

It was General Villa's break with Carranza that eventually led to his falling-out with the United States, and Wilson's declaration of support of Carranza came in October 1915. Now Villa's forces were fighting the *Carrancistas*, as Carranza supporters were known, under General Álvaro Obregón with tacit assistance from the U.S. military along the border. Indeed, the United States first alienated Villa in April 1915 in the battle for Matamoros when it allowed the Carrancistas to cross over into the protection of Brownsville while at the same time stopping Villa's forces from hot pursuit. General John "Black Jack" Pershing and his Buffalo Soldiers played a major role in border military politics at this time. With the United States now taking sides providing support for Carrancistas, Villa's forces suffered a number of losses in northern Mexico in the spring and summer of 1914. Villa's status changed from respected military general to U.S.-designated renegade bandit.

President Wilson's recognition of Carranza over Villa was probably an effort to end the internal strife within Mexico, which many in the United States felt was being fueled by Germany in its effort to draw the U.S. military into the Mexican Revolution, thereby keeping them out of the European war. Evidence of the German motive came later with the Zimmermann communiqué of May 3, 1916. Most likely Germany saw Villa's March 9, 1916, raid on the U.S. Army base in Columbus, New Mexico, as the likely catalyst for full U.S. involvement in Mexican affairs. Clearly, the resulting Punitive Expedition had the opposite effect, mobilizing the National Guard for the first time and transforming the U.S. military from the nineteenth-century horse cavalry to a mechanized force in the form of the highly successful Rainbow Division led by General Douglas MacArthur under the overall leadership of General "Black Jack" Pershing. Harsh reactions to the Plan de San Diego by the United States, notably the use of the Texas Rangers, also aggravated these issues, contributing to General Villa's cross-border raids.[14]

BORDERLANDS FOLLOWING THE MEXICAN REVOLUTION

The immigration situation from the early twentieth century until the Second World War was one where people of Mexican origin, living along the U.S./Mexico border, either fled south to Mexico to avoid the harsh repercussions associated with the Plan de San Diego or were deported during the Great Depression or they fled north into the United States to avoid the battles associated with the Mexican Revolution. Either way, this migration was mostly into the borderland region and, for many, was seen as being transitory. Moreover, the male drain in the United States due to the First World War, coupled with both the newly enforced restrictions on Asian immigrants and the rapid growth of the economic revolution in the United States, led to a labor shortage. Soon agricultural demands in the fertile fields of Texas, New Mexico, and California led to the black-market practice of smuggling illegal Mexican laborers into the United States.

Van Nuys estimated that 10 percent of the Mexican population fled to the United States during the Mexican Revolution, enriching the borderland region by at least a million immigrants from south of the border. This coupled with the United States' stereotype of the Mexican peon as a docile, ignorant, hardworking entity immune to the harsh desert conditions of the West, and the distrust of Asian workers at this time led to the special waiver provisions of the restrictions of the Immigration Act of 1917, eliminating the literacy test, head tax, and contract labor provisions for Mexican workers from May 1917 to March 1921.[15] De Leon in his work *Mexican Americans in Texas* indicates that tens of thousands of Mexican-born workers entered Texas during the period of 1900–1930 for a total of over 700,000. These migrations occurred during a time when the U.S./Mexico border was basically un-policed.[16]

These undocumented migrations occurred even though the U.S. Border Patrol was established in 1924. However, its initial function was enforcing customs laws against Asians as well as enforcing Prohibition smuggling laws—a function that involved the borders both north and south of the United States. De Leon noted that while most of these early immigrants stayed within the old territorial borders conceded to the United States in the nineteenth century, they were still perceived in racist terms. Speaking of what some termed the "Mexican Problem," even those advocating continued migration of Mexican laborers perceived them as being a degenerate people posing moral and political danger to the United States. But, they argued, this was outweighed by the fact that overall they were docile farm laborers who lived together in barrios and, therefore, could be easily controlled without posing a threat to the dominant white society.

Restrictionists, on the other hand, worried that some of the Mexican laborers might leave the agricultural fields and migrate to the industrial centers where they would replace white workers. They also argued that the Mexicans represented an inferior people who would spread disease and crime in the United States. Though thousands did enter the United States legally, *restrictionists* did win the battle during the hardship years of the Great Depression when most foreign laborers were being restricted entry into the United States, even those from Canada.[17]

The *Bracero Program* of 1942 was unique in that it allowed Mexico to establish the minimum standards for its workers in the United States. During the period covered by the initial Bracero Agreement, from 1942 until 1947, some 200,000 braceros came to the United States as agricultural workers under these international provisions. Ill feelings toward Mexicans certainly brewed during this time given that foreign migrant workers were guaranteed wages and benefits denied U.S.-born farm workers. With Texas boycotting the initial accord, its reliance on illegal Mexican migrant workers further fueled anti-Mexican sentiments, even among the rising Mexican American political class. While political opposition to the Bracero Program existed in the U.S. Congress, the fact that the program was under the auspices of the U.S. Department of Agriculture (USDA), and not Labor, gave the strong agricultural business lobby what it wanted—cheap labor.

Dissension from labor groups and the ensuing Korean conflict led to changes in the original Bracero Agreement for the period from 1948 until

1951. Again some 200,000 legal Mexican migrant laborers were recruited during this period with approximately twice as many undocumented workers recruited as well. This program existed in a state of flux during 1948–1951. The abuses were now directed toward American workers, while those Mexican citizens who crossed the border in search of work found that their home country was increasingly disenfranchised from protecting its workers.

The controversy over Mexican workers in the United States became heated in the 1950s with the conservative, anti-Communist McCarthyism movement. A major target of McCarthyism was racial and ethnic minorities who were grouped together with political minorities—Socialists and Communists—and identified as threatening to the American way of life. This phenomenon led to the heated bracero debate of 1951, which eventually fostered *Operation Wetback,* created to deport Mexican immigrants. Notwithstanding the fear incited by the McCarthy witch hunt, Public Law 78 passed on July 12, 1951, establishing the first effort at legislating the Mexican guest workers program. This arrangement again placed the bracero contracts at a government-to-government level, eliminating the blatant abuses that abounded during the interim 1947–1951 period. Agribusiness in general supported this effort at congressional oversight, if only to guarantee needed seasonal laborers for planting and harvesting U.S. crops, the exception being the sugar beet farmers of the Northwest. The caveat offered those opposed to the Bracero Program was the built-in six-month renewal clause, which meant that the law had to be reconsidered twice each year. Even then, Public Law 78 continued to regulate the Bracero Program unopposed for the next 13 years.[18]

In the 22 years of the official Bracero Program, Mexico was forced to reevaluate its own agricultural and rural communities—those from which guest workers originated. In the final analysis, while certain progress was being made, rural poverty persisted in Mexico while the *campesino* programs stalemated. In the end, over four-and-a-half million Mexican workers were involved in the exchange of labor sanctioned through the official Bracero Agreement. Ironically, the Bracero Program also contributed to a rush of undocumented Mexican workers into the United States. It is estimated that while a little over 200,000 guest Mexican workers were contracted for 1953, nearly 900,000 others that are known of also entered the U.S. workforce.[19]

Societal events in the United States during the 1950s and early 1960s spelled the end of the Bracero Agreement. Increased mechanization in harvesting agricultural products, notably cotton, led to a reduced need for the guest worker. The fact that the guest workers program existed from 1951 until the end of 1964 was due mainly to the efforts of the Mexican government. The end of Public Law 78 did not, however, stem the flow of undocumented Mexican workers into the United States, now to work in any venue where cheap labor was needed. In the final analysis, the anti-bracero groups included both Mexican American workers and Mexican American political action organizations, as well as other political and economic interests in the United States. The changes brought about since 1965 had seen an increase of immigrants from developing nations. Indeed, Mexico now became a corridor for entry into the United States for illegal migrants coming from Central and South America. Mexico now had to contend with human contraband entering the country at its southern border and exiting at its northern border. There was also increased opposition to nonwhites entering the United States under the new immigration rules.[20]

Industrialization and Internationalization of the Borderlands

Tougher environmental laws in the United States in the mid-1960s led to the proliferation of the *maquiladoras,* or twin manufacturing plants, where U.S. and other international firms would establish and operate plants in Mexico along the U.S. border in the borderland. The origins of Mexican industrialization extend back to the early years of World War II when Mexico began the process of preparing workers for industrial jobs. In 1944, the Mexican Congress passed legislation opening the door to foreign participation with the provision that Mexicans hold a controlling stock in any mixed corporation. This action led to the establishment of the maquiladora system which emerged along border. At the end of World War II, some 300,000 Mexican workers were employed by major U.S. industrial firms. The maquiladoras, in turn, led to a mass migration of mainly females from rural interior Mexico to the borderland. Both these migrants and immigrants contributed to the unique borderland culture.[21]

General Electric (GE) opened its first maquiladora in 1971 and soon expanded to eight plants within a decade. GE employed over 8,000 workers to produce circuit breakers, motors, pumps, and coils in its borderland Mexican plants. Soon General Motors followed suit, opening 12 maquiladora plants in Mexico while closing 11 factories in the United States, laying off nearly 30,000 workers. On the eve of the North American Free Trade Agreement (NAFTA), General Motors was the largest private employer in Mexico with 50 plants and 50,000 workers accounting for a tenth of Mexicans employed by some 2,000 maquiladoras. With this transformation of the U.S./Mexico border came rapid growth. Ciudad Juarez had a population of 250,000 in 1960 compared to well over a million today. The same phenomenal growth has affected every *maquilas* zone from Tijuana to Matamoros. In addition to the industrial pollutants came uncontrolled human waste and garbage that contributed to water and air contamination. Protected from U.S. environmental standards, the U.S. corporations operating in Mexico could pollute at will. By the time of NAFTA in January 1994, the Rio Grande was the most contaminated river in the North American region evidenced by high rates of childhood cancers, gallbladder problems, hepatitis, liver cancer, and even anencephalic births on both sides of the international border in the borderland. Moreover, Mexico's industrial accident and illness rate is among the highest in the world, with a rate of 23 per 100,000 workers. Yet, under Mexican law maquiladoras cannot be sued for work-related injuries or illnesses. The only recourse is a legally capped disability payment from the Mexican government. Under this arrangement, U.S. and other foreign companies have little incentive to clean up the work environment of their maquiladoras.[22]

The Mexican jobs along the U.S. border did not eliminate the influx of undocumented workers because the maquiladoras employed women, most of whom left the rural countryside to migrate to the border frontier of Mexico. This disrupted the traditional rural Mexican family and community system where women provided mostly unpaid labor. Soon young unemployed or underemployed men followed the migrating women to the borderland where many crossed into the United States illegally for work on farms, ranches, and in construction.

The North American Free Trade Agreement—NAFTA

Talks of a tripartite free trade agreement began in earnest in the early 1990s and by the fall of 1993, the United States Congress had approved the passage of NAFTA. In part, Mexico was being forced into the international free trade market by virtue of its overwhelming debt following the devaluation of the *peso* in 1976 and the stringent economic measures enforced to comply with the International Monetary Fund and U.S. conditions for economic aid. However, this drastic change in Mexico's international status did not resonate with everyone, especially with *campesinos* and Indigenous people who benefitted from the restoration of the *ejido system* (peasant communal-held land) following the Revolution. President Clinton insisted that as a condition for acceptance in NAFTA, the Mexican government abrogate Article 27 of the Mexican Constitution that protected Indian communal landholdings from sale or privatization. At the same time, the Clinton administration enforced the *Southwest Border Strategy* which was designed to shore up the most porous sections of the U.S./Mexico border, those areas adjacent to the major *borderland* centers: San Diego, California; Tucson, Arizona; and El Paso, Texas.[23]

With the dissolution of Article 27 of the Mexican Constitution, rural Indian and non-Indian communities that historically relied on their corn crop fell prey to the dictates of the big agricultural businesses in the United States. The unintended consequence of this was the unraveling of the traditional ejidos lifestyle, forcing young Indians and campesinos from the interior to the *borderland* maquiladoras.[24] Ironically, 1994 was the year when Mexico was to blast off on the path in modernization and join the other industrialized countries of the world. Instead it was the year of armed uprisings, political crimes, and economic crisis, as well as the rise of the Mexican drug cartels. In a sense, NAFTA was a major factor in the internal migration of working-class Mexicans from the interior to the *borderland,* and later, to industrial cities such as Toluca, Leon, and Puebla.[25] By the same token, poverty and discrimination against indigenous peoples in war-torn Central American countries was the main incentive for the migration of non-Mexican Hispanics into Mexico in transit to the *borderland* in their effort to enter the United States or Canada. While the maquiladora factories provided legitimate employment, the illicit businesses such as human trafficking, drug trafficking, and prostitution flourished as well.[26]

With the advent of a flood of young, single or unaccompanied females, the sex market in the *borderland* became a draw for Mexican and American men. According to the U.S. Department of State, *Human Rights Report: Mexico,* the most vulnerable groups to be exploited are women and children, indigenous persons, and undocumented migrants.[27] Since 1993, the period corresponding with the advent of the NAFTA accord, hundreds of teens and young women have been murdered or simply disappeared in the *borderland* region surrounding Ciudad Juarez, Mexico. The youngest victims from the maquiladora work pool are age 13, three years below the minimum legal age for this type of employment in Mexico. Civil rights groups in both Mexico and the United States fault the maquiladora administrators for these abuses since they obviously do not provide adequate protection for their female workers. Clearly, the United States bears some responsibility for this problem given that 40 percent of the maquiladora factories are U.S. owned. Drug and prostitution gangs, women haters, sexual sadists, and even those trafficking in body parts have come under scrutiny for the unsolved crimes.[28]

USA'S WARS ON DRUGS AND TERRORISM

The success of *Plan Colombia,* the tens of millions of dollars spent in Colombia to curtail that country's lucrative drug enterprise, opened the drug market in Mexico. Instead of eliminating the South American drug pipeline, U.S. antidrug efforts brought it closer to the United States by bringing this problem to America's southern border. This unintended consequence resulted in a new front on the *War on Drugs* along with a new battle strategy—*Plan Mexico.* Along with these strategies came a self-fulfilling prophecy, the transformation of Mexico from a small-time drug market to that of a major trafficking route to the United States starting in the 1990s. The U.S. Drug Enforcement Administration began its formal interventions in the Mexican drug war in 1996 with *Operation Reciprocity,* which addressed the distribution of cocaine and marijuana from Mexico to major U.S. cities. A year later, *Operation META* added methamphetamine to the drug battle. In 1999, *Operation Impunity* specifically targeted the Amado Carrillo Fuentes Cartel in Ciudad Juarez and in 2000 *Operation Tar Pit* was initiated to address the black-tar heroin trade 29.

This level of cross-border drug enforcement cooperation is linked to NAFTA through the Security and Prosperity Agreement of North America component. Not only did these actions increase the level of drug operations in Mexico, it promoted increased violence along Mexico's southern border with Guatemala and other entry points for illicit drugs driven north to the United States and Canadian markets. The establishment of a border fence was a major outgrowth of Clinton's NAFTA border strategy leading to the creation of *death corridors*. As a consequence of these actions, the U.S. government makes running the border gauntlet all the more deadly.

SUMMARY OF GEO-POLITICAL IMPACT OF BORDER CONFLICTS

At the northern border, U.S. interventions into Canada contributed greatly to the formation of the independent Canada that exists today (Newfoundland was the last to join the Union, doing so in 1949), while border disputes with Mexico during its revolution at the turn of the twentieth century aided the United States in the formation of its modern military. Not only did the Punitive Expedition help modernize the U.S. Army in its transition to a mechanized military, it also led to the federalization of state militias into National Guard units. These adaptations provided a better-prepared military as the United States entered World War I. It also set the stage for the continued militarization of the U.S.-Mexico border, a situation different from the "open" U.S.-Canada border. The porous U.S.-Canada border became evident during the Vietnam War, the only modern conflict that Canada did not endorse, when it became a safe haven for "draft dodgers" and deserters with many entering Canada from Buffalo, New York via the "Peace Bridge." Neither the anti–Vietnam War exodus nor the ensuing FLQ conflict (Front de Liberation du Quebec) of the 1960s and 1970s resulted in any substantial border reinforcement along the United States' northern border.

The North American Free Trade Agreement (NAFTA) of 1994 led to a more equitable border arrangement with the three North American partners. While resisted by the indigenous Mayan Mexicans fearing a loss of their traditional collective lifestyle, NAFTA helped grow the Mexican middle class, transforming it from a Third World country to an international economic partner with its North American neighbors. An international commerce emerged linking Mexico with Canada as well as opening up other direct routes within the United States. These connections continued despite the restrictions imposed on border security following the September 11, 2001 (9/11) terrorist attacks on the United States. NAFTA seems to have benefited Mexico economically, more so than Canada, despite the increased border barriers as a consequence of the terrorist attacks on the United States in 2001. Up until the 9/11/01 terrorist attacks, the Canada/USA border was a 5,525-mile porous and poorly policed barrier between two friendly, developed nations. This was in marked contrast with the 1,933-mile US/Mexico border which had a long tradition of increased border patrols. Prior to the terrorist attacks, a July 2000 federal report by the U.S. Department of Justice Inspector General noted that fewer than 4 percent of the total Border Patrol agents were assigned to the Canada/USA border; hence 300 agents were assigned to protect this 5,525-mile border while nearly 8,000 agents were assigned to the shorter border with Mexico. The U.S./Mexico border has been fortified to some degree since the War with Mexico (1846–1848) with capacity to hold those suspected of illegal entry. Along the U.S./Canada border, on the other hand, there has never been sufficient federal detainment facilities to house those attempting illegal entry, hence most have been merely released and allowed to retreat back to Canada.

BORDER PERSPECTIVE SINCE 9/11/01

The terrorist attacks of September 11, 2001 caught the United States and Canada off guard; forcing the North Atlantic Treaty Organization (NATO) partners to take a new look at border protection. At the time of 9/11/01 the United States saw Mexico as the major contributor to both illegal immigration (human trafficking) and the illegal drug trades. This was not an unreasonable focus given that it was estimated that the illegal immigrant count in the United States at the time of 9/11/01 was five million, about 2 percent of the total U.S. population, with the vast majority of these undocumented immigrants being of Hispanic heritage, the majority being Mexican. Most of the Hispanics came through Mexico, with the exception of Haitians and Cubans, while Eastern Europeans and Asians mainly came through the U.S./Canada border, along with nearly 100,000 illegal Canadians.

The group not being scrutinized carefully was Middle Eastern Muslims who entered the United States mainly from Canada. Even following the terrorists' attacks, increased border scrutiny was focused on the U.S./Mexico border and not the more likely terrorist entry point—Canada. Nonetheless, North American border security was dominated by the United States with Canada and Mexico compelled to comply. The terrorist attacks led to the creation of a new non-Cabinet-level administrative position, that of Homeland Security Director and the Department of Homeland Security (DHS). With the creation of the Department of Homeland Security, the Wars on Drugs and Terrorism were blended.

Given that most of the drug trade came from the southern border, post-9/11 security measures focused mainly on the Mexican border, the region known as *the Borderlands*. Since the establishment of DHS, over 95 percent of those arrested entering the United States illegally are arrested coming from Mexico—*the Borderlands*. Given the economic success of NAFTA, a dual system emerged, a "Fast Track" system for NAFTA business and a militarized zone in order to combat illicit business such as drugs and human trafficking, and to filter out potential terrorists. The major impact of these efforts to better secure borders while not hindering legitimate NAFTA trade was established in January 2009 under the *Western Hemisphere Travel Initiative* (WHTI). WHTI was intended to maintain the smooth flow of trade under NAFTA, while at the same time increasing security for "others" attempting trans-border entry into the United States. Now approved NAFTA groups have access to *FAST—Free and Secure Trade Express* passage but require official passports for all others.

NOTES

1. M.C. Meyer, W.L. Sherman, & S.M. Deeds. *The Course of Mexican History*, New York, NY: Oxford University Press, 2014.
2. Ibid.
3. F. Katz. *Riot, Rebellion, and Revolution: Rural Social Conflict in Mexico.* Princeton, NJ: Princeton University Press, 1988.
4. R.E. Ruiz. *Triumphs and Tragedy: A History of the Mexican People.* New York, NY: W.W. Norton and Company, 1992.
5. Ibid.
6. E. Krauze. *Biografia del poder: caudillos de la Revolucion Mexicana (1910–1940).* Mexico City, Mexico: TusQuets Editores, 1997.
7. F. Katz, op. cit. #3.
8. F. Katz. *The Secret War in Mexico: Europe, the United States, and the Mexican Revolution.* Chicago, IL: University of Chicago Press, 1981.
9. L.A. French, & M. Manzanarez. *NAFTA & Neocolonialism: Comparative Criminal, Human & Social Justice.* Lanham, MD: University Press of America, 2004.
10. R.F. Acuna. *Occupied America: A History of Chicanos.* New York, NY: Pearson Longman, 2007.
11. L.A. French & M. Manzanarez, op. cit. #9.
12. Ibid.
13. R.F. Acuna, op. cit. #10, p. 140.
14. F. McLynn. *Villa and Zapata: A History of the Mexican Revolution.* New York, NY: Carroll and Graf Publishing, 2000; & F. Tompkins. *The Last Campaign of the U.S. Cavalry.* Harrisburg, PA: Military Service Publication Company, 1934.
15. F. Van Nuys. *Americanizing the West: Race, Immigrants, and Citizenship.* Lawrence, KS: University of Kansas Press. 2002.
16. A. De Leon. *Mexican Americans in Texas: A Brief History.* Arlington Heights, IL: Harlan Davidson, 1993.
17. O.J. Martinez. *Mexico's Uneven Development: The Geographical and Historical Context of Inequality.* New York, NY: Routledge, 2016.
18. J.R. Garcia. *Operation Wetback: The mass deportation of Mexican undocumented workers in 1954.* Westport, CT: Greenwood Press, 1980.
19. Ibid.

20. R.B. Craig. *The Bracero Program: Interest Groups and Foreign Policy.* Austin, TX: University of Texas Press, 1971.

21. A. Navarro. *The Immigration Crisis: Nativism, Armed Vigilantism, and the Rise of a Countervailing Movement.* Lanham, MD: AltaMira Press, 2008.

22. K. Fatemi. *The Maquiladora Industry: Economic Solution or Problem?* New York, NY: Praeger Press, 1990.

23. V. Bulmer-Thomas, V. Nikki Craske, & M. Serrano. *Mexico and the North American Free Trade Agreement: Who will benefit?* New York, NY: St. Martin's Press, 1994.

24. A. Khasnabish. *Zapatistas: Rebellion from the Grassroots to the Global.* Halifax, Nova Scotia, Canada: Fernwood Publishing, 2010.

25. Ibid.

26. L. French & M. Manzanarez, op. cit. #9.

27. *Human Rights Report: Mexico,* 2008.

28. L. French & M. Manzanarez, op. cit. #9.

SIX

Twentieth-Century Factors

Border Security and Migration Trends

The Spanish-American War (1898) with U.S. acquisition of Spanish colonies in the Caribbean and the Pacific; the Punitive Expedition into Mexico during the Mexican Revolution (1911–1917); and the American Expeditionary Force during World War I (1917–1918) caused further chaos in America. The United States was now the colonial power over a substantial non-White population of Hispanics, Asians, and Polynesians who now had legitimate reasons to migrate to the U.S. mainland. Moreover, the large deployment of mainly White service personnel during World War I left a gap in America's rapidly growing industrial north leading to an internal mass migration of Blacks to urban industrial centers. At the same time, Asian workers, notably Chinese, Koreans, and Filipinos, were enticed to work in dangerous occupations like mining and railroad construction while Mexican laborers were drawn to farm and ranch jobs that Whites felt were beneath their dignity. This influx of non-Whites in American society fostered immigration legislation designed to curb the influence of these racial and ethnic minorities.

THE MEXICAN REVOLUTION AND ITS AFTERMATH

The Mexican Revolution at the turn of the twentieth century changed the dynamics of border politics and immigration from Chinese exclusion to turmoil at the southern border. Anti-Diaz discontentment grew despite a much improved Mexican economy mainly because the wealthy elite, both at home and abroad, were the main benefactors. The common folks, notably the Mestizos/peons and American Indians, did not benefit from this international economy. Indeed, they suffered under Diaz's long tenure. Diaz's political apparatus developed a strong national police and army, and a strong control mechanism that continued to suppress the populace until the 1940s, creating a brutal force that continued to manipulate national elections until the twenty-first century. During his 30-year reign, Diaz set the stage for national political control reversing the decentralization efforts put in place by his predecessor, President Benito Juarez, Mexico's first indigenous leader.[1]

After three decades of abuse, Mexicans revolted over the exploitations of Mestizo and Indian peasants (peons) as well as the restrictions placed upon the new emerging middle class, many of whom felt excluded from top business and political positions. The Maderista Revolt was launched on November 10, 1910 by Francisco Madero, a member of the Mexican elite. Madero ran against Diaz in the 1910 election and was arrested but escaped to the United States. On November 10, Madero and his forces crossed into Mexico at Piedras Negras Coahuila. In reaction to the revolution, some 20,000 U.S. troops mustered at the U.S./Mexico border. The revolution also brought forth two popular revolutionary leaders, Emiliano Zapata, a Mexican Indian, and Francisco "Pancho" Villa, a Mestizo. In May 1911, Madero's forces took Ciudad Juarez, the largest city in the Borderlands separating the United States and Mexico. This victory led to the Treaty of Juarez in which Diaz agreed to resign, leaving Mexico on May 25, 1911 effectively ending his long reign and setting the stage for Madero to ascend to the presidency.[2]

Madero's tenure as president ended when he and his vice president Pino Suarez were assassinated in a coup d'état under General Victoriano Huerta in 1913. In July 1914, Huerta was forced into exile and the revolution took on new dimensions with the competing forces of Generals Venustiano Carranza and Álvaro Obregón representing the "Constitutionalists" faction against the popular forces of Generals Emiliano (Emilio) Zapata and Francisco (Pancho) Villa known as the "Conventionists." The Constitutionalists represented a strong Mexican federal government free of U.S. controls but one that maintained the status quo of a highly stratified social structure that benefitted the elite at the expense of the campesinos, Mestizos, and Indians. The Conventionists also wanted an autonomous country free from international influence, notably the United States, but with a redistribution of the land and a return to the communal village system—the *ejido*. Nonetheless, the outcome of the Mexican Revolution was greatly influenced by President Woodrow Wilson.[3]

President Theodore Roosevelt set the stage for Wilson's interference in the Mexican Revolution with his aggressive and paternalistic view of Latin America. A critical factor was Roosevelt's 1904 Corollary where he determined the right to unilaterally intervene in Caribbean and Central American affairs if outside interests attempted to influence our nation. Roosevelt's "big stick" policy was an affirmation of the Monroe Doctrine with the President using the U.S. Marine Corps as America's international police force protecting U.S. business interests in the region. Clearly, Roosevelt's "big stick" tactics in Latin America (Cuba, Nicaragua, Haiti, Dominican Republic . . .), coupled with his strong support of the Philippine-American War (1899–1901) and its occupation and colonization, promoted suspicion among Hispanics relevant to U.S./Mexico border geo-politics.[4]

A consequence of the Mexican Revolution was the mass migration of hundreds of thousands of Mexicans to the United States for protection. It is estimated that nearly 900,000 Mexicans crossed the border between 1910 and 1920. Fearing that the situation along the border could worsen, President William Howard Taft (1909–1913) ended the U.S.'s non-intervention pact with the Diaz regime in 1911, sending in a division of Buffalo Soldiers to patrol the U.S. side of the Borderlands at San Antonio, Texas. Taft's successor, President Woodrow Wilson, continued and strengthened border security under his administration. Indeed, President Wilson took an even more active military approach toward border security and Mexican politics with his paternalistic "Wilson Critique." Wilson sided with the Constitutionalists since it seemed that they would continue to protect U.S. oil, mineral, and manufacturing interests in Mexico. When Mexicans objected to Wilson's intervention in their internal affairs, the president reacted by resorting to gunboat diplomacy. Like his predecessors, Presidents Madison, Polk, and McKinley, Wilson used a minor incident to justify military intervention into Mexico, changing the dynamics of the civil war. The "Tampico Incident" involved the arrest of nine U.S. sailors from the *USS Dolphin* while ashore in the Mexican port. President Wilson's reaction was to invade and occupy Veracruz, sending U.S. Marines to occupy the port city from April to November 1914.

Interestingly, President Wilson lent his support to General Francisco (Pancho) Villa during the early years of the conflict. Villa was a successful general during the Mexican Revolution whose troops once controlled all of Mexico north of Mexico City. Villa was a leading general under Carranza and the Constitutionalists and was popular in the United States when his forces seized the northern Mexican cities of Chihuahua and Juarez when battling Huerta's forces which the U.S. felt were being backed by Germany. Villa's attack on Ojinaga in January 1914 forced Huerta to cross over to the United States and surrender to the U.S. Army to avoid a greater defeat at the hands of Villa. Now the United States was responsible for a 5,000-strong Mexican force including 1,000 women, 500 children, and some 3,000 horses and mules being held at Fort Bliss in El Paso, Texas. Huerta's force was later transferred to Fort Wingate in New Mexico near the Navajo Nation. The victory at Ojinaga gave Villa control over northern Mexico including the entire U.S./Mexico border.[5]

Villa fell out with Carranza, which led to his loss of U.S. support. Villa's forces were now fighting Carranzitas under General Álvaro

Obregón who was aided by the U.S. military along the border. In April 1915, during the battle of Matamoros, the U.S. allowed Obregón's forces to seek shelter across the border in Brownsville, Texas while stopping Villa's forces at the border. Brigadier General John "Black Jack" Pershing and his Buffalo Soldiers played a major role in policing the border now that the United States took an active role in the revolution, first by aiding the Carranziatas in 1914 and then formally recognizing the Carranza regime as the de facto leaders of Mexico on October 9, 1915. Wilson's recognition of Carranza over Villa was seen as a means for ending the war in Mexico, which the U.S. felt was being fueled by outside forces, notably Germany which was attempting to draw America into the Mexican Revolution hence diminishing the likelihood of the U.S. joining the Allies in the on-going war in Europe—WWI. Evidence of this scenario was the Zimmermann communiqué of May 3, 1916.[6]

General Villa reacted to the U.S. changing sides in the civil war by his daring raid on the U.S. Army base in Columbus, New Mexico on March 9, 1916. This act did more to prepare the United States for its eventual involvement in the First World War than any other event in that it resulted in the unilateral 11-month Punitive Expedition into Mexico in pursuit of General Villa and his army. While Villa managed to escape capture by either the Americans or Carranza's forces, the Expedition transformed the U.S. military from the nineteenth-century horse-based Army to a mechanized force. It also federalized the state militias, known as the National Guard, into a coherent military force. This was the first time that the National Guard was utilized as part of U.S. border protection. Two National Guard units, the First New Mexico Infantry National Guard and the Second Massachusetts Infantry National Guard were among the federalized forces mustered for a supportive role during the Punitive Expedition. Barred from being used as a federal force within the United States by the Posse Comitatus Act, the National Guard units remained on the U.S. side of the border while the U.S. Army carried on the hunt for General Villa.

The Posse Comitatus Act, aka "Knott Amendment," was enacted in 1878 and signed into law by President Rutherford B. Hayes (1877–1881) as part of a deal between Republicans and Southern Democrats to allow Hayes to become president in exchange for removing the federal military as an occupation force in the defeated Confederacy protecting the newly gained civil rights of Blacks. Essentially, the Knott Amendment transferred federal civil protection for Blacks to state authority, hence endorsing the Jim Crow era along with its vigilante force, the Ku Klux Klan. The exception for federal military intervention in domestic affairs was the declaration of martial law. This restriction did not pertain to Indian Country given that the United States was at war with the tribes. Aiding Wilson's use of the military along the border was the fact that the Militia Act of 1903 determined that the various state and territorial militias were to serve as the primary organized reserve force for the U.S. Army, leading to the change from "State Militias" to the State National Guard which could now be federalized in times of crises allowing for the federalization of some 75,000 Guard members by President Wilson for border protection in support for the Punitive Expedition. This provided the prototype for the mass mustering of National Guard units for service in the First World War as part of the Expeditionary Forces under General Pershing.[7]

Wilson's war against General Villa into Mexico did much to demonize the Mexicans in the eyes of the American public. The Mexican Revolution also emboldened Mexicans residing on both sides of the borderland in Texas in 1915 to attempt to take back lands they felt were stolen from them by Anglo ranchers. U.S. interventions and interference in the Mexican Revolution helped precipitate the *Plan de San Diego,* a short-lived rebellion by a small radical element of Mexican revolutionaries attempting to regain territory lost to the United States since the end of the War with Mexico in 1838. While not endorsed by either the Constitutionalists or the Conventionists these radicals engaged in some 30 cross-border raids resulting in 21 U.S. (Anglo) deaths.

The race-based reaction by the Texas Rangers and local sheriffs resulted in a brutal reign of terror against all Texans of Hispanic descent, the Tejanos, notably Mestizos, as described by Benjamin Heber Johnson:

> Tejanos paid a high price for the newfound united state of Anglo south Texans. . . . Those suspected of joining or supporting the raiders constituted the most obvious of targets, as they had from the uprising's beginning. Ethnic Mexican suspects were lynched after nearly every major raid in 1915. Shortly after the attack on the Norias ranch house, for example, unknown assailants killed three Tejanos . . . presumably for suspicion of aiding or participating in the attack. The Texas Rangers who had arrived after the fight might have been responsible. In any event, the Rangers' actions encouraged such measures: the next morning, they posed with their lassos around three corpses, and the picture soon circulated as a postcard.[8]

U.S. soldiers were not permitted to summarily execute their prisoners and some acted to prevent the slaughter of anyone thought to be Mexican. Yet, some, like Lieutenant George S. Patton of World War II fame, apparently took delight in trophy killings: " . . . flamboyant young cavalryman George S. Patton would make a name for himself chasing Villistas south of the Rio Grande . . . bring(ing) three corpse back, tied to the hood of his car like hunting trophies to present to (General) Pershing."[9] Nonetheless, some soldiers turned Mexican or Tejanos (Texans of Mexican descent) suspects over to local sheriffs or the Texas Rangers knowing that they would execute them without trial. One practice of the Texas Rangers was to leave the bodies of those they hanged for public display often with empty beer bottles stuffed in their mouths. So feared were the Rangers that relatives did not dare cut down the bodies for a decent burial. The summary execution of Mexicans and/or Tejanos, without trials or due process, by the Texan Rangers and local sheriffs is estimated to be as high as 1,500. U.S. Army scout Virgil Lott noted: "How many lives were lost can not be estimated fairly for hundreds of Mexicans were killed who had no part in the uprising, their bodies concealed in the thick underbrush and no report ever made by the perpetrators of these crimes."[10]

The reign of terror at the hands of Texas lawmen in south Texas resulted in many Tejanos fleeing into Mexico despite having historical roots in what was now the United States. Ostensibly, this was the latent intention of the Anglo ranchers using the cross-border raids as a mere pretense for cleansing south Texas of Tejanos. Robert Kleberg, manager of the vast King Ranch, wanted martial law enforced in south Texas with Mexicans and Tejanos rounded up and placed in concentration camps. During this purge, the King Ranch increased its holdings from 500,000 acres to over one million acres, much of the land stolen from Mexican and Tejanos owners. The King Ranch, like its counterparts, was run, much like post–Civil War southern plantations, with sharecropper labor where the former Hispanic owners were kept as subservient laborers indebted to the "company store." Toward this end, the Texas Rangers and county sheriffs acted as the King Ranch's private police force. An unintended outcome of the reign of terror was the awakening of the Mexican-Americans and the beginning of political and social organizations such as the League of United Latin American Citizens (LULAC).[11]

Angry with President Wilson's change of allegiance in the Mexican Revolution and the harsh treatment of Mexican prisoners and civilians along the borderland, General Villa with a force of 485 men made an early morning raid on the 13th U.S. Cavalry at Camp Furlong near Columbus, New Mexico on March 9, 1916. Being only the second time the U.S. had been attacked by a foreign military force (since Washington, D.C. was burned during the War of 1812), the raid had a dramatic effect on U.S./Mexican relations due to its audacity. The raid killed 10 enlisted U.S. soldiers and eight civilians in Columbus. The aftermath of the raid had far more devastating consequences for both Mexicans and Mexican Americans with a reign of terror much like that occurring in Texas during the Plan de San Diego raids with over 100 Mexican civilians killed during the immediate "hot pursuit" carried out by Major Frank Tompkins. President Wilson's reaction was to unilaterally declare a mini-war against Villa by authorizing a force of some 12,000 U.S. military personnel during the 11-month Punitive Expedition.[12]

Now the U.S. military joined its civilian law enforcement counterparts in the reign of terror perpetrated against anyone Mexican. The treatment of alleged Villa soldiers did not follow the established prisoner of war protocol which Mexican forces adhered to regarding U.S. POWs. In the Columbus, N.M. raid, seven Mexican soldiers were captured, tried in civilian courts, and sentenced to death by hanging. Racial sentiments played a major role here as they did in south Texas. With anti-Mexican sentiments running high in New Mexico, the Deming, N.M. courts labeled the captured prisoners bandits instead of POWs. Another 19 of Villa's troops were captured by General Pershing's forces in Mexico, and they were also charged with murder and tried in civilian courts instead of following military justice protocol. Six Mexican soldiers were hanged in June 1916 while six of the seven men captured in the Columbus raid eventually received full pardons from the governor of New Mexico in November 1920. The governor's decision to pardon these men following harsh incarceration conditions was influenced by the 1907 Hague Convention concerning the laws and customs of war on land. These rules were adopted in response to the brutal treatment of the Dutch Boers by the British in South Africa during the Boer War (1899–1902) and the atrocities attributed to U.S. occupation troops in the Philippines in the aftermath of the Spanish American War. However, once pardoned, the Villa POWs were rearrested by the Luna County sheriff and again charged with murder, convicted by an Anglo jury and were again sentenced to prison in blatant violation of the U.S. Constitutional guarantee against double jeopardy.[13]

Wilson's support for Carrranza, while abandoning Villa, was not satisfactory in that concessions were made to the Conventionists in the 1917 Mexican Constitution that threatened U.S. business interests in the country. Nonetheless, U.S. recognition of the Mexican government was paramount and an obvious condition was the assassination of retired General Villa in 1923, an event that occurred during the Harding administration (1921–1923). Even then U.S. businesses, notably the petroleum industry, wanted the U.S. military to again intervene into Mexico to protect their interests. This diplomatic crisis was finally resolved by the Bucareli Conference in August 1923 when President Calvin Coolidge (1923–1929) departed from Wilson's unilateral intervention policies along with acceptance of the 1917 Constitution and its election process, regardless of how distasteful to U.S. business interests.

BETWEEN THE WORLD WARS: EUGENICS AND THE SEEDS OF ETHNIC PURIFICATION

World War I saw massive in-country migration of African Americans from their impoverished sharecropper conditions to the industrialized centers of the North, leading to the creation of massive urban ghettos alongside those created by the massive influx of White immigrants from eastern and southern Europe as well as French Canadians fleeing the punitive draft policies in Canada. This complex shift in demographics gave rise to a WASP (White Anglo-Saxon Protestant) backlash leading to both the eugenics movement and the rigid racial caste system in the Jim Crow South. The Great Depression also witnessed the migration of poor whites from the "dust bowl" regions of the Midwest to California further agitating the already fragile race relations between Anglos and those of color (Asians, Hispanics, Blacks, American Indians). An outcome of these demographic changes was passage of ethnic-based immigration laws designed to preserve the ethnic purity of America in the guise of legislating morality. Prohibition was a prime example of this political process followed by the promotion of White supremacy via the eugenics movement.

The combination of the economic devastation of the Great Depression and Prohibition along with the influences of the Bolshevik revolution in Russia led to the call for a stronger federal law enforcement presence leading to the birth of the Federal Bureau of Investigation (FBI). Both fears concerning communism and greater union membership such as the Industrial Workers of the World (IWW) sent fears throughout capitalist countries, including the United States. Moreover, many recent immigrants, notably those situated in urban ghetto clusters, resisted President Wilson's call to arms and openly defied the draft, joining the French Canadians fleeing south to avoid England's call to arms. A struggling Bureau of Investigation under the U.S. Attorney General's Office was overwhelmed and the vacuum was quickly filled by a special capitalist-led vigilante movement, the *American Protective League* (APL).[14]

The Bureau of Investigation's ranks of a few hundred men paled in comparison to the APL's membership comprised of hundreds of thousands of WASP operatives. This was the environment when J. Edgar Hoover took charge of the Bureau of Investigation and the investigation of both the May 1917 Selective Service Act (draft) and the May 1918 Sedition Act. One of his responsibilities was to catch enemy aliens. In doing so, Hoover put together a task force composed of local law enforcement agencies, APL operatives, National Guard units, and his Bureau of Investigation (becoming the FBI in 1935). On September 3, 1917, Hoover conducted a three-day raid in a multistate dragnet seeking draft dodgers and aliens resulting in some 50,000 arrests, leading to some of the first criticisms of J. Edgar Hoover and his extra-legal tactics.

Congressional criticism led to an investigation into Hoover's actions with a major declaration that vigilantism had no place in legitimate law enforcement, leading to the APL bring disbanded in February 1919. A contributing factor was the 1917 lynching of Frank Little in Butte, Montana. Little was a member of the IWW Executive Committee and was a leader in the mining dispute for better wages and working conditions. He was lynched by APL operatives despite the presence of federal troops who were deployed as "strike breakers" for the mining industry. This embarrassment led to the eventual end of the APL. Many former members of the APL now joined the Ku Klux Klan, an organization that received recognition from none other than President Wilson.[15]

The Great Depression fueled social unrest and conflict between the corporate elite and the often struggling working class forcing lawmakers to reexamine their laissez-faire support of big business and provide laws that improved the lives of the working class, many of these changes occurring during the administration of Franklin D. Roosevelt (1933–1945). The Dust Bowl migration from Oklahoma to California and the creation of federal relief for the unemployed, the Civilian Conservation Corps (CCC) and Works Project Administration (WPA), were prime examples of federal intervention into areas once the exclusive domain of corporate America. The National Labor Relations Act (Wagner Act) of 1935 represented the turning point for workers' protection including their right to organize and engage in collective bargaining, a far cry from the use of the National Guard and U.S. Army as strike breakers. The Social Security Act and Public Contracts Act (Walsh-Healey Act) followed, providing labor standards and setting minimum wages and overtime pay as well as child labor and safety provisions. Roosevelt and Congress also provided standards that checked exploitation during the Second World War such as the War Labor Dispute Act (Smith-Connally Act) that authorized federal plant seizures if industry did not comply with fair employment practices. These standards provided the smooth transition from the Depression economy to the thriving war production period of the 1940s.[16]

Ironically, these mass migrations and immigration movement facilitated America's transition from a rural to an industrial nation during the late nineteenth and early twentieth centuries. It also fueled its not so latent racist and sectarian bias, bringing these seething sentiments to the forefront in a renewed wave of White Supremacy. These sentiments and actions were no longer restricted to "poor Whites" who felt that people of color were undeservingly taking their jobs. The White Supremacy movement was now endorsed not only by U.S. presidents like Woodrow Wilson but by the White elite in their endorsement of the eugenics movement. The American Eugenics Movement became prominent at the turn of the twentieth century coinciding with the massive migration north of freedmen and the influx of non-Protestant immigrants from southern and eastern Europe.

Eugenics is defined as the study of hereditary improvement of the human race through selective breeding, a concept put forth by British psychologists Sir Francis Galton, a cousin of Charles Darwin. Galton coined the term eugenics as a method of achieving what he termed *Social Darwinism*—a social experiment designed to produce a highly gifted White race. His theory gained strong support in the United States where the concept of White supremacy dates back to the Puritans and the long-held concept of Manifest Destiny—the belief that White Protestant males were predestined by God to be superior to all others.[17]

Eugenics and racism are closely associated, providing a seemingly objective rationale for social discrimination under the guise of "intelligence testing" to determine "feeble minded" individuals. The flaw in this theory is that White Protestant men determined human suitability, even creating their own classification system of feeble-mindedness: Idiot, Imbecile, and Moron. Elitist blindness soon found many candidates for sterilization among people of color and sectarian ethnics, notably Jews, fueling negative stereotypes of hatred and anti-Semitism within American society. The eugenics movement gained support within America's White elite leaders including those in academia. Indeed, the White elite in American society found a champion for their cause at Stanford University with psychologist Lewis M. Terman.

Terman was influenced by his mentor, Francis Galton, who was considered to be the founder of "scientific psychology" setting the stage for objective measures determining a human classification continuum relevant to social Darwinism. The advent of psychological testing in measuring intelligence, while new, was seen as the predictive factor in determining social suitability, hence a critical factor in the selection of involuntary sterilization in order to cleanse society of its undesirables and allowing for a superior human gene pool. It was Lewis Terman who provided the seemingly objective measure of determining who was unfit. He was confident that his version of the 1908 French Binet-Simon test would accurately weed out the genetically deficient members of American society, those he labeled as being the "serious deviant." Terman joined his fellow academicians and White elite in using his test, the 1916 *Stanford-Binet,* to determine those slated for either life-long institutionalization or forced sterilization, or both. The main problem with his "scientific norm" with which to determine those of inferior status was that it consisted of the upper-middle-class White faculty and families of Stanford University. Teman describes his methodological epistemology in the *Stanford-Binet* test introduction:

> It is safe to predict that in the near future intelligence tests will bring tens of thousands of these high-grade defectives [morons] under the surveillance and protection of society. This will ultimately result in curtailing the reproduction of feeble-mindedness and in the elimination of an enormous amount of crime, pauperism, and industrial inefficiency. . . . Not all criminals are feeble-minded, but all feeble-minded are at least potential criminals. That every feeble-minded woman is a potential prostitute would hardly be disputed by anyone. . . . Considering the tremendous cost of vice and crime . . . it is evident that psychological testing has found here one of its richest applications.[18]

Terman's work coincided with the mass testing of American servicemen during the First World War where he and other American psychologists comprised a Committee on the Psychological Examination of Recruits, chaired by the then president of the American Psychological Association (APA), Robert Yerkes. What resulted was the development of two alternative tests, one for literate recruits (Army Alpha) and one for those deemed illiterate (in English)—the Army Beta test. Both used the new metric of intelligence, the *Intelligence Quotient* (IQ), initially utilizing the "ratio IQ" formula and later the "deviation IQ" format (with a standard deviation of 16 for the Stanford-Binet and 15 on later tests where the norm is 100). Yerkes, Terman, and the Committee described the objectives of the Army Alpha and Beta testing:

> The purposes of psychological testing are (a) to aid in segregating the mentally incompetent, (b) to classify men according to their mental capacity, (c) to assist in selecting competent men for responsible positions. . . . The success of this work in a large series of observations, some five thousand officers and eighty thousand men, makes it reasonably certain that similar results may be expected if the system be extended to include the entire enlisted and drafted personnel and all newly appointed officers.[19]

Now there was so-called scientific evidence of the inferiority of minorities and poor Whites in that they scored well below their better-educated White counterparts. A major flaw of these early IQ tests was that they only measured one's *verbal IQ*, one biased by the standard of the educated elite. It was not until 1939 and the introduction of the *performance IQ* subtests that a more realistic measure of *general intelligence* could be ascertained. The Wechsler-Bellevue scale and subsequent adaptations measured both the verbal and performance IQ leading to a general IQ. This method was introduced into the new Army General Classification Test (GCT) used during the Second World War and beyond.[20]

Yet, psychologists could not undo the damage already caused by the mass testing and classification of Americans using these inadequate "scientific" measures. Nonetheless, Terman and Yerkes were in good company with the eugenics movement joined by the Carnegie Institution, Rockefeller Foundation, Harriman Rails, Kellogg, Harvard University and other elite universities, and even the Smithsonian Institution, the National Geographic Society, and the U.S. Bureau of Ethnology. So strong was the eugenics movement and the effort to purify American society that by 1926, twenty-three states had enacted compulsory sterilization laws with the U.S. Supreme Court condoning these practices in its 1927 *Buck v. Bell* decision. The extremes of eugenics by Nazi Germany helped tone down the ethnic purification furor within the general public, but the practice continued in both state and federal programs until the 1970s with Blacks and American Indians the main targets.[21]

The sanctioning of eugenics and its basic theme of White supremacy served to embolden racism and the legitimatization of segregation in all aspects of society and human life, a process that institutionalized discrimination including in education, hence creating a self-perpetuating and self-fulfilling prophecy of White superiority and minority inferiority. The harsh reality of segregation was that it legitimized violence in the form of vigilantism and riots, including lynching and massacres. Lynching became a public spectacle in the South while the destruction of Black, Asian, and Hispanic communities by White vigilante groups carried on with impunity setting the stage for the Civil Rights movement in the 1960s and 1970s. It took a number of high-profile federal court cases to highlight the process of institutionalized discrimination in the United States via its public educational system—the major socialization agent second only to the family. While the long process of adjudication began in earnest in 1945 with the Hispanic challenge to segregated schools in Texas in *Mendez v. Westminster School District* it took the 1954 U.S. Supreme Court decision regarding segregation in Kansas schools, *Brown v. Board of Education,* to articulate this process of instituting shared psychological boundaries that provided the basis of America's racism.[22]

While Thurgood Marshall and the NAACP played a role in both cases, it was the work of Black psychologists Kenneth and Mamie Clark who unraveled the psychological underpinnings of institutional racism perpetrated through school segregation, a process that instilled racial inferiority not only among Whites but among Blacks and other minority groups as well. In their classic study, Kenneth and Mamie Clark devised their famous "doll test" whereby they presented young children with four identical dolls (Black male, White male, Black female, White female) asking them to indicate which doll was "best" and was "nice," which was "bad," and which would they prefer to play with. Regardless of race, a statistically significant number of the children rejected the Black dolls, instead preferring the White dolls. This was the study presented to the U.S. Supreme Court as proof that segregation had the intent, latent or manifest, to foster and maintain a racial self-fulfilling prophecy throughout the United States. The Clarks demonstrated that there are psychological borders associated with institutionalized racism such as slavery, indentured servitude, and segregation.[23]

A host of immigration laws emerged in the first half of the twentieth century, further highlighting the racial, ethnic, and sectarian divides within the country and efforts to manage the influx of "outsiders" to America. John Isbister noted that some 15 million immigrants entered the United States from the time of the War with Mexico and Reconstruction (1840–1870), the time of U.S. expansion and transitioning from a rural society to the mills of New England. These were the Irish, Scot-Irish, French Canadians, and Germans, as well as Mexicans and Asians. The next wave of immigrants, those entering the United States between 1880 until the borders closed during the Great Depression in 1930 equaled some 25 million people with many now from southern and eastern Europe—Poles, Italians, Russians, Greeks, Austro-Hungarians—those who were either Catholic or Jewish. It was a reaction to this wave that led to exclusionary legislation in 1882.[24] The immigration situation for Mexican migrants between the World Wars was spurred either by the harsh repercussions associated with the Plan de San Diego or the hostilities generated by the Mexican Revolution. Most of this movement involved the Borderland region along the U.S. southern border and, for the most part, considered to be transitory until the situation was resolved in Mexico. But the situation in the United States at the time of the male workforce drain was due mainly to the draft during the First World War. This coupled with both the newly enforced restrictions on Asian immigrants and the rapid economic growth in the U.S. led to a labor shortage in the areas of mining, railroads, and agriculture, opening these jobs to Mexican men. The agricultural demands in Texas, New Mexico, and California led to a black market of smuggled laborers from Mexico leading to a more favorable and formal process known as the Bracero Program, setting the stage for the migrant workers program initiated during the Second World War when, again, the draft created a major shortage of available men in the workforce. Indeed, Van Nuys estimates that 10 percent of the Mexican population fled to the United States during the Mexican Revolution, enriching the borderland region by at least a million immigrants. These conditions, plus the prevailing stereotype of the Mexican peons as docile, ignorant, hard workers who were well suited for harsh desert conditions of the West, coupled with the distrust of Asians at the time, led to the special waiver provisions of the restrictions of the Immigration Act of 1917, eliminating the literacy test, registration fee (head tax), and contract labor provisions for Mexican workers from May 1917 until March 1921.[25]

De Leon, in his work *Mexican Americans in Texas,* claims that over a half-million Mexican workers entered Texas alone during the first three decades of the twentieth century. These migration waves occurred following the end of U.S. military intervention during the Mexican Revolution, a time when the U.S./Mexico border was unpoliced much like the U.S./Canada border. When the U.S. Border Patrol was established in 1924 its main function was enforcing customs laws directed against Asians as well as enforcing Prohibition smuggling laws, a function that involved both the Mexican/U.S. and U.S./Canada borders. De Leon noted that while most of these migrant workers stayed within the traditional boundaries of Old Mexico before U.S. acquisition, negative stereotypes emerged with racist overtones, like *wetbacks*, and *greasers,* reflecting the anti-Mexican racial sentiments of the Anglos who now occupied their former homeland. This stereotype fueled the "Mexican Problem" where Mexicans were now seen as a degenerate people posing moral and political dangers to the United States, notably the border states.[26]

Clearly, the early U.S. immigration laws were directed toward Asians in general with particular focus on the Chinese. As noted above, the literacy requirement of the 1917 Immigration Act did not apply to Mexican migrants at the time. Indeed, the U.S./Canada border played a greater role in attempts to curtail Chinese immigrants entering the U.S. by circumventing Angel Island scrutiny. The 1893 "Canadian Agreement" allowed American customs agents to screen people, notably Asians, attempting to enter the United States prior to their departure on Canadian transportation. This agreement allowed U.S. immigration inspectors to be stationed at major Canadian ports of entry. This procedure continued into the Prohibition (1919–1933) era when Canada was a prime resource for illicit liquor under the Volstead Act. Subsequent immigration legislation also targeted the mass influx of Europeans as well. Nonetheless, there was a marked difference between the East Coast entry point at Ellis Island in the New York/New Jersey harbor and that of Angel Island Immigration Station in the San Francisco Bay. Angel Island operated from January 1910 until November 1940 on the eve of America's involvement in the Second World War. During its years of operation, Angel Island held hundreds of thousands of immigrants from China, Japan, the Philippines, India, and even Mexico. The largest island in San Francisco Bay, Angel Island was fortified soon after its acquisition from Mexico following the conclusion of the War with Mexico (1846–1848). It served as a military garrison during the U.S. Civil War and was used to process Asian immigrants even in the late nineteenth century.

However, it soon became clear that a more substantial processing center was needed, especially when the rising anti-Chinese sentiments began to surface along the West Coast. Hence, construction on the "Ellis Island of the West" began in 1905 and was completed in January 1910. The 1917 Immigration Act, with its "Asiatic Barred Zone," was seen as a filter to weed out undesirable Chinese (male laborers and females labeled as "prostitutes") attempting to enter the United States, with entry now greatly restricted to acceptable merchants, clergy, diplomats, and educators. Filipinos were more likely to be allowed to enter given their status as de facto territorial (colonial) wards of the United States subsequent to America's acquisition of the Philippines from Spain following the Spanish American War. Japanese immigrants were curtailed by the 1907 "Gentlemen's Agreement." The interrogation process for Europeans at Ellis Island and that for Asians at Angel Island differed greatly. While immigrants at Ellis Island were processed within a few days, Asians were often detained for months with many applications rejected. Changes for Europeans occurred in 1921, when Congress passed the Emergency Quota Act (Johnson Act) which was the first federal law restricting immigration from Europe. This was due to the influx of non-Protestants from southern and eastern European countries where many were Catholics or Jews. The law provided quotas based on 3 percent of the total number of immigrants per country already residing in the United States based on the 1910 U.S. census. Given the overwhelming proportion of Americans of western and northern European descent, the quota law had little effect on them while it greatly restricted the influx of those from southern and eastern Europe.[27]

Three years following the Emergency Quota Act, Congress passed the Immigration Act of 1924 further reducing the proportion of Europeans allowed into America while completely excluding Asian immigrants. The European quota was lowered to 2 percent of the group's representation within U.S. society according to an even earlier census—that of 1890 which predated the great influx indicated in the 1910 census. The 1924 Immigration Act excluded entry of any alien who by virtue of their race or nationality was deemed ineligible for U.S. citizenship. This provision, in effect, expanded the Asian Barred Zone to now include Japanese in violation of the 1907 Gentlemen's Agreement setting the stage for bitter relations between the United States and Japan which would erupt in hostilities 17 years later. Ironically, American Indians were officially recognized as federal citizens that same year, while Virginia passed its Racial Integrity Act further enforcing the anti-Black caste system that dominated the Jim Crow segregation in the Southern states. The total effect of the 1924 Immigration Act (Johnson-Reed Act) was to actually increase quotas for the British Isles and western Europe at the expense of southern and eastern Europe and Asians.[28]

Japanese immigrants came decades after the Chinese beginning in the 1880s, coinciding with the mass European migration from southern and eastern Europe, with the Japanese coming to Angel Island and not Ellis Island. The 1924 National Origins Act banned any future immigration of Japanese. This was seen by Japan as an "anti-Japanese" act in blatant violation of the 1907 "Gentlemen's Agreement" allowing for a bilateral resolution to the number of Japanese entering the United States. The anti-Japanese sentiments peaked on February 19, 1942, during the early years of America's entry into the Second World War, with President Franklin D. Roosevelt's Executive Order 9066 authorizing the mass incarceration of some 120,000 West Coast Japanese. This was seen as a preventive intervention stemming from the unfounded fear that people of Japanese descent would rise up to assist Japan in any attack on the United States. Japanese were classified at this time as immediate immigrants as *Issei* and *Nisei* was the term denoting first-generation Japanese born in the United States, while *Kibei* was the term assigned to those Japanese born in the United States but who went back to Japan for their education and then returned.

The forced internment of Japanese residing on the West Coast was similar to the forced removal of Indian tribes during the nineteenth century. Another parallel with the removal of American Indians was the pervasive negativity associated with a race and culture that departed from the majority U.S. society. There was little public outcry against Japanese internment, especially with the mass hysteria associated with the attack on Pearl Harbor and the Philippines in December 1941, forcing America's entry into the Second World War. Nonetheless, Sandra Taylor noted that negative stereotypes predated the December attacks:

> Hostility against the Japanese community was deeply rooted in racism. The Issei were denied the right of naturalization, the last group of immigrants who were discriminated against in this manner. In 1913, they were also refused the right to purchase land, based on their resident alien status, although many circumvented the law by putting the land in the name of their citizen children. Most white Americans had little to do with them, believing they were "too different" and unassimilable. . . . When Pearl Harbor was attacked on December 7, 1941, the Issei feared the worst, but assumed their children would be safe because of their citizenship. The Federal Bureau of Investigation (FBI) had already compiled a list of West Coast aliens considered dangerous, primarily community leaders—Buddhist priests, newspaper editors, Japanese language teachers, and the like. They were seized immediately and imprisoned in remote places in Montana and North Dakota. Neither they nor their families knew where they were taken. More than a month passed before the federal government, prodded by racist military leaders on the West Coast such as Colonel Karl Bendetsen and Lieutenant General John DeWitt, convinced President Franklin Roosevelt that all Japanese Americans should be removed.[29]

Japanese Americans were interned in ten concentration camps located at Poston and Gila Bend, Arizona; Jerome and Rohwer, Arkansas; Minidoka, Idaho; Tule Lake and Manzana, California; Topaz, Utah; Granada, Colorado; and Heart Mountain, Wyoming. From March through May 1942, Japanese Americans, including those with as little as one-sixteenth Japanese blood and foster children brought up in Caucasian families, were given a week to 10 days to prepare for internment with bedrolls and no more baggage than they could carry. As in Indian removal, the U.S. Army moved them to assembly centers located in converted livestock facilities and stadiums throughout the West. The camps were shoddily built and encircled by barbed wire with armed watchtowers manned by guards instructed to shoot anyone attempting to leave. Executive Order 9066 effectively installed martial law over those interned who had no constitutional recourse offered other Americans including habeas corpus writs. Ironically, while 120,000 West Coast Japanese Americans were interned, only about 1,000 of their counterparts in Hawaii were interned; this in a territory where they made up over one-third of the Islands' population. Even then, Hawaii, surrounding U.S. territories, and the Aleutian Islands of Alaska Territory were placed under martial law for the war's duration (some of the Aleutian Islands were briefly occupied by Japanese forces). In 1944, the U.S. Supreme Court validated President Roosevelt's Executive Order.[30]

EISENHOWER-ERA CONSERVATISM—COLD WAR PARANOIA AND ENSUING RACISM

On the surface the nationalist politics of the Trump administration appear to be a unique phenomenon in recent American history. It is not. A similar set of circumstances occurred over sixty years ago during the Eisenhower administration, providing a precedent for the current policies. Both administrations witnessed a marked turn toward the conservative political right as a reaction to a perceived national threat, real or imagined. In both situations, the curtailment of rights, especially that directed toward politically-defined "undesirable immigrants" and other "enemies" of the public, was enacted and justified under the pretense of "homeland security." A major difference, however, is that Canada was seen as America's staunchest ally during the Eisenhower era with the North American Air Defense (NORAD) agreement. President Donald Trump, on the other hand, has declared Canada to be a threat to the USA's security, hence his justification for unilateral tariffs on critical trade items. Currently, U.S. security is complicated by two concurrent security issues—the War on Drugs and the International War on Terrorism. During the Eisenhower era, the threat emerged from the paranoia associated with the Cold War and the incipient spread of Communism not only in the United States but through the Americas—the U.S.'s self-acclaimed domain defined under the Monroe Doctrine. These actions during the Eisenhower years actually contributed to the troubles in Central America that plagues the United States today with migrants attempting to escape violence initiated in their countries by the Central Intelligence Agency (CIA). Then, as today, the U.S. president was a Republican supported by a Republican majority in Congress (House of Representatives and U.S. Senate). The conservative influence also resulted in the diminishing of America's long-held secular stance when "under God" was added to the Pledge of Allegiance and was required at the beginning of every public school day. The 84th Congress also passed a Joint Resolution stating that the statement "In God we Trust" be placed on all U.S. currency. Moreover, public personnel, including schoolteachers, were compelled to take an anti-Communism, loyalty oath. The divisions within U.S. society were not as defined during the Eisenhower administration as they are today but were simmering, only to emerge as major civil disorder during the 1960s and 1970s. History is often repeated so it is important to look at the Eisenhower precedent in order to project to likely outcomes from the current Trump administration.

Operation Wetback: Operation Wetback emerged during the conservative anti-Communism era following the Second World War when the major Communist powers—the Soviet Union, dominated by Russia, and Red China—were vying with Western democracies for new converts among Third World non-aligned nations. Mexico and most of Central

America and the Caribbean islands were deemed potential candidates for Communist influences, especially among the mostly impoverished natives made up of American Indians and Mestizos (mixed Anglo/Indian). Mexico, with its high proportion of Indian blood among the vast majority of its citizens, notably the lower classes, was easily exploited and scapegoated by American agricultural and mining interests. Following the Second World War and the Korean Conflict, returning GIs (military veterans) needed the jobs that were occupied by U.S. Blacks, and Hispanics, including seasonal workers from Mexico.[31] The idea of using the U.S. military to enforce border security with Mexico surfaced during this time. First the U.S. government attempted to unilaterally militarize its border with Mexico in what became Operation Cloudburst. The harsh treatment of Mexican laborers and others attempting to enter the United States for work at the hands of the U.S. military (beatings, having their heads shaved . . .) was reported in both the American and Mexican press forcing the U.S. to soften its attempts at militarizing its southern border.[32] The United States realized that for any increased border security measure to work, it had to have the tacit acceptance of the Mexican government. Hence the birth of Operation Wetback, a scheme that replaced active U.S. military personnel with retired "civilian" Army generals like General Joseph M. (Jumping Joe) Swing. Swing, recently retired from the U.S. Army, was a classmate of President Eisenhower at West Point, and was part of General Pershing's Punitive Expedition into Mexico in 1917 in pursuit of General Pancho Villa where serious atrocities were committed by the U.S. military. Eisenhower appointed Swing Commissioner of Immigration in 1954 and placed him in charge of Operation Wetback where he had a blank check to conduct military-type tactics against undocumented Mexicans working in the United States. Swing's authority superseded that of the Border Patrol, which was thought to be too political at the time.

As an effort to neutralize the influences U.S. business and agriculture interests held along the Mexican border, General Swing had Border Patrol agents transferred from the southern border to the northern border with Canada thus neutralizing the influence of politicians in Arizona, California, and Texas interfering in Operation Wetback. Swing then added two fellow retired Army generals to his staff—Frank Pattridge and Edwin Howard. Now the border patrol system was consolidated into four districts with the southwest region along the U.S./Mexico border under the command of Operation Wetback. The military influence greatly improved border patrol operations creating direct communication networks, uniform data collection, and coordinated action within each section. This was the first time that federal, state, and local agents worked in concert greatly facilitating the extra-legal removal of Mexicans via massive airlifts, buslifts, trainlifts, and boatlifts for the purpose of transporting captured Mexicans not only away from the border but deep into its interior making return attempts difficult. Another innovation of Operation Wetback was the use of dogs to pursue targeted Mexicans. Indeed, this multifaceted approach toward rapid response, coupled with quick deportation, used yet another recent military innovation, that of air-to-ground and vehicle-to-vehicle communication networks setting the stage for the system still employed today in law enforcement. It also established the 100-mile entrapment radius for Border Patrol and other Immigration personnel.

While short-lived and expensive, Operation Wetback set the stage for future border-enforcement endeavors. It significantly changed the border patrol while soliciting cooperation with the Mexican government in the control of undocumented Mexican workers. In the two-month life of Operation Wetback some one million undocumented Mexican workers were deported, most from California and Texas. In addition to the fear and harm generated among Mexican and Mexican American workers was the demonization of Mexicans as subhuman, despicable characters who were prone to crime and violence. This campaign of fear-mongering generated by Operation Wetback forced many U.S. Hispanics of Mexican heritage to prove their citizenship with fear of being deported to Mexico without the benefit of due process. In this sense, Operation Wetback played into the racial and anti-communism fears generated by the McCarthyism movement of the time.[33] An unintended consequence of Operation Wetback was the unanticipated backlash of its anti-Mexican sentiments that led to the strengthening of Mexican advocacy groups like the League of United Latin American Citizens (LULAC) and the American G.I. Forum (AGIF) comprised of Hispanics of World War II and Korea.[34]

CIA INTERVENTION INTO CENTRAL AMERICAN

President Trump, in terminating protective status for Salvadorians as well as denying entry to those stranded at the Mexico/U.S. border, has publically demonized the entire population as vicious animals affiliated with the notorious MS-13 gang. Ironically, the violence culture that exists in El Salvador today has its origins during the Eisenhower administration and the secret CIA wars in Central America. Clearly, the seeds of Latin American unrest stems back to the Eisenhower administration and the Cold War. Eisenhower, in an unprecedented act, made John Foster Dulles, U.S. Secretary of State, and his brother, Allen Dulles, head of the Central Intelligence Agency (CIA). Together they were the architects of the unconventional and illegal attack on any perceived anti-American, pro-Communist governments in the Americas, notably those in Central and South America and the Caribbean.

Following the tradition of previous administrations that invoked the Monroe Doctrine as justification for unilateral intervention into hemispheric matters, the Eisenhower administration (1953–1961) ruthlessly intervened in South and Central American affairs with deadly consequences, an era of terror that continued until exposed during the Reagan administration (1981–1989). The Central Intelligence Agency (CIA) employed secretly trained U.S. allies in these countries in the methods of torture, assassination, and terror. During the period of 1952–1990, it is estimated that CIA-sponsored death squads killed hundreds of thousands in Latin American countries alone. The justification for instigating coups and the overthrow of democratically-elected leaders was America's labeling them as "Communists." The 1954 Guatemalan coup illustrates this situation. General Jorge Ubico, a U.S.-sponsored dictator since 1930, who gave large landholdings to the American United Fruit Company (UFCO) as well as allowing U.S. military bases to be stationed in Guatemala, was overthrown in 1944 during the country's first democratic elections. The ensuing administration under Juan Jose Arevalo disrupted these arrangements by breaking up large landholdings for the benefit of peasants, most of Mayan Indian or Mestizo descent, as well as establishing a minimum wage for the workforce. Both actions upset UFCO petitioning the U.S. government to take action. "Regime change" via coups began in 1954 when the Dulles brothers instigated the Guatemalan coup of 1954. Once Arevalo was ousted, the U.S. placed its puppet dictators in place. These coups, later justified as fighting communism, were to protect U.S. business interests like the American United Fruit Company (UFCO), hence the term for these countries—Banana Republics.

CIA-sponsored interventions continued throughout Latin America, in Honduras, Panama, Bolivia, Paraguay, Uruguay, Brazil, Costa Rica, El Salvador, Nicaragua, the Dominican Republic, and Haiti. In most instances, CIA-sponsored death squads targeted indigenous peasants, the working-class peons who were relegated to the lowest rungs of the social ladder. Much of this was hidden from the general public in the United States and the world until the Iran-Contra debacle under President Ronald Reagan. The U.S. Army School of the Americans (SOA), where these deadly tactics were taught, was finally expelled from Panama in 1984 and relocated to Fort Benning, Georgia. Much of the South and Central American operations used the Davis-Monthan Air Force base adjacent to the Tucson, Arizona civilian airport. Davis-Monthan played a critical role during the Cold War era where it was a major Air Combat Command and Headquarters of the 12th Air Force component of the U.S. Southern Command with responsibility for the Caribbean and Central and South America. It is also home to the 162nd Fighter Wing, the largest U.S. Air National Guard unit. Clearly, President Eisenhower quietly established these huge military units along the U.S/Mexico border as a deterrent to any military infiltration from Mexico or any other Latin American entity while supporting clandestine operations throughout the Southern Command, often in violation of international law. It was here that the CIA and

U.S. Army manuals detailing torture techniques originated and were used to train their Latin American operatives, notably in El Salvador, Guatemala, Ecuador, and Peru.[35] It is from these clandestine CIA operations that social unrest and violence became the norm in Central America leading to the emergence of an underground economy based on illicit activities including extortion and drug and human trafficking. One of the most notorious was the MS-13 Salvadorian gang. The U.S.-induced disruption in Latin America so totally changed these societies that a subculture of crime and violence emerged forcing many families to seek a better life outside their homeland, notably in the United States. This led to the influx of unaccompanied children flooding the U.S. border during the summer of 2014. Most were fleeing El Salvador, Honduras, and Guatemala. Regardless of the genesis of this social dishevel, these children escaping poverty and violence were perceived as a threat to America, a sentiment made more pronounced by President Donald Trump.[36]

ANTI-INDIAN POLICIES

The Trump administration's disregard for Indian rights evident in the Keystone XL pipeline controversy, his disregard for Indian sacred lands like the Bears Ears National Monument, and his reduction of aid to Indian education actually pale in comparison to the devastating laws enacted during the Eisenhower administration, laws that were specifically designed to rip up tribal boundaries and destroy Indian culture, *Termination* and *Relocation*. Things did not look good for American Indians when President Eisenhower appointed a former head of the Japanese American Relocation Camps, Dillon Myer, as Commissioner of the Bureau of Indian Affairs. Termination began with House Concurrent Resolution 108 on August 1, 1953. Here, the Republican Congress attempted to terminate federal supervision over American Indians ending their protective status. This sudden change in policy was strongly opposed by American Indian leaders. All Indian tribes in California, Florida, New York, and Texas, along with the Flathead Tribe of Montana, the Klamath Tribe of Oregon, the Pottawatomie Tribe of Kansas and Nebraska, the Chippewa Tribe of Turtle Mountain Reservation in North Dakota, and the Menominee Tribe of Wisconsin were the first to be terminated.[37] Public Law 280 augmented termination by extending state jurisdiction over offenses committed by Indians in Indian Country (reservations).

Again, a number of states were targeted for the initial stage of this experiment: California, Minnesota, Nebraska, Oregon, and Wisconsin.[38] Relocation was the other side of this new attempt toward cultural genocide. The plan was to entice young Indians off the reservation away from the cultural influences and language of the tribe. This process would serve to separate subsequent generations from their traditional language, culture, and customs.[39] During the Eisenhower era, the conservatives attempted to eliminate Indian Country through a blatant policy of "cultural genocide." The idea was to destroy the psychological boundaries linking modern Indians with their aboriginal heritage while, at the same time, instilling a sense of inferiority and psychocultural marginality due to their phenotype. A deliberate policy of cultural genocide within Indian Country was official policy from the early nineteenth century until the 1970s. Here, the government negotiated with various Christian sects in order to *Christianize* them. The missionaries worked diligently at stomping out Indian customs and practices mainly by forcefully separating Indian children from their "heathen" parents and relatives and therefore raising Indian youth up from their "savage" state of existence to the level of "civilized" Christian society. Absolutely everything that was even remotely identifiable as being Indian was uncompromisingly prohibited at the boarding schools, and the students were constantly reminded that they should be ashamed of their heritage, their culture, and their religion, and that Indians who failed to emulate white man's values, dress, customs, mannerisms are less than human.[40]

The practice of forced re-socialization via boarding schools and White adoption of Indian children and youth including a widespread practice of Mormons taking Indian children into their homes during the nine-month school year for the specific purpose of indoctrinating them into the Latter Day Saints (LDS) socio-religious perspective. This program, sanctioned under the Bureau of Indian Affairs' (BIA) effort during the Eisenhower administration, was designed specifically to "detraditionalize" Indian culture among the Navajo, Ute, and Pueblo tribes. The catalyst to significant change came following the recommendations put forth by the comprehensive American Indian Policy Review Commission with passage of the Indian Self-Determination and Education Assistance Act in 1975:

> An Act to provide maximum Indian participation in the Government and education of Indian people; to provide for the full participation of Indian tribes in programs and services conducted by the Federal Government for Indians and to encourage the development of human resources of the Indian people; to establish a program of assistance to upgrade Indian education; to support the right of Indian citizens to control their own educational activities and for other purposes (Public Law 93-638).[41]

The Indian Child Welfare Act of 1978 soon followed. It was a reaction to programs that sanctioned White adoptions of Indian children, including the Mormon school-year re-socialization scheme. This Act addressed the concerns the tribe had with the BIA and state authorities allowing for the adoption and placement of Indian children and youth without the consent of tribal authorities. Absent from the Indian Child Welfare Act were federal protections against child abuse including compulsory reporting laws that were imposed on all state jurisdictions at this time. These changes did not occur until 1990 following an exposé on the abuse of Indian children in tribal schools by BIA, notably White, teachers resulting in passage of the Indian Child Protection and Family Violence Prevention Act in 1990.[42] This was the same basis of instilling the idea of "White Supremacy" among Black Americans during the Jim Crow era. The idea was that *Indianism* and the *Indian Problem* would die with the remaining elders who were to stay on the reservations. What Relocation did was create urban Indian ghettoes forcing the U.S. government to ultimately institute Urban Indian Centers in an effort to correct this blatant injustice.

While the Trump administration's anti-immigrant and racist rants and actions seem severe today, they pale in comparison with those of the Republican-dominated Eisenhower administration. The difference was that Eisenhower entered the presidency as a popular war hero while Trump is the product of a culturally-divided America. Even then, the Eisenhower era saw the beginning of the militarization of law enforcement with the Border Patrol. This era also witnessed the attempt to dissolve Indian Country and the deliberate attempt to alienate young Native Americans through its cultural genocide policies of Termination and Relocation. President Eisenhower's decision to continue France's colonial war in Vietnam also contributed to the ensuing civil unrest of the 1960s and 1970s. Fortunately, American democracy survived the tactics of the Eisenhower administration, although it fueled a major social upheaval with the protests of the 1960s and 1970s. The Trump chapter is yet to be completed.

NOTES

1. R. Ali Camp. *Politics in Mexico.* New York, NY: Oxford University Press, 1993.
2. Ibid.
3. Ibid.
4. J.B. Bishop. *Theodore Roosevelt and His Time: Shown in His Own Letters,* Vol. 2. New York, NY: Scribner Press, 1920.
5. A. Brenner. *The Winds that Swept Mexico.* Meridian, CT: The Meridian Gravure Company, 1971; & C.C. Clendenen. *The United States and Pancho Villa: A study in unconventional diplomacy.* Ithaca, NY: American Historical Association, Cornell University, 1961.
6. E. Pinchon. *Viva Villa! A recovery of the real Pancho Villa—Peon . . . Bandit . . . Soldier . . . Patriot.* New York, NY: Harcourt, Brace and Company, 1933; & V.H. Taylor. *Memoirs of Pancho Villa.* Austin, TX: University of Texas Press, 1965.
7. F. Tompkins. *Chasing Villa: The Last Campaign of the U.S. Cavalry.* Harrisburg, PA: Military Service Publishing Company, 1934; F. McLynn. *Villa and Zapata: A History of the Mexican Revolution.* New York, NY: Carroll and Graf Publishing, 2000; & L.B. Hall, & D.M. Coerver. *Revolution on the Border: The United States and Mexico, 1910–1920.* Albuquerque, NM: University of New Mexico Press, 1988.

8. B.H. Johnson. *Revolution in Texas: How a Forgotten Rebellion and Its Bloody Suppression Turned Mexicans into Americans.* New Haven, CT: Yale University Press, 2003, pp. 113, 120.

9. M. Korda, *IKE: An American Hero.* New York, NY: Harper Perennial, 2008, p. 108; & L.B. Hall, & D.M. Coerver. Woodrow Wilson, Public Opinion, and the Punitive Expedition: A Re-assessment, *New Mexico Historical Review,* Vol 72 (#2), April 1997.

10. C.H. Harris, III, & L.R. Sadler. *The Texas Rangers and the Mexican Revolution: The Bloodiest Decade, 1910–1920.* Albuquerque, NM: University of New Mexico Press, 2004.

11. Op. cit. #7; & J. Hurst. *The Villista Prisoners of 1916–1917.* Las Cruces, NM: Yucca Tree Press, 2000.

12. Ibid.

13. A. Knight. *U.S.-Mexican Relations, 1910–1940: An Interpretation.* Monograph Series 28. San Diego, CA: Tinker Foundation, 1987.

14. P. Taft, & P. Ross. "American Labor Violence: Its Causes, Character, and Outcome," *The History of Violence in America: A Report to the National Commission on the Causes and Prevention of Violence,* H.D. Graham & T.R. Gurr (eds.). New York, NY: Bantam Books, 1969.

15. Ibid., "Lynching of Frank Little," pp. 333–36.

16. A.E. Alcock. *History of the International Labor Organization.* New York, NY: Octagon Books, 1971; & R.L. Filippelli. *Labor in the USA: A History.* New York, NY: Alfred A. Knopf, 1984.

17. F. Galton. *Hereditary Genius: An Inquiry into Its Laws and Consequences.* London, England: Macmillan, 1869.

18. L.M. Terman. *The Measurement of Intelligence.* Boston, MA: Houghton Mifflin, 1916, p. 26.

19. R.M. Thorndike, & D.F. Lohman. *A Century of Ability Testing.* Chicago, IL: The Riverside Publishing Company, 1990, p. 44.

20. *Ibis,* see Chronology, p. 155.

21. *Buck v. Bell,* 274 U.S. 200, 205, No. 292, U.S. Supreme Ct. 1927; & E. Black. *War Against the Weak: Eugenics and America's Campaign to Create a Master Race.* New York, NY: Four Walls Eight Windows, 2003.

22. *Mendez v. Westminster School District,* 64 F. Supp. 544 (C.D. Cal. 1946); *Brown v. Board of Education,* 347 U.S. 483 (1954); & E.C. Lagemann, & L.P. Miller. *Brown v. Education: The Challenge of Today's Schools.* New York, NY: Teachers College Record Series, 1996.

23. K.B. Clark. *Dark Ghetto: Dilemmas of Social Power.* New York, NY: Harper & Row, 1965; & D. Fellman. *The Supreme Court and Education,* New York, NY: Teachers College Press, 1969.

24. J. Isbister. *The Immigration Debate: Remaking America.* West Hartford, CT: Kumarian Press, 1996.

25. F. Van Nuys. *Americanizing the West: Race, Immigration, and Citizenship, 1890–1930.* Lawrence, KS: University of Kansas Press, 2002.

26. A. De Leon. *Mexican Americans in Texas: A Brief History.* Arlington Heights, IL: Harlan Davidson, 1993.

27. K. Allerfeldt. "Race and Restriction: Anti-Asian Immigration Pressures in the Pacific Northwest during the Progressive Era, 1885–1924." *History,* Vol. 88 (#289), January 2003, pp. 13–21; B. Wolfe. "Racial Integrity Laws (1924–1930)." *Encyclopedia of Virginia.* Virginia Foundation for the Humanities, 2009; & V.M. Briggs. *Mass Migration and the National Interest: Policy Directions for the New Century.* Armonk, NY: M.E. Sharp, 2003.

28. J. Higham. *Strangers in the Land: Patterns of American Nativism.* New Brunswick, NJ: Rutgers University Press, 1963; & C. Shanks. *Immigration and the Politics of American Sovereignty, 1880–1990.* Ann Arbor, MI: University of Michigan Press, 2001.

29. S. Taylor. "The Internment of Americans of Japanese Ancestry" (Chapter 22), *When Sorry Isn't Enough: The Controversy over Apologies and Reparations for Human Injustice.* (R.L. Brooks, ed.). New York, NY: New York University Press, 1999, pp. 165.

30. C. Daniel (editorial director). "Japanese-Americans Are Imprisoned," *Year by Year from 1900 to 2000: American Century.* New York, NY: Dorling Kindersley Publishing, Inc., 2000.

31. *The Official Bracero Agreement of August 4, 1942 with Modifications Agreed Upon on April 26, 1943* (Public Law 45—August 2, 1942–December 31, 1947).

32. J.R, Garcia. *Operation Wetback: The Mass Deportation of Mexican Undocumented Workers in 1954.* Westport, CT: Greenwood Press, 1980.

33. Ibid.

34. J.G. Quinones. *Chicano Politics: Reality & Promise, 1940–1990.* Albuquerque, NM: University of New Mexico Press, 1990.

35. G. Lesley, *The School of the Americas: Military Training and Political Violence in the Americas.* Durham, NC: Duke University Press, 2004; & J. Schirmer. *The Guatemalan Military Project: A Violence Called Democracy.* Philadelphia, PA: University of Pennsylvania Press, 2000.

36. Migrant Policy Institute. *Increased Central American Migration to the United States May Prove an Enduring Phenomenon,* 2016.

37. *House Concurrent Resolution 108,* U.S. Statutes at Large, 67: B132.

38. *Public Law 280.* U.S. Statutes at Large, 67: 588–90, August 15, 1953.

39. *Relocation of Indians in Urban Areas.* Annual Report of the Secretary of the Interior, 1954, pp. 242–43.

40. K. Kickingbird, & L. Kickingbird. "A Short History of Indian Education, Part 2," *American Indian Journal,* September 1979, pp. 17–21; A. Beuf. *Red Children in White America.* Philadelphia, PA: University of Pennsylvania Press, 1977; & M.C. Szasz. *Education and the American Indian: The Road to Self-Determination since 1928.* Albuquerque, NM: University of New Mexico Press, 1976.

41. *A National Tragedy: Report on Indian Education.* Senate Report No. 501, 91st Congress, 1st Session, Serial 12836-1, pp. xi–xiv, 1968; & Public Law 93-638. *Indian Self-Determination and Education Assistance Act,* 1975, U.S. Statutes at Large, 88: pp. 2203–14.

42. Public Law 101-630. *Indian Child Protection and Family Violence Prevention Act.* Title IV, 25 USC 1990: 3210.

SEVEN

Emerging Social Unrest and Its Aftermath

Civil Rights, War on Drugs, and the Militarization of Law Enforcement

The Cold War chaos during the Eisenhower era infected the entire hemisphere with right-wing coups in South America (Brazil, Argentina, Chili, Columbia . . .) and the Caribbean (Cuba, Dominican Republic, Haiti . . .) in addition to Central American nations and Mexico as well as a serious separatist's movement in Canada. The United States became embroiled in its civil rights and anti-war movements that involved not only people of color, notably Blacks, Hispanics, and American Indians including returning war veterans, but White college and university students as well.

THE BATTLE FOR CIVIL RIGHTS AND ITS IMPACT ON INCREASED FEDERAL POLICE OVERSIGHT

Economic woes overtook the brief post-war prosperity following the Second World War, a situation exacerbated by the heated Cold War anti-Communism rhetoric spewed by *McCarthyism* paranoia and fueled by J. Edgar Hoover's FBI secret wars against minorities and leftist student organizations, groups he labeled as being Communist sympathizers. The cost of Eisenhower's anti-Communism stance extended beyond the United States or the hemisphere with interventions in the Middle East, Africa, and Southeast Asia, notably Vietnam, which the U.S. willingly inherited from the defeated French.

The 1954 *Brown v. Board of Education* U.S. Supreme Court decision proved to be the catalyst for change in the Jim Crow South, casting a light on the biased institutions beyond education such as the judiciary and local law enforcement resulting in a harsh backlash—one that was prominently displayed worldwide via the mass media. The ensuing outcry of police brutality directed against non-violent Black protesters forced President Eisenhower to use federal troops to enforce the Supreme Court school desegregation law, a critical decision by a Southern-born president (hometown, Denton, Texas). In 1957–1958, President Eisenhower sent U.S. federal troops to Little Rock, Arkansas to protect Black students attending previously White-only schools. This required deploying regular army troops from Southern bases as well as federalizing local National Guard units comprised mainly of Southern White males, most who grew up and were socialized under the Jim Crow caste system. Here, Eisenhower had to invoke Section 502(f) of the U.S. Code under Title 32 which authorized the full-time federalization of the National Guard for limited, specified duty. He needed to do this to obviate Southern governors from deploying these same units to block integration under their Title 10 authority under the U.S. Code.[1]

On the civilian side, U.S. Marshals had to be deployed to provide similar services given J. Edgar Hoover's reluctance to use the FBI in these matters. Indeed, the FBI had to be compelled by U.S. Attorney General Robert Kennedy to investigate the murder of civil rights members in Mississippi. Eisenhower sent in the regular army to desegregate Central High School in Little Rock, Arkansas when Governor Orval Faubus ordered the State National Guard to block Blacks from enrolling in the high school. The president blocked the governor's action by federalizing the Arkansas National Guard and by bringing in a component of the 101st Airborne Army Division as well as U.S. Marshals to enforce the federal desegregation order. President Eisenhower used an exception to the Posse Comitatus Act of 1878 that allows for the use of military force when state authorities are either unable or unwilling to suppress violence that is in opposition to the Constitutional rights of citizens. This action is short of enforcing martial law in that it does not curtail Bill of Rights guarantees such as habeas corpus writs.[2]

Another key civil rights situation at this time was the much publicized 1955 murder of 14 year old Emmett Till, a Black youth from Chicago visiting relatives in Mississippi. The refusal of the FBI to get involved in the case was indicative of J. Edgar Hoover's racist biases. Nonetheless, Black civil rights groups continued to engage in non-violent protests, including economic boycotts, sponsored by the NAACP and the Southern Christian Leadership Conference (SCLC) and leaders such as the Reverend Martin Luther King, Jr. Not only did the FBI not investigate the abuses directed against Black protesters by Southern law enforcement agencies, it began its own clandestine campaign to infiltrate and provoke

Black protesters and investigate their leaders, notably Martin Luther King, Jr.:

> J. Edgar Hoover believed that the civil rights movement was being influenced secretly by the communists, that agents of the Soviet Union were using the civil rights movement to try to destroy the United States government. Hoover believed that the civil rights movement was neither spontaneous nor genuine, so in 1958, the FBI began watching Dr. King. Three years later, Hoover decided that watching wasn't enough. The bureau began an investigation.[3]

President John F. Kennedy (1961–1963) inherited his predecessor's problems, notably the brewing crisis in the Caribbean (Cuba and Dominican Republic), Vietnam, civil rights and draft protests—events that erupted into the massive social unrest targeting his and his successors, Presidents Lyndon B. Johnson's (1963–1969) and Richard M. Nixon's (1969–1974), administrations. Following President Eisenhower's example, President Kennedy federalized the Mississippi National Guard in 1962 to prevent White violence directed toward James Meredith, a Black U.S. Air Force veteran, from enrolling in the University of Mississippi. In the ensuing violence, spurred by state and local politicians and law enforcement, two people were killed and twenty-eight U.S. Marshals wounded. Conspicuously absent was the FBI. The following April witnessed the arrest of the Reverend Martin Luther King, Jr. in Alabama while on June 12, Medgar Evers, a Black NAACP field representative, was assassinated. The White suspects were subsequently acquitted by local all-White juries, as was the judicial standard during the Jim Crow era. President Kennedy had to federalize the Alabama National Guard to challenge Governor George Wallace from blocking Black students from entering the University of Alabama. Again, a Southern governor was denied the use of the National Guard as his own personal militia in order to enforce segregation.[4]

The Kennedy administration ended with his assassination on November 22, 1963 in Dallas, Texas. He most likely would have pursued civil rights legislation if not confronted with international crises like the 1961 Cuba "Bay of Pigs" fiasco and the 1962 Cuban missile showdown that almost ignited a nuclear war with the Soviet Union. Additional conflicts plaguing his administration were the invasion of the Dominican Republic and crises in Algeria and the Congo and the military buildup in Southeast Asia with violent unrest in Indonesia, Vietnam, and Taiwan. The Vietnam War added fuel to the civil rights movement at a time when events were being shown in "real time" on television. While President Lyndon B. Johnson took the blame for the escalating war in Vietnam, a stance that ended any hopes for reelection, he did get civil rights legislation passed by a divided Congress.

The landmark Civil Rights Act was passed by Congress and signed into law by President Johnson on July 3, 1964. The Act prohibits racial discrimination in public accommodations, employment, unions, and all federally funded programs and projects. The Civil Rights Act was preceded by the January 1964 ratification of the 24th Amendment to the U.S. Constitution prohibiting the use of a poll tax, or any other device, intended to prevent American citizens from their constitutional right to vote in federal elections. This was forty years since the last major racial class of people, the American Indian, was federally franchised. The poll tax was the primary vehicle used to disenfranchise impoverished people of color from voting during the Jim Crow era. In 1965, Congress added legislative teeth to the 24th Amendment by passing the Voting Rights Act, again due mainly due to President Johnson's urging and clout in Washington.[5]

RIOTS AND SOCIETAL REACTION—THE OMNIBUS CRIME CONTROL & SAFE STREETS ACT

Clearly, the anti-war movement served to overshadow the major civil rights advances during the Kennedy and Johnson administrations, including the Voting Rights Act, Medicare, Great Society programs, the Indian Civil Rights Act of 1968, and Dr. King receiving the Nobel Peace Prize. While many Blacks appreciated these efforts at desegregation, their sentiments were not fully shared by those long suffering from police brutality and the poverty of ghetto life. The litany of the ensuing chaos included: riots in New York City in the summer of 1964; the murder of three civil rights workers (James Chaney, Andrew Goodman, and Michael Schwerner) in Philadelphia, Mississippi in August 1964; the Free Speech movement at the University of California at Berkeley in the fall of 1964; Malcolm X's assassination in February 1965; the widely publicized police brutality during the "March to Montgomery" in March 1965; race riots in Watts, Los Angeles in August 1965; race riots in Atlanta and Chicago in September 1966 and in Detroit in July 1967 as well as the spontaneous mass rioting throughout the country following the assassination of the Reverend Martin Luther King, Jr. on April 4, 1968. College and university students added to the massive civil disobedience with antiwar protests including joint civil rights endeavors such as the "March on the Pentagon" in October 1967; campus takeovers in 1968; the riot at the 1968 Democratic Party Convention in Chicago; the coordinated antiwar protests in Washington, DC in 1969; and the American Indian Movement takeover of Alcatraz Prison in November 1969. These riots and protests culminated in the 1970s with the Kent State University (Ohio) and Jackson State University (Mississippi) protests that were met with deadly fire from National Guard units in 1970, and the deadly race riot at

Attica Prison in upstate New York in September 1971, and the Wounded Knee II uprising on the Pine Ridge Sioux Reservation from February to May 1973. These events demonstrated the depth of the divide in American society at the time, setting the stage for the "law and order" reactions that challenged the equal protection of all citizens, notably minorities of color, from biased policing.[6]

President Johnson also had to federalize a Southern state's National Guard in order to keep it from being used as a vigilante militia by a racist governor. Here he deployed the Alabama National Guard to counter the brutal beatings of protestors by state police and sheriff deputies. Johnson later federalized National Guard units in Michigan, Illinois, and the federal District of Columbia (DC) to assist police in patrolling streets to prevent rioting following the assassination of Dr. King. The reactions to civil rights and anti-war protests illustrated the need for an improved law enforcement apparatus in the United States including federal police, notably the FBI and Hoover's communist conspiracy theories regarding minorities. Toward this end, a number of "blue ribbon" investigations were launched. One, the comprehensive *Eisenhower Report*, looked at the history of violence in America:

> The President's Advisory Commission on Civil Disorder (Kerner Commission) sponsored a variety of social research studies that focused mainly on the attitudes of the public and the rioters. . . . From all sources, one conclusion emerges, namely the absence of organized conspiracy in commodity riots. However, the absence of organized conspiracy does not mean the absence of a pattern of events. . . . The difference from one outburst to another involved the extent to which each one proceeded through the various stages of increased and intensified collective behavior. . . . The new type of rioting is most likely to be set off by an incident involving the police in the ghetto where some actual or believed violation of accepted police practice has taken place. . . . There is some evidence that one index to National Guard effectiveness is the extent of integration of units. Because of its fraternal spirit, most National Guard units have been able to resist Federal directives and Negros accounted for less than 2 percent of its personnel in 1967. In those cases where integration took place, it meant that the units were seen as more legitimate by the local population. . . . In 23 disorders studied by the Kerner Commission, none were "caused by, nor were they the consequence of any plan or conspiracy." . . . The impact of the riots of 1967 on the civil rights movement was drastic in that it made the movement's demands more militant. But clearly the leaders of the civil-rights movement were not activists in these outbursts. If anything, they occurred because of the inability of the civil-rights movement to accomplish sufficient social change in the slums, although the movement made a decisive contribution in intensifying aspirations and group consciousness.[7]

Student campus protests, in contrast, appeared to reflect political action spurred on by the Vietnam War, and to a lesser extent, minority civil rights issues. On campuses, considerable damage was done during the occupation of administrative offices, an action known as "sit ins." Antiwar and civil rights groups coordinated their efforts in August 1968 in Chicago leading to the disastrous protests at the Democratic National Convention. The groups involved included: the mostly White, middle-class, National Mobilization Committee to End the War in Vietnam; the Youth International Party (Yippies); the Students for a Democratic Society (SDS); and the Black Panthers. The Eisenhower Report acknowledges that the catalyst for the ensuing violence was when Mayor Daley called out both the police and the National Guard, a force of some 23,000, to provoke and attack the 10,000 unarmed protesters. This event was widely publicized worldwide via the mass media and became known as the *Chicago police riot.* Nonetheless, President Richard Nixon ordered his Justice Department, which included J. Edgar Hoover's FBI, to prosecute the protest leaders with conspiracy and incitement to riot. These leaders, Abbie Hoffman, Tom Hayden, David Dellinger, Rennie Davis, John Froines, Jerry Rubin, Lee Weiner, and Bobby Seale, became known as the *Chicago Eight.* They were tried in February 1970 by Federal District Judge Julius Hoffman whose biases became readily known during the televised trials. One Black leader, Bobby Seale, was tried separately and was bound and gagged during his trial. The remaining "Chicago Seven" were found "not guilty" of conspiring to incite a riot, while five of the defendants were convicted of crossing state lines with intent to cause a riot. For these convictions, Judge Hoffman handed down the maximum sentence of five-year incarceration in a federal prison. These convictions and sentences were ultimately reversed on appeal.[8]

Emboldened by the conservative leanings of Richard Nixon's administration, J. Edgar Hoover embarked on his own CIA-type secret mission directed toward African Americans, notably the Black Panthers who initiated a successful community outreach program in the California Bay Area. The Black Panthers Party started in October 1966 in Oakland, California in the urban ghetto across the bay from San Francisco. They provided community programs such as a Free Breakfast for Children Program, school tutoring, and street health clinics. In two years these programs encompassed sixty-eight Black ghetto communities. Apparently, this infuriated J. Edgar Hoover so he engaged the FBI in a clandestine and illegal offensive targeting Black Panther leaders under his COINTELPRO program. J. Edgar Hoover's COINTELPRO-BLACK HATE initiative began while Martin Luther King, Jr. was still alive. Here, he targeted not only Dr. King but other nonviolent Black protest group leaders. Once the Reverend King was assassinated, Hoover was adamant that he would prevent the rise of another respectable Black leader, and in doing so, he created a scenario whereby he would use his leading role in law enforcement to denigrate Blacks in general and their leaders in particular. Hoover was able to team up with the CIA in these secret police activities, where they called their programs Operation CHAOS, attacking Black protestors including Dr. King. The FBI also worked closely with law enforcement in their clandestine and illegal activities including break-ins, planting incriminating evidence, vandalism, assaults, beatings, and assassinations. Hoover even used members of the Ku Klux Klan in these illegal and violent endeavors directed toward Black groups:[9]

> Hoover considered all black power groups extreme, so extreme tactics were called for. Hoover decided to implement COINTELPRO. COINTELPRO was the code name for Counter Intelligence Program. Counterintelligence meant that action would be taken to weaken these organizations. Convinced that these groups were out to harm the nation, Hoover set out to destroy them. The tactics that characterized COINTELPRO were the most extreme in the bureau's history. . . . FBI agents in the field were directed to take steps that would cause members of black radical groups to become fearful, mistrustful of one another, and confused. Agents were directed to exploit *all* avenues that might accomplish this and to recommend ideas. Organization leaders were arrested repeatedly for minor, and sometimes made-up, charges. The arrests were meant to drain the organization's personal and financial resources and hinder its ability to act. One COINTELPRO tactic had the odd-sounding code name "bad jacketing," and referred to a key individual becoming the subject of an FBI campaign to create suspicions about him or her within the organization. Once an individual was targeted for "bad jacketing," rumors were spread and evidence was made up. Sometimes there were attempts to convince other members that the targeted individual was an FBI informant. COINTELPRO tactics were used against all of the black power groups active in the late 1960s and early 1970s. In all, there were 360 separate operations. But the most unrestrained use of these tactics was aimed at the Black Panther party.[10]

Hoover also applied his COINTELPRO tactics against the newly emerging American Indian Movement (AIM), the outgrowth of the failed policies of Termination and Relocation during the Eisenhower administration. Indian youth relegated to urban Indian ghettos grew up with the knowledge that they were American Indians but without the benefit of being socialized within their particular aboriginal culture, a phenomenon that led to Pan-Indianism—the process of identifying with recognizable Indian traits that transcends those of any particular culture per se. This included attributes of the Siouan, Algonquin, and Athabasca groups—feather head dressings, silver and turquoise jewelry, sweats, peyote use, and fancy dancing, as well as seasonal meetings known as the "Pow Wow Circuit." This movement also popularized the Native American Church and its peyote ceremony. These once marginalized individuals were also attracted to the American Indian Movement which led to the

Wounded Knee II debacle on the Pine Ridge Sioux Reservation in South Dakota. Not well known or publicized by the FBI is its jurisdictional mandate in Indian Country secondary to the 1885 Major Crimes Act. Once the domain of the U.S. Marshals' office, these duties associated with policing felonies in Indian Country were transferred to the FBI during the early days of its inception. Now the Federal Bureau of Investigation is the primary federal law enforcement agency policing major felonies, known as "Index Crimes," on all federally-recognized tribal entities in the United States. It was in this capacity that the FBI played a major role in monitoring AIM activities including the 1969 takeover of Alcatraz Island and the 1972 march on Washington, DC, known as the *Trail of Broken Treaties* and subsequent occupation of the Bureau of Indian Affairs (BIA) headquarters, and most notably, the 1973 Wounded Knee II uprising.

At Wounded Knee II the AIM protestors endured the onslaught of federal troops, SWAT teams, FBI agents, and U.S. Marshals equipped with Vietnam-era weapons including armored personnel carriers and helicopters for seventy-one days. The U.S. Army coined this operation "Garden Plot." Indian casualties included two dead and many wounded, but more significant was the later death of two FBI agents in 1975 resulting in the imprisonment of Leonard Peltier. Yvonne Bushyhead, a noted American Indian lawyer, describes the extent of FBI misconduct unveiled at the 1974 Wounded Knee II trial of AIM leaders Dennis Banks and Russell Means:

> The misconduct by the FBI in this case included withholding and doctoring FBI files, the placing of an informer (Douglas Durham) within the defense team, and subornation of perjury. These actions were part of the Bureau's arsenal of techniques for the disruption of groups during the official span of COINTELPRO, although they occurred three years after COINTELPRO allegedly ended. Attorney William Kunstler further described the prosecution's misconduct as including failure to verify the testimony of a key witness in light of overwhelmingly contradictory information; failure to inform the court of the FBI's intervention in a rape investigation of the same witness; offering testimony which was directly contradicted by a document in its possession; and failure to provide relevant information regarding the extent of the United States military involvement in the occupation. (Based on this misconduct) the trial judge, Chief Justice Fred Nichol, dismissed charges against the defendants after concluding that the prosecution had acted in bad faith. One of the instances of improper conduct that particularly troubled Judge Nichol was the misrepresentation of [FBI] Special Agent Trimbach that there were no wiretaps at Wounded Knee.[11]

FEDERAL OVERSIGHT OVER LAW ENFORCEMENT: THE OMNIBUS CRIME CONTROL BILL

The massive civil unrest of the 1960s and 1970s, with its cost in human lives and extensive property damage, led to Congressional actions resulting in passage of the *Omnibus Crime Control and Safe Streets Act of 1968.* The forerunner of this Act was the "Law Enforcement and Criminal Justice Assistance Act of 1967" resulting from President Lyndon Johnson's President's Commission on Law Enforcement and Administration of Justice Task Force reports. The unrest of the time drew attention not only to racism and corruption within state and local law enforcement but at the federal level as well. The riots and unrest undermined the weakness of America's highly decentralized law enforcement and the need for universal training standards. At the time of the riots the only Constitutional national police force was the National Guard which emerged from the British-mandated provincial militias during the colonial era. This is why Presidents Eisenhower, Kennedy, and Johnson deployed federalized National Guard units to quell riots as well as to keep racist governors from using them to counter federal laws. The essence of the Omnibus Crime Control and Safe Streets Act was to provide a uniform standard of training for all law enforcement agencies. Even then, corrective action was delayed until after Hoover's death in 1972 at age seventy-seven. The Watergate debacle and President Nixon's resignation further fueled investigations into Hoover's FBI resulting in the disclosure of his secret files in 1975:

> Washington, DC, Feb. 27: J. Edgar Hoover, the late director of the Federal Bureau of Investigation, made improper use of files that he collected on political activists, a House of Representative subcommittee was told today. Attorney General Edward Levi said that Hoover, who died in 1972, kept documents with derogatory information on presidents, on congressmen and on a variety of prominent people. The Attorney General's testimony indicated that at least three Presidents—John Kennedy, Lyndon Johnson and Richard Nixon—had data collected regarding congressmen and senators who opposed them (May 19, 1976).[12]

Abuses by the Central Intelligence Agency (CIA) were also disclosed at this time:

> C.I.A. is accused of domestic spying: Washington, DC, June 10: The Central Intelligence Agency whose charter bans:internal security functions, systematically spied on alleged radicals during the administration of Presidents Johnson and Nixon. According to the report of an eight-man panel headed by Vice President Nelson Rockefeller, the agency amassed 13,000 files on domestic dissidents by illegally scrutinizing mail from the Soviet Union. It used wiretaps and breakins to police its own employees and held a defector in solitary confinement

> for three years. But the panel blames the Presidents, not the C.I.A. Johnson, for one, insisted that foreign money was behind the student anti-war effort. Rockefeller says the violations were "not major." But Senator Frank Church, who is investigating the C.I.A. on foreign assassinations, disagrees. "Ours is not a wicked country," he said, "and we cannot abide a wicked government" (May 19, 1976).[13]

These exposés led to a cry for police standards and oversight which the Omnibus Crime Control Bill purported to provide through block grants to every state, resulting in a standardized curriculum for police academies throughout the country. These grants were administered under the "Law Enforcement Assistance Administration" (LEAA) with each state establishing a Governor's Crime Commission. The country was further divided into ten funding regions in order to better accommodate geographical differences and needs. Hence, the LEAA block grants provided the incentive for a more standardized criminal and juvenile justice system, establishing standards for police academies as well as training for judges and prosecutors. Ironically, the provision for training for riot control also introduced military apparatus into civilian law enforcement, a phenomenon that led to many minority communities viewing law enforcement as an occupational force within the ghettos and barrios of America.

Nonetheless, the LEAA transformed the haphazard array of police, courts, and correctional facilities into more recognizable institutions. Prior to this, local and state law enforcement and judiciaries had their own regional customs dictating their actions, many blatantly racist as was the case throughout the Jim Crow South. Many criminal justice personnel were ill-trained for their positions, with many selected based on racial, ethnic, and cultural factors than on qualifications. Recent U.S. Supreme Court decisions during this time also provided boundaries and guidance for the administration of justice, especially in the area of capital punishment. *Furman v. Georgia* (1972); *Gregg v. Georgia, Jurek v. Texas, Proffit v. Florida* (1976) established protocol for the death penalty limiting it to first degree murder cases, while *Gideon v. Wainright* (1963) guaranteed access to counsel. *Miranda v. Arizona* (1966) required law enforcement to read suspects "their rights" and *in re Gault* (1967) set the standards for juvenile justice.[14]

Another condition of LEAA funding was that states were compelled to join the federal effort in its *War on Drugs*, a fallback to Hoover's contention linking violence and minorities. A major tool for combating the drug trade was passage in 1970 of the *Racketeer Influenced and Corrupt Organizations* statute known as RICO. RICO reflected a major revision of the 1934 Anti-Racketeering Act (Hobbs Act) in the federal arsenal used to combat organized crime during the Prohibition era. RICO penalties included property and money forfeiture, divestiture, and corporate dissolution and reorganization. Toward this end, LEAA allowed, and even encouraged, the acquisition of military gear including assault rifles, armored personnel carriers, bullet-proof vests, and the like.

AMERICA'S WAR ON DRUGS AND MINORITIES

Substance abuse has long plagued American society, with rum during the colonial and early republic era to the Whiskey Rebellion, Prohibition, and repeal. Drugs other than alcohol also played a role in how the United States defined acceptable behaviors, hence acceptable members of society. The Chinese were defined by their opium use while African Americans and Hispanics were closely associated with the use of hemp products leading to the 1914 Harrison Narcotic Act and the 1937 Marijuana Transfer Tax Act, both laws directed at American minorities. The United States was complicit, along with Great Britain, France, and Russia, in sowing the seeds of the current drug crisis when it participated in the Opium Wars of 1839–1858 when China was forced to open its ports to U.S. and European trade, notably the opium trade which it banned in 1799. The United States, using its "gunboat diplomacy," became a signee to the 1844 Treaty of Wanghai and the 1858 Treaty of Tientsin. These treaties went beyond the opium drug trade; they also opened the door for cheap Chinese labor for the development of the American West, especially the transcontinental rail system. America also joined its European allies in the Boxer Rebellion in 1900 when China attempted to purge itself of foreign influences. Again, the U.S. Marine Corps was used as America's international police in protecting the interests of big business under the guise of the Monroe Doctrine.

Anti-Chinese sentiments led to federal restrictions on immigration beginning with the Chinese Expulsion of 1882 under President Chester Arthur (1881–1885) which led to additional quota restrictions such as the Immigration Act of 1882 which soon followed, imposing a head tax on those seeking entry into the United States as well as restrictions of certain classes of peoples. The Naturalization Act of 1906 during Theodore Roosevelt's administration (1901–1909) added the further restriction of learning English as a condition of U.S. residency status. Moreover, American women who married foreign men automatically lost their U.S. citizenship unlike their male counterparts married to foreign women. This double-standard did not change until 1922 with passage of the Cable Act. These restrictions on immigration went hand-in-hand with the prevailing stereotype of non-Whites as being inferior humans susceptible to violence and drug abuse.

America's first "Drug Czar" was Harry J. Anslinger, a colleague of J. Edgar Hoover, and it is his legacy that influenced the racist nature of drug enforcement in the United States. Policing illicit substance use in the United States dates to 1920 during Prohibition with the Prohibition Unit under the U.S. Bureau of Internal Revenue that then became the Bureau of Prohibition in 1927. Three years later, in 1930, it became the Federal Bureau of Narcotics (FBN). Harry J. Anslinger started his career in 1929 as Assistant Commissioner of the U.S. Bureau of Prohibition and moved up to the commissioner's position in the newly minted FBN. The focus changed from alcohol to other substances, notably marijuana, when Prohibition was repealed in 1933. Like his colleague, J. Edgar Hoover, Anslinger promoted the myth of the "dangerous minority drug fiend" associated with marijuana use, especially among Blacks and Hispanics, despite opposition to this claim by both the American Bar Association (ABA) and the American Medical Association (AMA).[15]

Both Hoover and Anslinger were adept at using the mass media to promote their racist views. Anslinger used the 1936 movie *Reefer Madness* to promote his views to the public and Congress leading to passage of the 1937 Marijuana Transfer Tax, which was a de facto federal ban on hemp products with a devastating effect on minority members, many who served long sentences for marijuana possession and/or distribution. What is often lost in the marijuana debate is the involvement of American capitalists such as Randolph Hearst, Andrew Mellon (whom Anslinger was linked through marriage), and the powerful DuPont family in the hemp conspiracy. With the advent of the decorticator machine, hemp, a common agricultural product, was seen as threatening the paper pulp industry in the newspaper business where Hearst and others had large timber holdings. Equally significant was the advent of a new synthetic fiber, nylon, produced by DuPont. But for nylon to be successful, it needed to replace hemp. Toward this end, Hearst used his newspapers to spread stories of rape, murder, and violence by Blacks, Hispanics, and Asians committed under the influence of the evil drug marijuana. What resulted was not only the rapid decline of hemp farming but the fostering of negative stereotypes of people of color through Hearst's yellow journalism—the true fake news of the time.[16]

The race/drugs/violence profile of minority males was widely promoted through the joint efforts of both Harry J. Anslinger and J. Edgar Hoover in their capacity as heads of the FBN and FBI respectively. Anslinger was forced to resign in 1962 during the Kennedy administration while Hoover continued until his death ten years later. The Bureau of Drug Abuse Control became the Bureau of Narcotics and Dangerous Drugs in 1968 coinciding with passage of the Omnibus Crime Control and Safe Streets Act and became the Drug Enforcement Agency (DEA) under President Nixon who coined the term *war on drugs.* President Ronald Reagan (1981–1989) is credited with further militarizing the drug enforcement agencies by involving the FBI, CIA, and U.S. military in the U.S.-led international anti-drug operations. Clearly, the *war on drugs,* from its mandate stemming from the 1968 Omnibus Crime Control and Safe Streets Act to the present time, has been responsible for the increased militarization of civilian law enforcement in the United States.[17] The illicit drug trade presents a unique form of capitalism in that it involves classic market conditions of supply and demand. The problem with the U.S. is that it attempts to punish both elements of the supply and demand relationship without sufficiently addressing the root causes for this demand among Americans. Clearly, the adversarial criminal justice model is applied to American minorities and those within the lower classes while a pseudo-treatment agenda is available for White middle-class drug users. This differential is noted with both the use of marijuana and cocaine. These differences were not adequately studied until the Obama presidency (2009–2017) when he addressed the differential incarceration rates for drug offenses between people of color and Whites. Another factor is the opioid crisis in America, a situation forcing American society to seek out prevention and treatment alternatives to arrest and incarceration.

VIETNAM WAR AFTERMATH—NEW IMMIGRATION LAWS

The Vietnam War stirred unrest beyond U.S. borders with a deadly student riot in Mexico City in 1968. Turmoil existed in Mexico during the turbulent 1960s resulting in the Tlatelolco Square student massacre in Mexico City where hundreds of unarmed pro-democracy protestors, mostly students, were killed on the eve of the Olympics in Mexico City. The October 1968 incident coincided with the emergence of the *Bronze Power* movement and Cesar Chavez's *La Causa* movement and his leadership over the National Farm Workers organization. At the same time, Canada, which did not join the United States in the Vietnam War, became a safe haven for draft dodgers and AWOL service personnel, a reversal of the First World War when French Canadians fled south to the U.S. to avoid the blatantly prejudicial Canadian draft. Canada was experiencing its own "Quiet Revolution" with Quebec separatists who wanted independence from the Confederation, redrawing its own borders. The "Quiet Revolution" became violent at the height of the Vietnam War with the armed faction of the *Parti Quebecois* (PQ), the *Front de Liberation du Quebec* (FLQ). International attention was drawn to the separatist movement when the FLQ resorted to bombings, kidnapping, and assassinations during the "October Crisis" in 1970.[18]

The influx of refugees from Southeast Asia during and following the Vietnam War set the stage for the latest immigration wave. Beginning in 1965, this wave is characterized by a smaller percentage of European immigrants and a larger Hispanic influx from Mexico, the Caribbean, Central and South America, and Asia. The European exception was Hungarian refugees escaping the ill-fated 1956 Hungarian Revolution with nearly a half-million allowed in. The Cuban Revolution inflated the Caribbean migrant flow with affluent, mainly "White" Cubans allowed into the United States. This reflected a serious racial bias in Caribbean refugees in that Haitian and other Black or Mestizo refugees were greatly restricted from entering the United States. The 1966 Cuban Adjustment Act provided permanent resident status to Cubans who resided in the country as refugees for at least one year. These differences aside, it was the Civil Rights laws of the mid-1960s that changed the racial quota element of previous laws. Like the Magnuson Act of 1943 that repealed the 1882 Chinese Expulsion Act during World War Two when we needed China as an ally, the aftermath of the Vietnam War brought about changes in the racial nature of immigration laws. Notable here was passage of the Hart-Celler Immigration and Nationality Act of 1965 which replaced the ethnic quotas with preferential categories based on family relationships and occupation, giving preference to those with relatives in the U.S. and with occupations deemed critical by the U.S. Department of Labor.

Adding to the 1965 changes, the Refugee Act of 1980 amended the Immigration and Nationality rules to allow for a substantial number of refugees, notably Vietnamese, seeking asylum in the United States. The American Homecoming Act of 1989 gave preferential immigration status to mixed-ethnic Vietnamese children born to U.S. fathers, mainly those who served in the Vietnam War. A year later, the Immigration Act of 1990 expanded on the 1965 Immigration and Nationality Act by expanding the number of applicants to 700,000 per year while providing a diversity visa component to low-admittance countries. These new rules opened the doors to family members of American citizens and permanent resident aliens regardless of racial/ethnic origin. In 1996, Congress passed the Illegal Immigration Reform and Immigrant Responsibility Act (HRIRA) spelling out conditions for those undocumented immigrants who were caught and deported. Those who were in-country between 180 and 364 days were compelled to wait outside the U.S. for three years, unless pardoned, to apply for legal entry; while those caught and deported who were in-country over a year had to wait ten years before being eligible to apply for legal entry.

The 1997 Nicaraguan Adjustment and Central American Relief Act (NACARA) provided conditions for immigration benefits and relief from deportation for certain classes of asylees from Nicaraguans, Cubans, Salvadorans, and Guatemalans from Central America as well as those from former Soviet-bloc nations, providing they were registered asylum seekers and had resided in the U.S. for at least five years. The major problem was that this law did not positively impact upon Mexican immigrants given that the *Bracero* agreement between Mexico and the United States ended in 1964. Being omitted from the 1965 immigration law resulted in a new influx of illegal Mexicans entering the United States labor market due to the continued demands for their labor, especially in the agriculture segment of the U.S. economy. Another factor at this time was the emergence of the *maquiladoras*, the "twin-plant" system. The maquiladoras scheme was to have production components produced right across the border in Mexico, in what is known as the *Borderlands*, while the assembly of these items would occur in the United States. In the initial plan both systems would be close to the border in order to keep transportation costs to a minimum. But the United States never moved its manufacturing plants from the industrialized Midwest to the Borderland region. Instead, the U.S. established warehouses to store the products manufactured in Mexico at a reduced cost given the marked differential in labor costs as well as skirting stricter environmental standards enforced in the United States.

General Electric (GE) opened its first maquiladora in 1971 in a complex that expanded to eight plants within a decade. General Motors (GM) soon followed GE, opening twelve maquiladora plants while closing eleven factories in the United States and laying off nearly 30,000 workers. Indeed, on the eve of the North American Free Trade Agreement (NAFTA) in January 1994, GM was the biggest private employer in Mexico with 50 plants and 50,000 workers accounting for about a tenth of the Mexicans employed by some 2,000 maquiladoras, many of them from other countries. Ironically, the maquiladoras did not stem the tide of illegal crossings of Mexican men seeking employment in the United States. Instead it created an environment whereby families in the interior would send their women and girls to work in the maquiladoras and not the men and boys. Nonetheless, the high female ratio in the Borderlands also acted as a magnet for Mexican males and subsequently a staging area for illegal passage to the United States. The jobs and migration of young females caused a disruption to the traditional rural Mexican family and community system where women provided unpaid labor. Consequently, young unemployed or underemployed men followed the young women to the Borderland where many crossed into the United States illegally to work in agriculture, on ranches, and on construction. While the de facto quotas from legal entry rose from a half-million in 1961 during the concluding days of the Bracero Program to over another million spots on the eve of NAFTA, this did not satisfy the demand for a docile, low-paid workforce that Mexico easily provided.[19]

Another factor associated with the rapid growth of the maquilas zone was pollution. In addition to industrial pollutants came uncontrolled human waste and garbage and the proliferation of *colonials* (unregulated shanty communities) that contributed to water and air contamination. In addition to access to cheap labor, another major attraction for companies was the protection from United States environmental standards. Now U.S. companies could pollute at will. By the time of NAFTA, the Rio Grande, the major divide for most the Borderlands, was the most contaminated river in North America with marked increases in otherwise preventable diseases such as childhood cancer, gallbladder ailments, hepatitis, liver cancer, and anencephalic births in communities on either side of the Borderlands. Yet, under Mexican law, maquiladoras cannot be sued for work-related injuries or illnesses.[20]

INTERNATIONAL MARKET FORCES AND TRADE: GATT AND THE WTO

The relationship between labor demands and immigration has long been a major determinant in the market economy from colonial times to the present. The dynamics changed markedly with the nearly-universal prohibition on slavery during the nineteenth and twentieth centuries leaving nations to find other enticements to draw outsiders to their workforce. The other side of this equation is when peoples initiate entry due to unfavorable conditions in their homeland. This category includes those seeking asylum including from violence and chaos. These dynamics became magnified as the post–WWII economies became more international leading to the emergence of the World Trade Organization. Both World Wars and the Great Depression, along with the advent of improved mass communication, set the stage for a number of events that would greatly alter the world community, challenging both despotism and isolationism as well as colonialism.

The frenzy of neo-colonialism following WWI resulted in not only the realignment of previous European powers but also the creation of the Soviet Union. Mass communication, on the other hand, was greatly improved by the advent of FM (frequency modulation) radio in 1933, better phone networks, and later, television and eventually, satellites. These advances not only allowed for rapid cultural diffusions, but laid the foundation for the information revolution and the establishment of the World Wide Web (internet). Economic woes and rapid industrialization played a significant role in human displacement and cross-national movements. Post–WWII events led to attempts to better control the world economy, which was seen as a principal factor in world harmony. Here, the United Nations played an important role. Also critical at this time was the establishment of the General Agreement on Tariffs and Trade (GATT). Initiated in 1947, GATT was eventually replaced by the World Trade Organization (WTO) in 1995 creating an international marketplace with a semblance of stability. What resulted from these combined influences was an opening of world markets and cultures making political isolation more difficult. Indeed, attempts to maintain closed, oppressive societies within the current world economy met with harsh reactions and condemnation from others.[21]

The United States played a major, if ambiguous, role in these developments going back to WWI and its aftermath. Following the massive destruction, in both human and economic losses, the victorious Allies established the *League of Nations,* the forerunner to the United Nations, following the Second World War. The League of Nations represented the first world body attempting to address the pitfalls of colonialism. Prominent world leaders, such as Jan Smuts, Lord Robert Cecil, Leon Bourgeois, and U.S. President Woodrow Wilson, were involved in its development. Unfortunately, while President Wilson is credited with providing the basic philosophy for the League with his *Fourteen Points,* the U.S. Congress failed to ratify the League thus diminishing America's influence in its implementation. In addition to national reorganization (including neocolonialism), Item III set the stage for the emergence of the World Trade Organization. Here, Wilson suggested the removal of economic barriers and the establishment of trade equality. Item V addressed the colonial issue where Wilson suggested an impartial adjustment of all colonial claims with a balance between the interests of those subject to continual colonialization vis-à-vis the economic-political interest of the colonizing nation (oil, rubber, gold . . .).

The Articles of the League's Covenant included the establishment of a World Court (Articles 11–17), while Article 21 provided a concession to the United States allowing it to continue to be the dominant influence in the Americas via its Monroe Doctrine. Article 22 established Mandatories to oversee the development of autonomous or semi-autonomous states emerging from the defeated Turkish (Ottoman) Empire, as well as territories in Africa and the South Pacific Islands. And Article 23 provided the foundation for human justice where it attempted to establish fair and humane working conditions for men, women, and children, as well as the protection of native inhabitants of territories under member nations' colonial authority, leading to the establishment of the International Labor Organization and the foundation for the World Health Organization created under the United Nations. Also addressed in this Article was human trafficking and the international drug trade.[22]

The League's successor, the United Nations (UN), emerged following the devastation created by the Second World War, a conflict that involved American forces on both the European and Pacific fronts. The main difference was that in its aftermath the Allies, notably the United States, pursued a policy of reconstruction instead of punitive reparations. Now America was a willing participant in a world body designed to monitor events that might mitigate yet another devastating conflict—one that would involve nuclear weapons. With the United States now on board, the United Nations main office was located in New York City. The health concerns articulated earlier by the League of Nations were now forged in the UN through the World Health Organization (WHO) while a related area, labor conditions, was also addressed with the International Labor Organization (ILO) absorbed by the UN. Its main purpose when initiated in 1919 was to expose labor exploitation, especially within colonized regions of the globe, a role it continues to play in checking labor exploitation within the World Trade Organization.

The International Labor Organization was an outgrowth of the International Association for Labour Legislation founded in 1901 predating WWI and the establishment of the League of Nations. The primary purpose of the International Association for Labour Legislation was humanitarian concerns for workers worldwide, a mandate continued by its successor, the ILO. The ILO is a unique organization with a tripartite structure comprised of workers, employers, and government partners. This unique partnership prompted political and economic cooperation in finding solutions to international labor issues making it one of the longest-operating and respected agents of social justice. It has survived both World Wars and the Great Depression and continues to play a major role relevant to labor concerns stemming from the WTO.

The ILO Constitution became part of the Treaty of Versailles with the American Federation of Labor (AFL) as a partner despite the U.S. not being a member of the League of Nations. In 1934, President Franklin D. Roosevelt made the U.S. a formal member of the ILO, and five years later, John Winant, first head of the U.S. Social Security System, became director of the ILO. During WWII, the ILO added the Declaration of Philadelphia to its Constitution, stating that poverty constitutes a danger to world prosperity. This declaration articulated the fact that poverty needed to be addressed, especially in Third World countries and particularly the economic practice of exploitation of women and children in the workforce.

The ILO grew rapidly following WWII under the leadership of David Morse. During his twenty-two-year tenure as Director, the ILO established the International Institute for Labor Studies in 1960 and the International Training Center in 1965. In 1969, at its 50th anniversary, the ILO was awarded the Nobel Peace Prize. Despite the success of its American directors, President James (Jimmy) Carter (1977–1981) pulled the U.S. out of the ILO in 1977 until reinstated by President Ronald Reagan (1981–1989). With the U.S. withdrawal, the ILO lost one-fourth of its budget. As a leading advocate of human rights, the ILO is credited with the emancipation of Poland, thus playing a role in the fall of the Soviet Union.[23]

Another significant outgrowth of the League of Nations was the establishment of the Permanent Court of International Justice established in 1921 under Article 14. The current manifestation of the World Court is the International Court of Justice (ICJ). The International Court of Justice replaced the defunct League's international court and is situated at the Peace Palace in The Hague, Netherlands. Like its predecessor, the ICJ provides both judicial and advisory findings. The 15 permanent judges serve nine-year terms with only one judge per nationality. The ICJ's rulings are final and without appeal. In addition to its judicial and advisory functions, the Court established a Chamber of Summary Procedure in

1982 and a seven-member Chamber to address environmental cases in 1993. It holds time-limited jurisdiction over Genocide and Crimes against Humanity relevant to events in Rwanda and the former Yugoslavia in the 1990s. These were the International Criminal Tribunals—ICT-R and ICT-Y.[24]

A year following the creation of the UN, the General Agreement of Tariffs and Trade (GATT) was established in 1947 providing the foundation for the emergence of the World Trade Organization (WTO) that replaced it in 1995. GATT was an international organization designed to reduce trade barriers via multilateral negotiations. It emerged from the failure of the UN to establish a broader International Trade Organization (ITO), due mainly to the failure of the U.S. Senate to ratify the UN's ITO. Out of GATT came the *most-favored nation* principle requiring that a nation that grants trade privileges to another country needs to provide the same standard to all GATT (later WTO) members. Another trade principle is that of *national treatment* requiring nations to give equal treatment to foreign imports and services as it does to its domestic goods and services. The World Trade Organization emerged in 1993 as the result of the GATT Uruguay Rounds of Multilateral Trade Negotiations. The WTO officially replaced GATT when it was approved by the U.S. in November 1994, ten months after approving the North American Free Trade Agreement (NAFTA).

The WTO emerged more powerful than GATT due to its enforcement authority and the fact that it shifts trade authority from national governments to a global agency run by unelected bureaucrats whose decisions are binding. According to the final results of the Uruguay Rounds of Multilateral Trade Negotiations, all members of the WTO are also members of the Ministerial Conference and the General Council. The Dispute Settlement Body and Trade Policy Review Body are components of the General Council. Clearly, the WTO has emerged as the most powerful economic entity in the world, giving it powers to influence other competing international agencies such as the World Bank and the International Finance Corporation. China's entry into the WTO expanded its domain to include 90 percent of world trade.[25]

GLOBAL ECONOMY AND SOCIAL PROTEST

Immigration is a crucial component of the global economy. Industrialization and capitalism both contribute to mass migrations, first from the industrialized states to their Third World colonies and later from the Third World to the industrialized states. War also contributes to significant displacement of peoples. John Isbister makes a compelling argument linking capitalism, immigration, and justice. He notes that industrialization challenged the status quo in eighteenth-century Europe, changing forever the village lifestyle and replacing it with a system based on supply and demand market forces. Consequently, industrialized Europe created an environment with a growing demand for food and raw materials from abroad, mainly from the new colonies in the Americas, Australia, and Africa. Hence, the first transatlantic immigrants came from Britain, Spain, France, Holland, and Portugal. Later, at the end of the nineteenth century, migrants came to the United States from southern and eastern Europe. In the twentieth century, mass migration was often the outcome of war and poverty afflicting Latin America, Asia, and the former Soviet bloc.[26]

Under the WTO, global economics appear to be based on Adam Smith's concept of a "free market place" regulated by "supply and demand" without political influence or geographic boundaries. While this approach is appealing to many, it does not take into account geo-political factors based on "collective human behavior" driven by sectarianism, and racial/ethnic/gender factors as well as "nationalism." Clearly, the WTO's attempt to promote a "rational" model for human economic intercourse fails to account for the human psyche and its own demand for boundary maintenance and status relative to its cultural/social audience. It is little wonder that those most likely to benefit from a global economy were the privileged elite, regardless of racial composition.

The lower classes, many marginalized, comprised the bulk of the lower-echelon workers in the global economy. And with the diminishing authority of geo-political boundaries, many workers were attracted to economic opportunities in new cultural milieus. The WTO marketplace stimulated international migration once curtailed during the period between the two World Wars. It was renewed industrial growth in Western Europe, North America, and Oceania that opened the doors to international migration from less developed Third World countries. This era of international migration lasted from 1945 until the oil crisis of 1973 and the ensuing worldwide recession. International migration from the mid-1970s to the 1990s shifted from the traditional industrialized nations to emerging economies in southern Europe, Gulf oil countries, South America, Africa, and Asia. Accordingly, migrants fall into seven classifications: (1) temporary migrant laborers (guest workers); (2) highly skilled migrants (brain-drain migrants); (3) irregular migrants (undocumented or illegal migrants); (4) war refugees (forced migrants); (5) asylum seekers (political migrants); (6) family reunification migrants; and (7) return migrants.

Migration for economic reasons has again focused on the technologically developed nations in Western Europe, North America, notably the United States, and Australia. This migratory trend has also witnessed a sectarian/geo-political mix of Muslims and Orthodox Christians entering traditionally Christian countries comprised of Catholics and/or Protestant sects. For example, the largest groups of migrants in Germany are from Turkey and Eastern Europe, while Italy has witnessed an influx of asylum seekers and irregular migrants from Albania, North Africa, and the former Yugoslavia. Great Britain and France have migrants from their former colonies and the United States has seen increased migrant flow from Mexico and Latin America, while Australia has been overwhelmed by Asian migrants in addition to Anglo migrants from New Zealand and Great Britain.[27]

The UN tracks migratory trends, especially those involving refugees, doing so via the United Nations High Commission for Refugees (UNHCR). During the Balkan Wars of the 1990s that involved the break-up of the former Yugoslavia, the UNHCR estimated that over one million refugees migrated from Bosnia-Herzegovina in addition to another million-plus displaced through *ethnic cleansing* operations carried out by all the warring parties—Catholic Croats, Muslim Bosniacs, and Serb Orthodox. Roma were also impacted by ethnic cleansing. At the same time, there was a decline in asylum seekers in Western Europe and North America due mainly to greater stability within Southeast Asia following the Vietnam War and the end of Apartheid in South Africa. The break-up of the Soviet Union in 1991 resulted in a flow of migrants to the Russian Federation, which held a higher standard of living than many of its Union counterparts. Spain, with its close proximity to North Africa, has witnessed an increase in international migrants, mostly irregular migrants, especially since the fall of Libya subsequent to the Arab Spring revolts. The aftermath of the breakup of both the USSR and the former Yugoslavia and continued conflict between Serbia and Kosovo has resulted in increased displacement of peoples within Kosovo, Macedonia, Montenegro, and other Albanian-ethnic and Roma groups in the Baltic region. The United States' long military engagement in Afghanistan and Iraq has also fostered an influx of refugees seeking to escape these seemingly never-ending conflicts.[28]

The WTO shares some of the blame for the alarming rate of climate change now being seriously addressed in the twenty-first century. However, other factors contribute to the situation. There is a clear link between rapid industrialization during the twentieth century and environmental damage due to mining, deforestation, and the burning of carbon fuels with some of the worst environmental damage occurring within the former Soviet Union and Third World countries that continue to defoliate the earth like Brazil. A consequence related to the newly expanded world marketplace is the readily available cheap transportation even for the working poor. Mopeds and motorcycles are rapidly replacing man-powered devices such as pedicabs and bicycles. Another widely available item is the gas-operated portable generator allowing for modern appliances such as televisions even in the most remote underdeveloped regions of the world. These advances associated with improved economic development have compromised the ozone layer and most likely contributed to the rising temperature of the earth itself in addition to lowering both air and water quality levels. The UN has been instrumental in brokering a number of international treaties designed to reduce the exploitation and contamination of the environment; however, this means little if the largest economies, the United States and China, do not fully comply with, or endorse, these treaties.

The United Nations assesses globalization in terms of its promise and consequences. While it tends to promote liberal democracy, this has resulted in serious backlashes from failed pro-democracies from China to Egypt, Libya, and Syria. . . . The UN notes that the loosening of control in authoritarian regimes such as the former USSR and Yugoslavia, coupled with an emerging free market, has also fostered an increase in criminal cartels and international criminal activity. The WTO has contributed to the increasing gap between the rich and the poor, consolidating the wealth among the already wealthy elite at the expense of poorer groups and countries. This is due to the fact that capitalism has become international, transcending national borders and increasing fiercer competition in environments where not everyone has an equal chance. The "conditionalities" placed on Third World economies by the International Monetary Fund (IMF) and World Bank, deregulation, privatization of public enterprises, and a marked reduction of state expenditures make matters worse when the global economy falters. These failures, like in Greece, Ireland, Iceland, and Italy, not only disrupt the state's economy, it also disrupts traditional social forces and cultural traditions. The UN notes that the WTO has transformed some markets from production to service economies leaving some, like President Trump, activating his base by promising to "Make America Great Again" by returning to a long-lost industrial production economy like that of the twentieth century. More powerful computers and satellite communication have transformed the workforce in such a way that there is little chance of returning to the workforce environment of the twentieth century. Associated with these technical advances is consumerism which, in itself, stimulates the service market. Cell phone technology coupled with the World Wide Web (www) transcends cultures and borders tending to homogenize peoples so that they are readily, and instantly, aware of current events and trends making it more difficult for authoritarian societies to control their populace.[29]

Prior to the U.S.'s declaration of its "War on Terrorism" following the attacks by hijacked commercial airlines on September 11, 2001 (9/11), anti-globalization protests addressed the exploitation of workers and the environment. In the spring of 2001, Western Hemisphere leaders met in Quebec, Canada where they drafted a blueprint for an American Union free-trade zone affecting 33 of the 34 states in the Americas. This was designed to create another economic unit like the European Union (EU) within the WTO. The United States' insistence on excluding Cuba along with the collapse of the Argentine economy in 2001, the second-largest economy in South America, doomed this initiative. Major protests also occurred in Brazil, especially following the death of Ademir Federicci in October 2001, the vocal labor leader opposed to the exploitation of the rain forests by loggers, soybean farmers, and cattle ranchers. A month earlier, major protests against U.S. business interests in the Middle East occurred with the September 11, 2001 terrorists' attacks on the World Trade Twin Towers in New York City and the Pentagon, and attempted attack on the Capitol by radical Islamic groups representing one of the most conservative of Third World protest groups.

The most significant protest in North America surrounded passage of the North American Free Trade Agreement (NAFTA). While NAFTA passed in the United States with little fanfare, numerous protests erupted in Canada among those in opposition to its implementation. However, it was the Mexican reaction that was the most pronounced. On the day NAFTA went into effect, January 1, 1994, the Ejercito Zapatista de Liberacion Nacional (Zapatista Army of National Liberation—EZLN) declared war on Mexico. The EZLN is comprised mainly of Mayan Indians living in one of Mexico's poorest states—Chiapas, which is located on the Mexico/Guatemala border. The EZLN took its name from the revolutionary leader Emiliano Zapata who led the Army of the South during the Mexican Revolution. The EZLN were concerned that NAFTA would undermine the revolutionary efforts for land distribution and support for the traditional communal land system known as the ejidos. A major concern was NAFTA's attempt to override Article 27, Section 7 of the 1917 Mexican Constitution guaranteeing land reparation, especially to indigenous Indians and Mestizo. Under NAFTA, these small units could not compete with U.S.-subsidized agribusinesses for corn, the mainstay of the Indigenous lifestyle.

The EZLN war was short-lived, ending on January 12. The ceasefire was arranged by Bishop Samuel Ruiz of the Catholic diocese in San Cristobal de las Casa, resulting in the "Zapatistas" retaining some of the lands they occupied in the short war. Eventually, even these holdings were lost when the Mexican army occupied the region beginning in February 1995. The Mexican army failed in its efforts to capture the leaders of EZLN, most notably, "Subcomandante Marcos." International outrage forced the Mexican government to negotiate with the EZLN making the "Zapatistas" an international symbol for the anti-globalization movement. Both the WTO and NAFTA became the targets of this opposition. In 1996, the Intercontinental Encounter for Humanity and against Neoliberalism was held in Chiapas. Pro-Zapatista support groups soon emerged in the United States, Argentina, Austria, Britain, France, Italy, Spain, and Switzerland. Mexican recognition for EZLN came in 1996 with the signing of the San Andres Accords reinstating the autonomy and special rights of the indigenous populations. By 2003 these autonomous ejidos had created their own local governments (Juntas) where they established and maintained traditional communal programs, one that eventually spread to all 31 Mexican states setting a model for Indians and Mestizos throughout the Americas.[30]

September 11, 2001 changed the World's perception of the role of capitalism within the international marketplace. The previous Cold War that existed between the First World (democratic free-market states) and Second World (communist states) was now replaced with a capitalist versus Muslim conflict. Since 9/11, global geo-politics are deeply rooted in on-going Muslim wars, a particular section of the Third World that feels both left out of and threatened by the new global economy and its associated trans-cultural influences. In November 2001, the 142-nation membership of the WTO, in its meeting in Doha, Qatar, changed its economic model to address the unmet needs of poorer Third World economies with concessions from the wealthier neo-colonial nations including the United States. Clearly, the United States was incentivized by its need for a world consensus for its pursuit of its *War on Terror*, providing the justification for the second phase of the Gulf War in Iraq and Afghanistan.

Operation Iraqi Freedom was promoted as a necessary preemptive action to quell the War on Terrorism, skirting GATT and WTO rules by claiming this unilateral action was necessary to counter the "direct and imminent threat" Iraq presented to the United States and others. The emotions surrounding the 9/11 attacks allowed this action by the U.S. and Britain to bypass UN weapons inspections. In order to give the semblance of substantial support, President Bush used a tactic used by his father, President George H.W. Bush, during the First Gulf War; that of aligning a "coalition of the willing," a listing of some 40 nations lending their support to the invasion of Iraq. Despite this alleged support, the U.S. and Britain provided the bulk of the military personnel with other nations fielding far lower numbers. Conspicuously absent from this coalition were the two NAFTA partners, Canada and Mexico, as well as three permanent members of the UN Security Council (Russia, France, and Germany). These nations opposed the war opting for more time for authorized weapons inspections. Among the "coalition of the willing" were Albania, Romania, Hungry, Estonia, Latvia, Lithuania, Slovakia, Bulgaria, Macedonia, Georgia, Philippines, Uzbekistan, Colombia, El Salvador, Nicaragua, Dominican Republic, Costa Rica, Honduras, Eritrea, Ethiopia, Rwanda, Uganda, and Mongolia . . . former Soviet Bloc and Third World nations, many with questionable human rights records. Those who opposed or questioned the United States' action, even traditional allies like France and Germany, were severely castigated by the Bush administration. When no weapons of mass destruction were uncovered, the war's supporters diminished as well. Indeed, many saw this incursion as yet another colonial-style resource war with Iraqi oil the real objective.

President George W. Bush was able to integrate the War on Drugs into the worldwide War on Terrorism—merging law enforcement and military components as well as presenting numerous legal challenges to martial law standards such as the status and treatment of prisoners (enemy combatants versus prisoners of war). The economic drain of these wars and worldwide initiatives in the combined wars on drugs and terrorism clearly contributed to the ensuing worldwide "Great Recession" of 2008. Many of President Trump's policies mimic those of George W. Bush, notably those actions that support the "resource war" concept including the Trump administration's "Trade Wars" tariffs, given that the ensuring trade imbalance has its roots linked to the admission of China (December 2001) and Taiwan (January 2001) into the World Trade Organization—two Asian giants that changed the trade balance, notably in the United States. And like George W. Bush, Donald Trump skirted GATT/WTO rules by claiming that these actions were justified under the "threat to national security" clause. This included labeling Canada as a country threatening the United States when, in fact, it is one of America's staunchest allies.[31]

NOTES

1. S. Brackin, J. Cole, W. Hester, C. Pena-Guzman, R. Schroeder, J. Taylor, & M. Young. *U.S. Southwest Border Security: An Operational Approach.* Fort Leavenworth, KS: U.S. Army Command and General Staff College, 2012.
2. L.A. French. Civil Rights during the Eisenhower Era. *The History of Policing America: From Militias and Military to the Law Enforcement of Today.* Lanham, MD: Rowman and Littlefield, 2018, pp. 113–115.
3. B. Denenberg. Hoover and the Civil Rights Movement. *The True Story of J. Edgar Hoover and the FBI.* New York, NY: Scholastic, Inc. 1993, pp. 138–139.
4. Op. cit. #2.
5. J.W. Kirshon (ed.). The Eagle Ascendant 1946–1999. *American Century: Year by Year from 1900–2000.* New York, NY/London, England: Dorling Kindersley Publishing, Inc. 2000.
6. Op. cit. #2.
7. H.D. Graham, & T.R. Gurr. *Violence in America: Historical and Comparatives* (Eisenhower Report). New York, NY: Bantam Books, 1969, pp. 419–20, 424, 427.
8. D. Farber. *Chicago '68.* Chicago, IL: University of Chicago Press, 1988.
9. T. Weiner. *Enemies: A History of the FBI.* New York, NY: Random House, 2012.
10. Op. cit. #3, pp. 165–168.
11. Y. Bushyhead. In the Spirit of Crazy Horse: Leonard Peltier and the AIM Uprising. *Winds of Injustice: American Indians and the U.S. Government* (L.A. French). New York, NY: Garland Publishing, 1994, pp. 84–85.
12. Op. cit. #5, p. 326.
13. Ibid., p. 328.
14. *Furman v. Georgia* (408 U.S. 238, 345, 1972); *Gregg v. Georgia* (428 U.S. 153, 96 S. Ct. 2912, 1976); *Jurek v. Texas* (428 U.S. 262, 96 S. Ct. 2950, 1976); *Proffit v. Florida* (428 U.S. 242, 252, 1976); *Gideon v. Wainwright* (372 U.S. 436, 1963); *Miranda v. Arizona* (384 U.S. 436, 1966); *In re Gault* (387 U.S. 1, 1967); & *Omnibus Crime Control and Safe Streets Act of 1968*, Public Law 90-351; 82 Stat. 197/42 USC.; ch. 46 (June 19, 1968).

15. J.C. McWilliams. *The Protectors: Anslinger and the Federal Bureau of Narcotics (1930–1962).* Newark, DE: University of Delaware Press, 1990.

16. L. Sloman. *Reefer Madness: A History of Marijuana in America.* Indianapolis, IN: Bobbs-Merrill, 1979.

17. Ibid.

18. E. Poniatowska. *Massacre in Mexico.* (H.R. Lane, trans.). New York, NY: Viking, 1975; P. Desbarats. *Rene: A Canadian in Search of a Country.* Toronto, Canada: McClelland and Stewart-Bantam United, 1977; & M. Richler. *Oh Canada! Oh Quebec! Requiem for a Divided Country.* New York, NY: Viking. 1992.

19. J. Gonzalez. Nightmare on the Border. *Harvest of Empire: A History of Latinos in America.* New York, NY: Viking, 2000.

20. Ibid.

21. K.W. Dam. *The GATT: Law and International Economic Organization.* Chicago, IL: University of Chicago Press, 1970.

22. T.L. Deibel. *Struggle for Cooperation: The League of Nations Secretariat and Pro-League Internationalism in the United States, 1919–1924.* Geneva, Switzerland: Graduate Institute of International Studies, 1970; & B.V. Dexter. *The Years of Opportunity: The League of Nations, 1920–1926.* New York, NY: Viking Press, 1967.

23. G.H. Bartolomei de la Cruz. *The International Labor Organization: The International Standards Systems and Basic Human Rights.* Boulder, CO: Westview Press, 1996; & L.A. Compa, & S.F. Diamond (eds.). *Human Rights, Labor Rights, and International Trade.* Philadelphia, PA: University of Pennsylvania Press, 1996; & C.W. Jenks. *Social Justice in the Law of Nations: The ILO's Impact after Fifty Years.* New York, NY: Oxford University Press, 1970.

24. A.D. Sofaer (ed.). *The United States and the World Court.* Washington, DC: U.S. Department of State, Bureau of Public Affairs, Office of Public Communication, 1985; H.B. Tolley, Jr. *The International Commission of Jurists.* Philadelphia, PA: University of Pennsylvania Press, 1994.

25. W.J. Clinton. *GATT Uruguay Round of Multilateral Trade Negotiations: Communication from the President of the United States.* 103d Congress, 2d Session, 103, 195. Washington, DC: U.S. Government Printing Office, 1994; & K.W. Dam, op. cit. #21.

26. J. Isbister. *The Immigration Debate: Remaking America.* Westport, CT: Kumarian Press, 1996.

27. J. Isbister. *Capitalism and Justice: Envisioning Social and Economic Fairness.* Bloomfield, CT: Kumarian Press, 2001, pp. 201–215.

28. Ibid.

29. J. McMurtry. *Unequal Freedoms: The Global Market as an Ethical System.* West Hartford, CT: Kumarian Press, 1998; F. Rajaee. *Globalization on Trial: The Human Condition and the Information Civilization.* West Hartford, CT: Kumarian Press, 2000.

30. D.E. Lorey. *The U.S.-Mexican Border in the Twentieth Century: A History of Economic and Social Transformation.* Wilmington, DE: A Scholarly Resource Book, 1999.

31. R. Gunaraatna. *Global Terror: Unearthing the support networks that allow Terrorism to survive and succeed.* New York, NY. New York University Press, 2002; M.T. Klare. *Resource Wars: The New Landscape of Global Conflict.* New York, NY: Metropolitan Books, 2001; A. Rashid. *Taliban: Militant Islam, Oil and Fundamentalism in Central Asia.* New Haven, CT: Yale University Press, 2001; & R. Mahajan. *The New Crusade: America's War on Terrorism.* New York, NY: New York University Press, 2002.

EIGHT

Border and Immigration Issues in the Twenty-First Century

THE WAR ON DRUGS' IMPACT ON BORDER SECURITY

The renewed emphasis on border security since the early twentieth century and the Mexican Revolution, notably the militarization of the U.S./Mexico border, began with the administration and Operation Wetback. This operation made creative use of the military, skirting the 1878 Posse Comitatius Act restricting the use of the military in domestic affairs except in certain circumstances by placing "retired" generals in charge and using military procedures to standardize the Border Patrol. Hence, the foundation for increased military-type security at the United States' southern border was already in place when President Nixon (1969–1974) declared his "War on Drugs." President Reagan (1981–1989), in turn, provided greater authority to prosecutors with passage of the Anti-Drug Abuse Act, including the Drug Kingpin Act reinstating the federal death sentence since the 1972 Supreme Court decision in *Furman v. Georgia.*

The plan for increased border security was part of President Clinton's (1993–2001) NAFTA plan, what he called his Southwest Border Strategy. Clinton's plan was to secure the most porous sections of the Borderlands, designating sites adjacent to San Diego, California; Tucson, Arizona; and El Paso, Texas. On the Mexican side of the international border, there was increased U.S. involvement in law enforcement in funding, equipment, and training. This started out as part of the NAFTA effort to fight the war on drugs as well as curtail undocumented entries into southern Mexico from those using Mexico to transit from South and Central America and the Caribbean. This joint international effort created in 1995 is known as the "Mexico-US Plenary Group on Law Enforcement." It coordinated efforts between the U.S. FBI and the Mexican Federal Agency of Investigation (AFI). Since then, thousands of AFI agents have been trained by the U.S. Drug Enforcement Administration and the French National Police. In 2000, hundreds of Mexican law enforcement personnel were trained within the newly created Border Patrol Search, Trauma, and Rescue Teams (BORSTAT). This effort was to create a North American secure perimeter around the entire NAFTA zone. Pre-9/11, Canada was skeptical of this plan and only joined in when forced by the United States following the terrorist attacks.[1]

In 1989, President George H.W. Bush (1989–1993) created Joint Task Force-6 (JTF-6) at Fort Bliss in El Paso, Texas. JTF-6 was created in order to provide military support to the War on Drugs and was later expanded to keep undocumented immigrants from entering the United States. Under JFT-6, the U.S. military provided free support in terms of personnel and equipment to domestic law enforcement agencies in federally designated "High Intensity Drug Trafficking Areas." Military personnel and federal funding were/are used to provide training maneuvers and support to the Border Patrol and other federal, state, and local law enforcement involved in joint border security endeavors. JTF-6 was the longest joint task force in U.S. history, with over 70,000 military personnel from 30 states involved in 3,300 missions for the period 1990–1997 alone. The killing of a U.S.-born Mexican American teen, Esequiel Hernandez, by a U.S. Marine squad in 1997 drew national and international attention to the JTF-6 forcing them to modify, not curtail, its operational standards. JTF-6 is responsible for the Border Patrol blockage operation initiated in 1993 where common urban entry points along the U.S./Mexico border were saturated by law enforcement along with the construction of blockade fences, actions that forced undocumented aliens to take more perilous routes through the desert known as "death corridors." The underlying principle of these actions was that a marked increase of the likelihood of a torturous death would be a deterrent to others attempting to enter the United States "illegally." Operation Jump Start was the forerunner of Plan Mexico that soon followed.[2]

Since its inception during the Nixon administration, tens of millions of U.S. dollars were spent in combating the cocaine problem with special interest in Colombia. This initiative became known as Plan Colombia under the Reagan and Clinton administrations. Once Colombia became somewhat stabilized, President George W. Bush's administration's focus turned to Mexico and the Merida Initiative, also known as Plan Mexico. Now tens of millions of U.S. dollars were being pumped into Mexico and Central America in the effort to stem the flow of cocaine, methamphetamine, marijuana, and heroin into the U.S. market. Plan Mexico was a security agreement put forth by the United States with the government of Mexico and countries of Central America with the specific purpose of combating drug trafficking, transnational organized crime, and money laundering. The reality is that Mexico and Latin American nations, while not cocaine-producing countries like Colombia, were transit countries for contraband, like cocaine, to reach the lucrative U.S. market. President G.W. Bush found an ally in Mexican President Felipe Calderon and the Meridan Initiative (Plan Mexico) became effective June 30, 2008. From Fiscal Year 2008 until Fiscal Year 2015, the U.S. Congress appropriated over two billion dollars for this program which included tens of millions for the Central American Regional Security Initiative (CARSI) and the Caribbean Basin Security Initiative (CBSI). This aid included military equipment and training, hence militarizing law enforcement on either side of the U.S. southern border. The equipment deployed included Bell 412 and Black Hawk helicopters, transport aircraft, a Reconnaissance Dornier Jet, inspection equipment, and telecommunication equipment as well as firearms. The ATF's *Project Gunrunner* was part of Plan Mexico, hence its secrecy even today. Another major criticism was that torture techniques and methods were being taught to Mexican law enforcement and military personnel by U.S. security firm instructors, much like the torture being conducted during the Gulf War and that taught to South and Central American death squads during the Cold War era. It is important to note that the Merida Initiative continued to be funded and implemented during the Obama administration.[3]

NORTH AMERICA BORDER SECURITY SINCE 9/11

The terrorist attacks of 9/11 initiated America's worldwide war on terrorism creating havoc with its wars in Iraq and Afghanistan, and the subsequent Arab/African migrant wave through Europe. It also dramatically changed border security along both the U.S./Mexico and U.S./Canada borders as well as changing the dynamics of the borders of the over 500 recognized tribes comprising America's Indian Country. September 11, 2001 provided an added incentive to continue militarizing the U.S./Mexico border. The 9/11 attacks led to the creation of a new federal agency—the Department of Homeland Security (DHS)—established on March 1, 2003. DHS gained oversight over the U.S. Customs and Border Enforcement (CBE), the U.S. Citizenship and Immigration Services (USCIS), and the U.S. Immigration and Customs Enforcement (ICE). Now the U.S. Border Patrol falls under CBE while ICE has jurisdiction over deportation. The U.S. Coast Guard is also now a part of DHS. Since its inception, DHS data shows that 95 percent of all those attempting to enter the United States illegally were arrested along the U.S.'s southern border—the Borderlands. With DHS in place, President George W. Bush authorized *Operation Jump Start* in 2006 which enticed the governors of the Borderland states, California, Arizona, New Mexico, and Texas, to deploy their National Guard units under Title 32, with federal reimbursement, thereby skirting the prohibition of the use of federal troops within the United States for domestic purposes.

Interestingly, the justification for this use of military forces along the U.S. border is found in an official report put forth by the U.S. Army Command and General Staff College:

> Joint Task Force Six (JTF-6) was established November 13, 1989 at Fort Bliss, Texas, to support local, state, and federal law enforcement agencies within the Southwest border region in order to counter the flow of illegal drugs into the United States. The terrorist attacks of September 11, 2001 brought changes through passage of the 2004 National Defense Authorization Act. The Act authorized DOD to expend funds for counter drug operations to support counterterrorism task forces in an effort to mitigate the risk from the potential relationship between the illegal narcotics trade and terrorism. On September 28, 2004, JTF-6 was officially renamed Task Force North (JFT-N) and its mission was expanded to include homeland security support to the nation's federal law enforcement agencies. To date [2012], JTF-N has completed 600 missions in support of U.S. law enforcement and counter-drug task forces.
>
> JFT-N has also undertaken multiple engineering projects along the Southwest border and deployed soldiers for short-term operations. Military units deploy through JFT-N on a strictly volunteer basis, as JFT-N has no assigned or apportioned units. These Title 10 deployments concentrate support on military unique skills and capabilities that domestic law enforcement agencies lack, or cannot practically replicate.
>
> Title 10 counterdrug support must also provide a training opportunity that contributes to combat readiness and cannot be used for continuing, on-going, long-term operational support commitments at the same location. The use of Title 10 forces is effective in large scale engineering operations and in other areas where their Mission Essential Task List (METL) and critical capabilities intersect with law enforcement requirements.
>
> Under Title 32 of the U.S. Code, National Guard members may be ordered to perform full-time duty under section 502(f). For example, National Guard units were deployed during OPERATION JUMP START (OJS) and OPERATION PHALANX (OP) under 32 USC 502f. In OJS, National Guard units were divided into Entry Identification Teams (EIT) and deployed at fixed interdiction sites specified by Customs and Border Protection (CBP). These sites were high visibility and served as a deterrent to help interdict illegal activities. Units deployed under Title 32; 502f worked under the same guidelines as Title 10 soldiers. This arrangement tied both the EITs and Border Patrol Agents to static pre-determined locations regardless of the evolving tactical situation on the ground.
>
> Under Title 32, section 112 of the U.S. Code, the National Guard Counter Drug program is authorized up to 4,000 National Guard members performing drug interdiction or counterdrug activities in all 54 states and territories. Units deployed under Title 32; 112 Counter Drug Sup-

> port (CDS) fall under the command of the State Governor and the Adjutant General (TAG). This allows for a much more flexible use of military assets and capabilities, as they are not restricted by Posse Comitatus Act (PCA) under the federal exemption offered to them. National Guard units deployed under Title 32; 112 have the authority to conduct surveillance operations within their States to support Federal agencies operating along the southwest border. These soldiers are working in the states they reside and are able to fully integrate into the law enforcement operational rhythm, as the length of their service both in time and location is far greater that their Title 10 & Title 32; 502f counterparts (report in public domain).[4]

With this ploy in action, subcomponents of *Operation Jump Start* were implemented. *Operation Hold the Line* was the name of the operation at the Juarez, Mexico/El Paso, Texas border crossing; *Operation Gatekeeper* was the name of the Tijuana, Mexico/Imperial Beach–San Diego border entry; while *Operation Safeguard* was the name for the operation at the Nogales, Mexico/Douglas-Tucson, Arizona border crossing. *Operation Jump Start* was a contemporary version of *Operation Wetback* 50 years earlier. The National Guard units worked in conjunction with a reinforced Border Patrol in these efforts to stem illegal entry into the United States. That same year, 2006, the U.S. Bureau of Alcohol, Tobacco, Firearms and Explosives (aka ATF) initiated its five-year (2006–2011) sting operation, *Project Gunrunning,* where ATF purposely allowed licensed U.S. firearm dealers to sell assault rifles and high-capacity weapons to persons known to be representing the Mexican drug cartels ostensibly to trace the weapons through Mexico. This sting operation process was known as *gun walking* with *Operation Fast and Furious* its largest project. Of the 2,000 weapons distributed during this particular project, only 710 were effectively traced as of February 2012 while both the George W. Bush and Obama administrations have stonewalled any viable investigation into the operation. The exposure of this operation did little to improve Mexican/U.S. relations given that the ATF deliberately armed Mexican drug cartels with more lethal weapons resulting in tens of thousands of drug-related deaths, many involving innocent civilians.[5]

The post-9/11 War on Terrorism impacted the northern border with Canada as well, if not as severely. Even then, Canada's post-9/11 efforts at increased border security were met with widespread public outcry despite the increased security on the U.S. side. Canada's attempt at creating military security zones in order to curtail potential terrorist attacks on its country fell short of U.S. expectations. Drafted as Public Security Act C-42, it was withdrawn in April 2002 due to mounting criticism from civil libertarians who claimed that the Act provided excessive powers to cabinet ministers when issuing emergency decrees and defining "military security zones," an action seen as tantamount to martial law. It was replaced with a modified antiterrorism, C-55, which omitted the martial law component associated with designated security zones. Unlike the United States' convoluted use of the National Guard, C-55 does not allow military involvement when quelling civil disobedience. Instead, C-55 allows the Royal Canadian Mounted Police (RCMP) to scan air passenger manifests for potential terrorists or for anyone with an outstanding felony warrant. Canada, the North American country with the smallest population, has allocated over a billion Canadian dollars toward its national security, immigration control, customs, and the military since 9/11.

The 9/11 terrorist attacks on the United States caused both the United States and Canada to reassess the security along what is the longest open border in the world. The difficulties associated with increased border security, especially its economic impact, is that Canada is the United States' largest trading partner. The increased security effort by the NAFTA partners has been costly with considerable economic impact as trade initially slowed between Mexico, Canada, and the United States. Tourism is another area impacted by these increased security measures with new passport requirements at international border crossings. NAFTA arrangements for a more fluid crossing were replaced under the Western Hemisphere Travel Initiative (WHTI) which took effect on June 1, 2009. WHTI resulted from the Intelligence Reform and Terrorism Prevention Act of 2004 (IRTPA) which affects both land and sea travel into the United States. IRTPA requires a valid passport in order to enter the USA from either Canada or Mexico. Given its reciprocal arrangement, the Canadian Border Service Agency (CBSA) now requires a valid passport for anyone age 16 or older, or an equivalent travel document such as a NEXUS card, a WHTI-approved Enhanced Driver's License (EDL), or a Free and Secure Trade (FAST) Express Card in order to enter Canada legally via any USA border entry point. Friendly border relations were seriously challenged when President Obama proposed a $5.50 entry fee for Canadians entering the U.S. as part of his 2012 budget plan. If implemented, this would have affected millions of Canadians who enter the U.S. regularly given that the two countries constitute the largest trading bloc in the world with daily bilateral trade worth about two billion U.S. dollars.[6]

9/11'S IMPACT ON INDIAN COUNTRY

U.S. "Indian Country" currently comprised of 565 federally recognized tribes (reservations, bands, boundaries, and other specific tribal entities), each with its own boundary denoting its semi-autonomous status and federal protection from outside intrusion and exploitation. Some are small rancheros in California while the largest is the Navajo Nation which covers 17.5 million acres, an area larger than New England. The Navajo (the Dineh) have some 260,000 enrolled members. Other reservations are known for post–Indian Wars conflicts, most notably being the

Pine Ridge Sioux Reservation in South Dakota. This is where both the last major battle of the Indian Wars of the nineteenth century (Wounded Knee) and the battle in the 1970s known as Wounded Knee II occurred. Both battles were considered military actions given that the Posse Comitatus Act apparently did not apply to these situations, hence the use of military interventions. Wounded Knee is a community on the Pine Ridge Reservation which comprised of 2.8 million acres and an enrollment of about 28,000 members.[7]

Accordingly, tribal members share a psycho-cultural identity with its own historical significance, hence forging their own psychic boundaries known as their psychological reference. The boundaries for these 563 entities, from the largest to the smallest, provide a needed barrier to keep out external influences, many designed to destroy and exploit their cultural heritage. Their semi-autonomous status allows for some semblance of tribal governance with federal protection, for the non–Public Law 280 states, from local and state interference. Currently, the United States Supreme Court has a case from a Creek Indian sentenced to death in Oklahoma within the state jurisdiction for the death of a fellow Indian. This case before the nation's highest court is to discern between "Indian reservations" and the larger entity—Indian Country—given that Oklahoma was designated as the original Indian Territory. Even then, border restrictions stemming from the post-9/11 security measures have complicated the treaty arrangements protecting Indian Country. As stated earlier, the inhabitants of Indian Country are known as "American Indians" or "Alaska Natives" (AI/AN) whose tribal membership is determined by official tribal enrollment rolls. U.S. Department of Homeland Security (DHS) measures challenge the long-held 1794 Jay Treaty allowing for the free cross-border travel for Indigenous peoples whose tribal/linguistic heritage and traditional homelands transcended Euro-American geo-political boundaries.

Transnational tribes have historically been allowed intra-tribal movement to its traditional tribal lands. This has long been a condition between tribes sharing traditional lands across the United States/Canada border, a practice extending to the early days of the U.S. Republic as a condition of the 1794 Treaty of London (Jay Treaty). These rights were later extended to tribes transcending the U.S./Mexico border as conditions of both the 1848 Treaty of Guadalupe Hidalgo ending the Mexican War and the 1854 Gadsden Purchase that took more Mexican land along the now New Mexico and Arizona border. In 1924, the same year that American Indians/Alaska Natives gained federal citizenship (June 2), the U.S. Congress passed a law exempting American Indians born in Canada from the dictates of the *Immigration* Act of 1924—To wit: That the Immigration Act of 1924 shall not be construed to apply to the right of American Indians born in Canada to pass the border of the United States: Provided, That this right shall not extend to persons whose membership in Indian tribes of families is created by adoption (April 2, 1928). The new "passport" and Real ID requirements now in effect exempts many tribal members whose only means of identification is their tribal enrollment card or the older version of a state driver's license. Both of these new standards for border crossing require an official birth certificate, something many North American Indians lack given home births. Since 9/11 the federal government has further intruded into the limited autonomy of tribal governance within Indian Country whereby the U.S. military can unilaterally enter any Indian entity in the name of homeland security.

The U.S. reservations most impacted by homeland security are those closest to the international borders. The historical Jay Treaty applied to the U.S./Canada international divide although not specifically to its most eastern boundaries given that the Maine/New Brunswick border dispute was not settled until 46 years following the Jay Treaty. The major cross-border tribes in Maine are: (1) the Houlton Band of Maliseet Indians with the U.S. tribe called the Passamaquoddy while their Canadian counterparts are known as Maliseet, linguistic cousins to the Micmac tribe; (2) the Penobscot Nation of Indian Island; (3) the Passamaquoddy tribes located at Princeton Perry; and (4) the Aroostook Band of Micmac Indians. These tribes are part of the Abenaki (Wabanaki) Confederacy whose membership numbers in the thousands. There are seven Maliseet bands in Canada (New Brunswick and Quebec) and 28 Canadian bands within the Micmac Nation. In 1980, the Maine tribes won a landmark decision, initiated on their behalf by the Native American Rights Fund (NARF), resolving an eight-year suit over land taken illegally by White settlers. In return for the 12 million acres stolen, the Maine Indian Settlement Act with the Passamaquoddy and Penobscot tribes provided a cash settlement with the monies used to improve the historically poor living conditions of these tribes.[8] Moving westward, New Hampshire, and to a lesser degree Vermont, engaged in a vicious policy of ethnic cleansing through extermination and forceful removal of the traditional Abenaki tribes so that there are no state or federally recognized tribes in either state. The remnants of these disposed tribes exist in Canadian reserves in Quebec at St. Francis and Becancour while the St. Francis-Sokoki Band of the Abenaki Nation in northern Vermont has petitioned for U.S. federal recognition to join Indian Country.

New York, on the other hand, is home to Iroquoian tribes, notably the Mohawk, Tuscarora, Cayuga, Onondaga, and Oneida. Iroquois tribes also reside across the international border in Ontario and Quebec provinces. Accordingly, there are currently two Great Councils maintaining two Council Fires; one at the Onondaga Reservation in New York and the other at Grand River in Ontario, home to the Six Nation Reserve. The St. Regis Mohawk (Akwesasne) reservation is significant in that it crosses the U.S./Canada international border with its 23,000 acres straddling New York State and Quebec and Ontario provinces. The U.S. portion of the tribe is governed by three chiefs and three sub-chiefs while the Canadian Council is administered by a chief and 11 councilors. The Mohawk have been active in the American Indian Movement (AIM) protests during the 1960s and 1970s and in an intra-tribal cross-border gaming dispute in the 1990s. The gaming issue divided the Akwesasne following passage of the Indian Gaming Regulatory Act in 1988. The intra-tribal dispute was between the AIM Warrior Society and the followers of the Longhouse tradition. In July 1989, the FBI and New York State Troopers raided a gaming house in Akwesasne at the request of the Longhouse faction. Tensions were high leading to protest and vandalism that erupted in violence in the spring of 1990 resulting in the death of two Mohawk Indians, leading to a police occupation by the New York State Police and the Royal Canadian Mounted Police (RCMP). Leaders of the Mohawk Sovereignty Security Force were arrested, convicted, and imprisoned as a result of their militant action since 9/11. This particular intra-tribal border region continues to be monitored.[9]

In the Great Plains region, the Sioux tribes dominated both South and North Dakota. Sitting Bull's home, Standing Rock reservation, lies in both Dakotas as does the Lake Traverse Sisseton reservation. Devils Lake and Fort Berthold reservations are further north. The reservation closest to the international border with Canada, however, is the Chippewa Turtle Mountain Reservation. The Chippewa (Ojibway) are Algonquian, not Siouan. While they are represented in both Canada and the United States, Turtle Mountain is the reservation closest to both countries.[10]

Montana has a number of tribes that have cross border-members residing in Canada. These groups include the Sioux, Cheyenne, Crow, and Flathead. The Cheyenne joined up with the Sioux in the defeat of Custer at the Little Bighorn battle in 1876. Peaceful Cheyenne were murdered by the Colorado militia at the Sand Creek Massacre in 1864 during the early years of the Indian Wars. The Blackfoot Confederation once extended well into Canada from Alberta province to the Missouri River in Montana. They are called "Blackfoot" in Canada and "Blackfeet" in the United States. Their name reflects their traditional footwear, moccasins dyed black. Today, the Northern Cheyenne and Crow reservations lie in the lower eastern part of the state while the Flathead reservation is the most western reservation. The four Sioux reservations, Rocky Boys, Fort Belknap, Fort Peck, and Blackfeet, are those closest to the international border with the Blackfeet reservation right on the Canadian border. The largest reservation in Montana is the Crow reservation with 2.5 million acres, followed by the Fort Peck reservation with 2.1 million acres, and the Blackfeet with 1.6 million acres.[11]

Washington, the furthest western state along the U.S./Canada border, is host to two large reservations, Colville and Yakima, as well as a host of smaller coastal reservations. The Colville lies close to the international border and is home to the Confederated Tribes which includes the Nez

Perce, which also has a reservation in Idaho bordering on Washington. Chief Joseph is the Nez Perce chief who when captured attempting to escape across the border to Canada, stated: "I will fight no more forever." Of the reservations in Washington is the most western entity in what constitutes Indian Country in the lower 48 states—Makah Reservation. The Makah people are also unique in that they have no linguistic association with any other tribe in the United States. Their culture is similar to other Northwest Coast Indians and that of their Canadian neighbors, the Nootka on Vancouver Island.[12]

The 1,933-mile southern United States border is less than half that of its northern counterpart, running from east to west with Texas, New Mexico, Arizona, and California. As noted earlier, the Texas cession from Mexico in 1836 resulted in an open policy of physical genocide directed against all Indian tribes within the Texas Republic while the purge of Mestizos at the time of the Mexican Revolution destroyed any remaining semblance of groups of indigenous heritage. While the state with the longest border in the Borderland region, Texas, currently has only three federally-recognized tribes: the Alabama-Coushatta Reservation, north of Houston; the Texas Kickapoo tribe situated along Eagle Pass on the Rio Grande River on the Mexican border; and the Ysleta Del Sur Pueblo reservation along the Mexican border near El Paso. The border tribes are small in both members and tribal lands with the Kickapoo only recently federally-recognized and still in the process of acquiring tribal lands. The Ysleta Pueblo, on the other hand, was part of the Indian gaming scam, *Gimmie Five,* perpetrated by Tom DeLay, Jack Abramoff, and Mike Scanlon, during the George W. Bush administration.[13]

New Mexico is home to 19 Pueblo tribes and two Apache tribes (Jicarilla and Mescalero) and is part of the Navajo Nation, but it has no Indian lands near the international border although there is a link to the Pueblo peoples in northern Mexico. Arizona, on the other hand, is home to the bulk of the Navajo Nation as well as the Grand Canyon Havasupai Reservation, the Hopi Pueblo tribe, Fort Apache and San Carlos Apache reservations, and a number of smaller Mohave, Apache, Pima, Yaqui, and Hohokam tribes. The two major border tribes are the Cocopah/Fort Yuma cluster near the intersection of the international and California borders along the Colorado River. The largest tribe on the international border is the Tohono O'odham (Papago) Reservation comprised of four entities (Maricopa, Gila Bend, San Xavier, and Sells) encompassing 2.8 million acres and some 20,000 members whose families reside on either side of the Borderlands. They are part of the Hohokam cultural group with links to the Aztecan linguistic groups of South America. Tribal members have traditionally crossed the border via "The Gate," a gap in the barbed-wire international boundary. There have been increased incidents of police brutality leveled against the Tohono O'odham since the Department of Homeland Security increased border surveillance along the United

States' southern border, including deaths at the hands of the Border Patrol. Tribal members are also harassed by right-wing White supremacist militia groups. The tribe is resisting Trump's wall and has formed a political action group known as the Voice Against the Wall Project.[14] The most western state along the Borderland is California, a Public Law 280 state, with over 60, mostly small, federally-recognized entities. The array of tribes include rancherias and reservations. Noted among the Southern California tribes is Agua Caliente Reservation, home to the Palm Springs Resort frequented by U.S. presidents, and the Cabazon Reservation which was one of the original plaintiffs leading to the U.S. Supreme Court decision legalizing Indian gaming. Fort Yuma transcends the California/Arizona border and lies on the international border.[15]

Cross-border tribes encountered considerable hardships in their attempts to visit relatives residing on the other side of the international line. This is especially the case for those Indians living along the U.S./Mexico border. Since 9/11 and the creation of the Department of Homeland Security (DHS), the federal government has further intruded into Indian Country restricting tribes' already limited autonomy. The current situation allows for the U.S. military and federal security forces to enter and occupy tribal lands under the DHS's Tribal Consultation Policy. Major components of the Tribal Consultation Policy include these actions and rationales:

> B. The Department of Homeland Security (DHS) is committed to strengthening the government-to-government relationship between the United States and Indian Tribes. DHS recognizes that agency policies, programs, and services may directly or indirectly impact Indian Tribes and is committed to regularly and meaningfully, collaborating, communicating, and cooperating with Indian Tribes with regard to policies that have Tribal Implications. . . .
>
> D. Thus, in accordance with Presidential Memoranda issues in 1994, 2004, and 2009 and Executive Order 13175, "Consultation and Coordination with Indian Tribal Governments." (Nov. 9, 2000), *65 Fed. Reg.* 67,249, DHS adopts this DHS Tribal Consultation Policy.
>
> E. This DHS Tribal Consultation Policy outlines the guiding principles under which DHS is to engage with governments of Indian Tribes. The DHS Tribal Consultation Policy is intended to be continually updated and refined to reflect our ongong engagement and collaboration with Tribal partners.
>
> II. Definitions
>
> a. "Communication: refers to the verbal, electronic, or written exchange of information between DHS and Indian Tribes.
> b. "Consultation" involves the direct, timely, and interactive involvement of Indian Tribes regarding proposed Federal actions on matters that have Tribal implications.

c. "Exigent Situation" refers to an unforeseen combination of circumstances or the resulting state that calls for immediate action in order to enforce or uphold the law; to provide for the national defense; or to preserve life, health, national security, national resources, tribal resources, property, rights, or interests.

d. "Indian Tribe" refers to an Indian or Alaska Native tribe, band, nation, pueblo, village, or community that the Secretary of the Interior acknowledges to exist as an Indian Tribe pursuant to the *Federally Recognized Indian Tribes List Act of 1994,* 25 U.S.C. 479a.

e. "Tribal Government" refers to the recognized body of an Indian Tribe, including any Alaska Native Village defined in or established pursuant to the *Alaska Native Claims Settlement Act* (85 Stat. 688).

f. A "Tribal Implication" exists when a DHS policy or action causes a substantial direct effect on 1) the self-government, trust interests, or other rights of an Indian Tribe; 2) the relationship between the Federal Government and Indian Tribes; or 3) the distribution of rights and responsibilities between the Federal Government and Indian Tribes. . . .

V. General Provisions

A. DHS will periodically consult with Tribal Government to review the effectiveness of this DHS Tribal Consultation Policy and make revisions as necessary.

B. This document has been adopted for the purpose of strengthening government-to-government relationships, communications, and mutual cooperation between DHS and Tribal Governments. This document is not intended to, and does not, create any right to administrative or judicial review, or any other right or benefit or trust responsibility, substantive or procedural, enforceable by a party against the United States, its agencies or instrumentalities, its officers or employees, or any other person.

C. DHS adopts this DHS Tribal Consultation Policy pursuant to Executive Order 13175. This DHS Tribal Consultation Policy does not replace or change any existing Co-obligations of DHS under the *National Environment Policy Act,* the *National Historic Preservation Act,* Section 102 of the *Illegal Immigration Reform and Immigration Responsibility Act,* or any other statute.[16]

Not only are North American Indians and Native Alaskans now greatly restricted in their travels to relatives residing outside the U.S. border, the United States now has free access to militarize and occupy Indian Country in the name of homeland security. These unilateral actions come under the authority of the Director of Tribal Government Homeland Security. The Director's role is to ensure Indian tribes with jurisdiction over lands adjacent to the Canadian and Mexican borders are sufficiently armed to protect the United States from outside influences. President Trump's "border wall" falls within the DHS jurisdiction relevant to Indian Country without regard to environmental concerns or considerations for the preservation of ancestral sites.

President Trump's "Wall of Intolerance" and Renewed Racism in America

Secure borders, like walls and fences, are erected for various reasons but mostly to either keep undesirable people and material out or to keep people contained. Market demands, on the other hand, often transcend these barriers due to unmet needs. Illicit trade occurs when acceptable, reciprocal trade agreements fail to satisfy market demands. Clearly, the United States is the major market for goods and services in North America. With a population of over 318 million it has nearly three times the population of Mexico (124 million) and ten times that of Canada (37 million). In size, the United States has the world's fourth-largest land mass followed by Canada with Mexico listed as the fifteenth-largest country. The 1994 North American Free Trade Agreement (NAFTA) and its proposed modifications under the United States, Mexico, Canada Agreement (USMCA), or "NAFTA 2.0," articulate "legitimate" trade between these countries. Nonetheless, the United States continues to represent one of the world's largest drug markets including illicit agents. The U.S. "War on Drugs" has done little to suppress this appetite. And while the United States has long supported Israel's "right-to-return" policy regarding its increasing incursions into Palestine, it fights indigenous peoples of the Americas attempting to reside in lands once theirs but stolen by the United States. If the "right-to-return" policy has any foundation anywhere, it would be Mexicans, notably those of Indian descent, freely entering those lands that once were part of their aboriginal heritage prior to European contact and especially since the creation of the United States of America. Clearly, race, ethnic, cultural, sectarian, and class biases play a role in how a society and its government define membership "acceptability."

The Trump presidency has witnessed a divided society not seen since the turbulent 1960s and 1970s. Some were shocked at the intensity of this divide thinking that we, as a society, had moved on from the race, ethnic, and class biases of the past. In reality, these divisions were merely suppressed as other issues dominated our lives. It took the election of a non-White as U.S. president to bring out the latent racial/ethnic bias simmering in our collective psyche. It took the Obama presidency to stir the White supremacy nationalistic fervor that lay latent all these years and the Trump presidency to re-ignite these flames of hate and distrust. Discontent is a fact of social interaction from dyadic interpersonal interactions to international relations. It is the nature of the human psyche to test the boundaries of acceptable behaviors in social situations. This phenomenon of "boundary maintenance" applies to all social settings up to and including international geo-politics. The ultimate goal, for therapists to politicians, is to minimize the damage resulting from our discontent. At the personal level we attempt to resolve cognitive dissonance while at the societal level the goal is to come to some acceptable compromise. The major intervening variable within this equation is chaos. Personal chaos such as mental distress or societal chaos like race, class, gender, sectarian conflicts, if not adequately resolved, can lead to a worsening of the presenting crisis. Georg Simmel noted that chaos can be functional in that out-group hostilities tend to solidify in-group cohesion. Hence, fostering conflicts can shore up all parties involved in what Simmel termed reciprocal antagonism. In-group/out-group perceptions are then enhanced by the confirmation bias whereby each group's propaganda attributes disproportionate cause for each group's behaviors, leading to differential interpretations for similar behavior resulting in different social and even criminal outcomes, relevant to which group is judging the other. Some leaders welcome continued chaos in that it allows for greater control over its people including martial law. While presenting a constant "outside" threat or enemy, internal disputes which would likely surface are suppressed.[17]

The nineteenth century was one of seemingly endless conflict within the Americas as the colonies broke away from their European masters. The United States was especially afflicted with its expansionism and ethnic cleansing of its indigenous peoples to its end of slavery and exploitation of other race/ethnic groups to harvest the untapped riches of their new empire. Not only were these actions justified under a unique interpretation of White Supremacy, the Covenant of Divine Providence, allowing White Americans to dehumanize Blacks, Indians, and other non-WASP (White Anglo-Saxon Protestant) peoples. This ideological reasoning was presented as *Manifest Destiny* and soon was expanded beyond the United States to include territories in the Caribbean and the Pacific. It also justified incursions into Central and South America and Mexico in the pursuit of their raw materials. While *Manifest Destiny* reflected the U.S.'s White Supremacy ideology, the *Monroe Doctrine* was its enforcement arm within the Americas.

Manifestations of these nineteenth-century practices continued into the twentieth century leading to the post–Civil War *Jim Crow* era where White Supremacy continued to thrive despite the end of slavery and the so-called extension of the Articles of the U.S. Constitution. Racism was now promoted under the guise of eugenics and the pretense of improving the human race. As we noted earlier actions of two U.S. presidents, who also served as presidents of Ivy League colleges: Woodrow Wilson was president of Princeton University, and Dwight D. Eisenhower served as president of Columbia University. Although started during the Reconstruction era in the South, the Ku Klux Klan flourished under Wilson following his endorsement of a racist 1915 movie, *The Making of America*, leading the way for the legitimacy of the *Jim Crow* South and its political arm, the Dixiecrats (Southern Democrats, replaced later by Southern Republicans). Lynching was an ugly era in American history with Blacks mutilated, tortured, hanged, and burned alive. It was at the end of Wilson's second term that the 1921 Tulsa Massacre occurred when angry Whites attacked and destroyed the prosperous Black Greenwood neighborhood with impunity, resulting in hundreds of Blacks murdered. The proliferation of Confederate statues were a stark reminder of the *Jim Crow* era and the subjugation of Blacks in the South. Three decades later, terror was perpetrated on mainly indigenous peoples in Central America under the Cold War interpretation of the Monroe Doctrine. These people continue to suffer from that chaos with many attempting to escape the violence and poverty it perpetrated.

The twenty-first century witnessed acts of contrition aired by former European colonial powers following the post–World War II succession of autonomous nations emerging from former colonial empires. The United States has been reluctant to admit errors of the past, including slavery or Indian genocide. Yet, it has supported corrupt governments that have been allies in America's Cold War era providing access to U.S. citizenship to "White" Cubans who were part of Batista's corrupt and discriminatory elite while, at the same time, making every effort to curtail entry to Haitian Blacks or Central American Indians. These are the peoples that should be given priority to enter the United States. All American Indians, from Central America, Mexico, and Canada, should have automatic free-entry rights to the land that once was theirs. Restorative social justice will not be truly administered until their countries agree to the *Indigenous Ancestral Rights of Intra-America Free Movement.*

Obviously this is not the case during the Trump administration. Instead of welcoming these peoples, President Trump has promoted a hate campaign against people attempting to gain entry into the United States, even criminalizing their efforts to enter the country. It is apparent that Donald Trump would not have become U.S. president if not for the simmering undercurrents of class, race, and elitism within America. This phenomenon is best explained on two continuums: 1) the horizontal continuum of color supremacy; and 2) the vertical continuum of class/cast stratification. "White Supremacy" falls on the horizontal continuum and was predominant among the European colonial powers as well as the United States. "Whiteness" was used to classify one's class/cast acceptability in the U.S. with Jews being excluded from the "White race" and White Hispanics labeled as "other Whites." Sectarianism was also used to define non-Protestant ethnics as "lesser Whites." Whiteness or even "lightness" was not universally applied to all groups. American Indians, Asians, and Africans usually based their hierarchical standards of superiority/inferiority on genetic purity which often referred to "lightness" as a contaminating factor. The stratification continuum denotes societal ranking of acceptability with those at the top being the "elite." Class stratification occurs among all race/ethnic groups with those at the top showing distain for their members at the lower strata. Here, the "class ceiling" is more significant that the much acclaimed "glass ceiling" that upwardly mobile women and minorities allude to. The "class ceiling" most closely reflects the current divide within America. Indeed, those like Hillary Clinton attempting to break the "political glass ceiling" do it while standing on the "class ceiling," often unaware of this phenomenon that separates the elite and aspiring elite from the rank-and-file working-class American. Wealth and status generally go hand in hand in this scheme of things regardless of sectarian doctrine. That said, Max Weber, among other scholars, noted that the Protestant Ethic established intellectual and moral superiority with one's social status. Others, like John Dollard and Oscar Lewis, wrote on the class structure among American Blacks and Mexicans.[18]

White Supremacy influenced the U.S. Constitution which was written exclusively for White, Protestant males (WASPs). Its inclusiveness evolved over the course of history but a strong sub-culture of White Supremacy persisted and survived following the U.S. Civil War and the U.S. Civil Rights, a century later. Attacks by radical White groups during the 1980s to the present brought this phenomenon to light, especially with the reactions to having a Black American president. The Trump presidency added fuel to this radical White nationalism resulting in a backlash culminating in current movements to remove Confederate statues from their prominence through the South. A closer look at the Confederate statue controversy uncovered the existence of the well-planned, long-term, process of promoting White Supremacy and its not so subtle message of Black and minority inferiority.

Brian Palmer and Seth Fred Wessler uncover this phenomenon in the December 2018 issue of *Smithsonian* noting how a program defending the "virtues" of the Confederacy has been institutionalized and funded by both state and federal monies. The introduction to the article, *The Costs of the Confederacy*, states: "In the last decade alone, American taxpayers have spent at least $40 million on confederate monuments and groups that distort U.S. history and perpetuate racist ideology."[19] Southern states continue to indoctrinate their children, regardless of race or ethnicity, with sanctioned, compulsory, field trips to Confederate sites, where they are subjected to lectures on the moral superiority of the Confederacy ethos that supports White Supremacy and Black inferiority. Palmer and Wessler debunk the proposed "historical and cultural' value of this indoctrination:

> To address this explosive issue in a new way, we spent months investigating the history and financing of Confederate monuments and sites. Our findings directly contradict the most common justifications for continuing to preserve and sustain these memorials.
> First, far from simply being markers of historic events and peoples, as proponents argue, these memorials were created and funded by Jim Crow governments to pay homage to a slave-owning society and to serve as blunt assertions of dominance over African-Americans.
>
> Second, contrary to the claim that today's objections to the monuments are merely the product of contemporary political correctness, they were actively opposed at the time, often by African-Americans, as instruments of white power.
>
> Finally, Confederate monuments aren't just heirlooms, the artifacts of a bygone era. Instead, American taxpayers are still heavily investing in these tributes today. We have found that, over the past ten years, taxpayers have directed at least $40 million to Confederate monuments—statues, homes, parks, museums, libraries and cemeteries—and to Confederate heritage organizations.[20]

These efforts are seen as a continued effort at maintaining the Jim Crow philosophy despite the evidence denouncing this practice when the devastating past social indoctrination, presented to the U.S. Supreme Court, led to the 1954 *Brown v. Board of Education* decree ending Jim Crow school and social desegregation. The White Supremacy carry-over effect addresses all groups considered "outsiders," including people of color and different gender identification or religious affiliation. The physical borders and boundaries that separated Whites and Blacks during the Jim Crow era may no longer be enforced, but the psychological and social implications are clear in the neo–Jim Crow South. The on-going focus on White Supremacy has fueled an increase in extremist groups including militias. Added to the "alt-right" list within the Sovereign Citizen and Lost Cause groups are the Citizens for Constitutional Freedom (C4CF); the Nationalist Front (NF); the Proud Boys; the Patriot Prayers; and the Oath Keepers, most who openly wear Trump and his MAGA hats.[21]

Another issue is the "privileged elite" who are targeted by the working classes. It also became evident that not all those who voted for Donald Trump were "racist." For some, especially those that voted for Barack Obama, voting for Trump was as much a vote against Hillary Clinton who many associated with the "privileged elite" and the trend toward enforced "political correctiveness." Racial bias is not restricted to members of the non-elite in America. The difference lies in the manner in which racial sentiments are expressed. The "elite" uses a more subtle, patronizing method of expressing their racial biases, including terms that are not considered to be vulgar, using instead a lexicon of "political correct racism." The irony is that Donald Trump is also part of the privileged elite, but his attraction to the "common man and woman" was his disdain for political correctness. Candidate Clinton alienated many with her reference to "basement dwellers" and "the basket of deplorables" implying that the working class represented a lower caste of Americans than her group of educated sophisticates. One argument is that the educated elite, in maintaining the "class ceiling," was attempting to impose their rules of speech and deportment on all Americans, a practice long used by elites historically in order to distinguish themselves from the proletariat. This process included using Greek and Latin in the preferred elite professions like law and medicine, languages not readily accessible to the lower classes. Donald Trump's appeal to many was his blunt talk and personal attacks on others, especially those already held in low esteem by working-class Americans.

The current national divide is a mix of White nationalism with its foundation in America's long-simmering racial bigotry and the pervasive fear of terrorism generated out of the 9/11 attacks. Together, these sentiments have emerged as a formidable challenge to America's domestic tranquility. These problems existed prior to Trump's presidency but it is his rhetoric that has served to inflame deep-rooted sentiments within the American public, most notably his insistence of building a "Wall" to keep out unwanted Latinos from Mexico and Central America. The "Wall" denotes a physical barrier designed to exclude certain people from entering the United States even for time-honored reasons such as seeking asylum. President Trump has employed a propaganda technique from the pages of authoritarian regimes by fear-mongering and demonizing and stereotyping a visible group as "outsiders," providing a classic example of Simmel's thesis that out-group hostility increases in-group cohesion. In Trump's case, this technique is to solidify his popularity among his self-defined followers who, in effect, represent a minority (35 percent–40 percent) of the American populace. Indeed, the forced partial-shutdown of the U.S. government over Christmas in 2018 is presented as an ultimatum over building his "Wall of Intolerance." A substantial portion of Trump's followers are military veterans, a sentiment voiced by U.S. Representative Clay Higgins (Republican—Louisiana) in the January 2019 issue of *The American Legion Magazine*:

> For too long, the United States has neglected its responsibility to defend the sovereignty of our borders. Our laws have gone unenforced, and we have failed to provide front line defenders with the infrastructure and resources necessary to combat illegal immigration. This is why I have co-sponsored House Majority leader Kevin McCarthy's Build the Wall, Enforce the Law Act [author's note: House leadership changed from Republicans to Democrats in January 2019]. While America will always be a land of compassion, we cannot compromise the safety of our citizens. Previous administrations have allowed illegal immigration to threaten the fabric of the nation. Parts of our southern border are controlled by criminal cartels that traffic weapons, drugs and humans. These dangerous elements operate in direct violation of

> our immigration laws and pose real threats to our national security. Border security is national security, and it is our border enforcement agents who are tasked with detecting, deterring and responding to these criminal elements. However, they cannot carry out their mission if we neglect top border security priorities. I've spoken with the boots on the ground. The evidence is clear: walls work. Physical barriers delay or stop illegal border crossings, allowing border agents greater response time. Further, catch and release loopholes and sanctuary policies endanger local, state and federal law enforcement. We must end these policies and stand with those who enforce our immigration laws. The Build the Wall, Enforce the Law Act funds President Trump's border wall, cracking down on sanctuary policies and increasing penalties on deported criminals who try to re-enter the United States. These are steps we must take to restore our sovereign borders and combat illegal immigration.[22]

This rationale is similar to that of past attempts to restrict entry for certain groups via restrictive immigration laws. Like in the past, these symbolic crusades fuel hate groups. A report in the Fall 2018 issue of *Intelligence Report,* a special issue of the Southern Poverty Law Center (SPLC), indicates that a year following the Charlottesville alt-right riot, there was a 12.5 percent rise in hate crimes in the 10 largest U.S. cities; 12 percent rise in hate crimes overall for 38 jurisdictions reviewed; the fourth year in a row with a rise in hate crimes in the U.S.; 1,038 hate crimes in the 10 largest cities; and hate crimes against Muslims up 99 percent in 2014–2016. The SPLC also put forth a special issue providing an in-depth analysis of attacks on civil rights by the Trump administration, *America the Trumped: 10 Ways the Administration Attacked Civil Rights in Year One.*[23]

1. Promoting White Nationalism: President Trump's refusal to even use the phrase "alt-right" has many white supremacists gleefully praising him as their ally in the White House;
2. Slashing Civil Rights Enforcement: Former U.S. Attorney General Jeff Sessions and the U.S. Department of Justice scaled back Obama-era efforts to hold police departments accountable for abuses, stopped investigating discriminatory voting laws, and rescinded policies protecting transgender children and workers with disabilities;
3. Revving Up the Deportation Machine: Trump started his campaign by calling Mexican immigrants rapists and killers and made a proposed border wall the centerpiece of his candidacy;
4. Banning Muslims: Trump called for a total and complete shutdown of Muslims entering the United States. Federal courts blocked President Trump's travel ban, but the U.S. Supreme Court allowed the third version to go into effect;

5. Attacking Voting Rights: President Trump created a commission to investigate what he claimed was widespread voter fraud after contending, falsely, that he lost the popular vote because millions voted illegally despite studies showing such fraud nonexistent;
6. Shedding LGBT Protection: Trump's rollback on Obama-era protections include ousting LGBT within the military;
7. Encouraging Police Abuses: Former Attorney General Jeff Sessions reversed a number of policies designed to rein in police abuses such as the numerous shootings of unarmed Black men in recent years;
8. Reviving Debtors' Prisons: Trump's U.S. Justice Department retracted Obama-era policies designed to eliminate abusive municipal judicial practices resulting in the jailing of poor people who cannot afford to pay escalating fines and fees for minor offenses including traffic tickets;
9. Undermining Public Education: The U.S. Department of Education under Trump deliberately starved monies for public schools in order to fund privatization schemes that benefit the wealthy; and
10. Eroding the Rights of Students With Disabilities: Education Secretary Betsy DeVos has gutted guidelines that help ensure children with disabilities adequate services within school settings.[24]

The major arguments concerning President Trump's promised "Wall" surround national security, an issue addressed by his predecessors—George H.W. Bush, Bill Clinton, George W. Bush, and Barack Obama. Indeed, the *Secure Fence Act of 2006* established measures that addressed both land and sea security as its full title attests: *An Act to establish operational control over the international land and maritime borders of the United States.* This Act also amends the *Illegal Immigration Reform and Immigrant Responsibility Act of 1996.* With passage of this Act, the effort to reinforce the U.S./Mexico border with physical barriers was accelerated under President George W. Bush, calling for hundreds of miles of double fencing. However, the idea of installing two-layer reinforced fencing over the various terrain that constituted the international Borderlands was deemed impractical, hence the current collection of fencing, physical barriers, perimeter roads, lighting, cameras, sensors, and most recently, drones. Even then, these border security efforts caused habitat problems that adversely affected wildlife. More significantly, these barriers forced migrants to take more dangerous routes to the United States resulting to at least 2,000 additional deaths in the border region as well as intensifying battles between competing drug cartels.[25] An article in the September 2017 *National Geographic Magazine,* by Richard Misrach, questioned the utility of increased border security as long as the market demands continue within the United States:

> Functionally speaking, a border wall attempts to do two things. One is to stem migration—people coming into this country for greater opportunity. But only when we stop hiring will they stop coming. The other is to keep out drugs—but Americans are the ones creating the demand. Until we address the problem successfully on our end, the cartels will find ways to get through. A wall doesn't stop the reasons that this is happening. . . . To me the building of walls seems more symbolic than anything, a desperate gesture.[26]

America has long been seen as a haven for impoverished peoples, especially those escaping violence. In the case of Central American Indians and Mestizo this has been due to America's interventions during the Cold War, a policy that shored up brutal dictators who fought Castro-type Communism while supporting America's business interests. Before the "migrant caravans" there was the Obama-era Deferred Action for Childhood Arrivals (DACA) which initiated a wave of unattended children from Latin America flooding the U.S./Mexico border. In November 2014, President Obama initiated his *Immigration Executive Action* that expands the number of undocumented immigrants allowed to stay and work, providing deportation relief for many Hispanics. This led to the onslaught of thousands of unattended children from Guatemala, El Salvador, and Honduras drawing attention to the United States' double-standard, one for Cubans versus others from Latin America and the Caribbean (notably Haiti). Using President Obama's amnesty for Mexican children and youth, many families, and *coyotes* (human traffickers), saw this as an opportunity to escape the poverty and violence in their countries. However, the public reaction to this phenomenon and the president's solutions to it have been mixed, again showing the polar divides (and racial biases) still evident in the U.S.A. Seeing Obama's action as a green light, desperate families in Guatemala, Honduras, and El Salvador sent their children and youth unattended to the U.S. border. The number entering the U.S. grew to more than 57,000 in 2014, up from 27,884 in 2013.

These children are fleeing the horrors and violence, extreme poverty, and gangs and their governments' failure to protect them. The flood of unaccompanied children and youth from impoverished Latin American countries, those nations beset with violence, adds a new dimension to the human trafficking dilemma as well as reawakening the racial biases of anti-Indian/Mestizo prejudices in the United States. The current demographics show that most of the unaccompanied children and youth arriving at the U.S. border via Mexico—are females. The Pew Research Center indicates that apprehensions of unaccompanied teenage girls are up 62 percent to 9,597 in 2014 compared with 5,916 in 2013 while there's been virtually no increase among their male counterparts. Most of the female teens (2014 data) crossing into the U.S. are from Honduras, followed by Guatemala, El Salvador, and lastly, Mexico. For male teens, Mexico is first, followed by Guatemala, El Salvador, and Honduras.[27] The DACA provision allowing some individuals brought to the United States illegally as children a two-year renewable deferred action from deportation, which is a major issue within the Trump administration's immigration policy, has not been resolved as of January 2019. One could ask why immigration, especially those from Mexico, is such a hot topic among Trump's followers when the Pew Research Center data indicates that the unauthorized immigrant total continues to decline to its lowest level in a decade. The decline, according to government data, is due mainly to a sharp decrease in the number of Mexicans entering the U.S. illegally. According to the December 2018 Pew report, there were 12 million immigrants from Mexico residing in the U.S. in 2016 with less than half of them illegal. Nearly 90 percent of children living with unauthorized immigrant parents were born in the United States. The report goes on to note that Mexico is the primary source of immigrants accounting for over a quarter of all U.S. immigrants. These trends are indicative of a number of factors including the effectiveness of the existing composite border security measures in place as well as the long-term positive effects of NAFTA on the Mexican economy.[28]

Trump's rants against immigrants, first as a candidate and later as president, focused on Mexicans. These hostile sentiments were then easily transferred to Latin American Hispanics when the "caravans" made their way from southern Mexico to the U.S. border. The harsh backlash from the Trump administration echoes that of the militarized expulsion of Mexicans, legal and illegal, conducted during the Eisenhower administration with Operation Wetback. President Trump has expanded on the Eisenhower policy by greatly restricting the availability of official border sites for those seeking asylum while "criminalizing" those attempting to gain entry through any means so that they can seek asylum. By making attempts to gain entry for the purpose of seeking asylum a criminal offense, the administration uses this ploy in order to justify the mobilization of the U.S. military, sending thousands of active duty troops to augment the 2,100 National Guard personnel already deployed at the border during the 2018 Christmas holidays.

Another policy that has brought worldwide condemnation is the separation of families in separate detention centers resulting in thousands of children and youth placed in "contract" detention centers without consideration of the psychological significance of such actions of separating young children from their parents and then not allowing them to communicate with each other. Indeed, some parents were deported without knowing the status of their children and vice versa. This deliberate action was justified by the Trump administration as a deterrent for others attempting to enter the United States from its southern border. Surveys of these contracted detention centers, especially those holding children and youth, have shown them to be lacking in basic accommodations needed for the care of minors. These facilities are managed much like concentration or POW camps with little or no privacy, lights on 24/7, open sleeping and toileting areas, and virtually no social or human services. Language is also a barrier where asylum seekers are compelled to sign statements written in English, and the recent death of two "Caravan" children showed that addressing them in Spanish is inadequate when their native language is Mayan. The seriousness of this issue came to light in December 2018 with the death of a seven-year-old Guatemalan girl, and a week later, the death of an eight-year-old Guatemalan boy in U.S. custody. These deaths prompted the administration of medical checks for all children in the custody of the Border Patrol. The Trump administration's policy of systematically denying medical care for migrants, notably those of indigenous groups, is explored by researchers from the University of Texas at El Paso (UTEP) and the University of Arizona:

> The death of seven-year-old Jakelin Amei Rosemery Caal Maquin in December of 2018 while in US Border Patrol custody has led to outrage, frustration, and a host of unanswered questions. We know that she and her father were apprehended at 9:15 p.m., but Jakelin was not admitted to Providence Children's Hospital in El Paso until 8:51 a.m. the following morning. . . . Beyond this tragic case, our research—which consists of more than 1,100 post-deportation surveys with unauthorized Mexican migrants—suggests that the denial of medical attention to migrants in US custody is a widespread and systemic problem, and one that appears to affect indigenous language speakers disproportionately. . . . Asylum seekers are being bottlenecked at ports of entry, where they are admitted to the United States in extremely limited numbers or stopped from initiating their asylum request entirely. As a result, they are attempting to cross the border in risky ways, and at remote places in order to initiate an entirely legal request for asylum. This new pattern of government-created risk to asylum seekers reproduces a previous death- and injury-generating policy in which concentrated enforcement infrastructure and resources push unauthorized migrants into dangerous desert and mountain terrains.[29]

In another tactic in its attempt to avoid legal responsibility, Trump has made arrangements for Mexico to detain the Central American "caravan" asylum seekers in shelters near the U.S. border to wait for their applications to be processed.

Many of the president's actions are being challenged within the courts, especially the administration's efforts to defy the Flores Consent Decree which forbids holding migrant children in criminal detention centers. Under the Flores settlement migrants without travel documents cannot be held in detention for more than 20 days. Otherwise they are recorded by border personnel and then released and allowed to live freely in the United States until their status hearing, although some are provided with GPS ankle bracelets. The Trump administration wants to override the Flores settlement and instead allow for undocumented migrants, individuals or families, to be held in indefinite detention. This is Trump's compromise to the administration's intention to immediately turn back all undocumented migrants without the benefit of any judicial review. Former U.S Attorney General Jeff Sessions' "zero-tolerance" mandate in 2018 resulted in the jailing of thousands of migrant parents while forcefully separating some 2,500 children from their families and in a number of civil lawsuits. Public support for a militarized and walled border is strongest among President Trump's conservative Republican base (30–40 percent) and among active military troops (65 percent) but is not otherwise widely endorsed by the general public as a whole.[30]

CANADA'S ROLE IN THE AMERICAN IMMIGRATION CRISIS

Greater security along the 5,000-plus-mile borders with Canada (lower 48 and Alaska) increased following both the implementation of NAFTA and 9/11 but nothing like that along the shorter (1,933) international border with Mexico. Increased scrutiny along both borders occurred during the Trump administration. Even then the differential between the United States' southern and northern international borders remains with greater focus placed on the border with Mexico. As previously mentioned, a major problem with both international crossings affects American Indians in that tribal border issues pertain not only to the 563 federally-controlled indigenous groups comprising *Indian Country*—but to those 40-plus tribes that transcend the U.S./Canada and U.S./Mexico borders—creating both internal and international sovereignty issues. As stated earlier, the largest of these international cross-border tribal areas exists along the U.S./Mexico border where the Tohono O'odham (aka Papago) share their three million acre reservation between Arizona USA & Sonora Mexico. The stopping of "suspected illegal" immigrants brings back the horrors of the Indian Removal era; the Geary Act of 1892, forcing Chinese in America to produce documentation of legal status on demand; and the roundup and internment of Japanese during World War Two. Using law enforcement and the military in these search and seizure operations fueled existing race and ethnic animosities as well as making minorities in America feel that their communities are under siege and their lives endangered by the police.

The anti-immigrant rhetoric and the attempt to impose checkpoints in the north like those along the southern border have divided both the general public and law enforcement agencies. This current conflict along the northern border is actually rooted in the Eisenhower era dictate calling for a semi-militarized 100-mile zone throughout the United States, a policy historically only enforced along the southern border, especially since the Nixon/Reagan "War on Drugs." The expansion of the 100-mile militarized zone stems from Trump's seeming support for racial and sectarian hostility within American society, where the president has sent a strong message to those who support these sentiments as well as to those likely to be targeted for legal and extra-legal prosecution and persecution. Color and ethnicity, along with religious background, simplifies the "out-groups" in President Trump's America sending fear, especially for those who reside here as undocumented, or with temporary visas. Here, the NAFTA highway to Canada plays an increasingly significant role in the exodus north. The Canadian attraction is strong for African and Middle Eastern peoples from Islamic cultures as well as for Mestizos and Haitians from Mexico, Central America, and the Caribbean. An August 10, 2017 Associated Press article described the scene at a remote New York/Quebec border crossing:

> Seven days a week, 24 hours a day, migrants who came to the U.S. from across the globe—Syria, Congo, Haiti, elsewhere—arrive here where Roxham Road dead-ends so they can walk into Canada, hoping its policies will give them the security they believe the political climate in the United States does not. . . . The passage has become so crowded this summer that Canadian police set up a reception center on their side of the border in the Quebec community of Saint-Bernard-de-Lacolle, about 30 miles south of Montreal, or almost 300 miles north of New York City. It includes tents that have popped up in the past few weeks, where migrants are processed before they are turned over to the Canada Border Service Agency, which handles their applications for refuge.[31]

Ethnic Muslims as well as Hispanics and Haitians sought refuge in Canada is order to escape harassment by law enforcement and vigilante groups in the United States, forcing the Canadian Border Services Agency (CBSA) to bolster their border surveillance at popular Quebec crossings. The marked increase among those seeking asylum or refuge in Canada is straining social services along the entire border region, especially entry points in Quebec and Manitoba provinces. Canada's Interior Minister cites the need to provide better screening for those seeking entry into his country based on an existing Canada-U.S. Safe Third Country Agreement. This agreement compels Canada to turn back refugees, forcing them to attempt to enter Canada illegally along its porous border region. According to this agreement, asylum seekers are to be turned back and told to file a claim while in the United States. Canada opened Montreal's Olympic Stadium to house asylum seekers while tent cities hold many of those who have already crossed. The incentive for many seeking refuge is to reach Canadian sanctuary cities. The rush of those seeking refuge in Canada to escape Trump's toxic anti-immigrant atmosphere has led to predatory behavior in the U.S. with taxi drivers fleecing those trying to get rides to the international border. New York Attorney General's office has filed charges against taxi companies for price gouging refugee clients.

President Trump's trade and tariff war with Canada has led to greater support for refugees regardless of existing agreements.

Enforcement of the Eisenhower-era 100-mile enforcement zone is that it encompasses entire states like New Hampshire where U.S. Immigration and Customs Enforcement (ICE) has set up unannounced roadblocks interrupting the flow of traffic to and from Canada. There is a steady flow between the French in Canada and the Franco-Americans in New Hampshire where the latter represent the largest minority group in the state. Some 500,000 French Canadians visit New Hampshire annually making valuable contributions to its economy. The potential for these searches exists along the entire northern international border but is unique in New Hampshire in that this federalized police authority encompasses the entire state. The problem is further exacerbated by the conservative "law and order" nature of New Hampshire politics. In 2016, the then Republican-led legislature (House and Senate) passed a law giving federal Border Patrol officers the same jurisdictional authority as the New Hampshire State Police in its most northern county, Coos County. Under this arrangement the State Police would accompany ICE at these roadblocks where they also searched for drugs resulting in the arrest of legal individuals with small amounts of marijuana either for medical or personal use. Again we see the merging of the War-on-Drugs and the War-on-Terrorism, especially with New Hampshire having one of the highest opiod-related death rates in the nation. Marijuana busts further highlighted the differences between New Hampshire and surrounding states and Canada where personal use of marijuana is legal. The dilemma is that only medical marijuana is legal in New Hampshire while marijuana possession remains a federal offense.

The authority to stop someone based on their physical appearance merely emboldened other law enforcement agencies through the state's other nine counties and 234 public entities that were eager to detain suspected illegal immigrants for ICE and/or subsequently arrest those stopped for drug infractions. The legal challenge surrounded the use of the ICE stops to search for illicit drugs and then turning these people, who are legal U.S. citizens, over to local law enforcement for prosecution. This action led to an intervention by the New Hampshire American Civil Liberties Union (ACLU). Under judicial scrutiny, New Hampshire prosecutors dropped the drug cases when a circuit judge ruled that this action exceeded the federal authority under the 100-mile zone: Essentially, the court's argument was that the U.S. Supreme Court affirmed the authority for the U.S. Border Patrol to lawfully stop motorists, with no suspicion required, at checkpoints away from the border to determine the citizenship of a vehicle's occupants and found it is consistent with the Fourth Amendment and not for other reasons, especially those that would violate laws.

The irony of the current double standard regarding drug crimes is that drug cartel leaders are prosecuted to the fullest extent of the law, including the potential for using the Reagan "Drug Kingpin Death Sentence," while big pharmaceutical officials are allowed to make civil deals without any disclosure relevant to premeditated plans designed to "hook" Americans on opioid medications. This has long been the practice within American justice where white collar crime is seen as an acceptable part of capitalism distinguishable from organized crime which is adjudicated to the fullest extent of the law. The "catch and release" practice for white collar crimes has a long history within American society, extending to the colonial era, where breaking the law is seen as a legitimate element of capitalism. The practice is to exercise illicit practices until caught and brought before a civil hearing where you are allowed to make a satisfactory monetary compensation with the proviso that allows your company to deny any claim of guilt. The important factor here is that no one is held personally accountable for any premeditated criminal activity unlike with organized crime cases where the alleged offender (Mexican drug lord) is adjudicated to the fullest extent of the criminal law including the threat of the death sentence. If the American drug supply problem is to be adequately addressed, then all parties (big pharmaceutical officials and Mexican drug lords) need to be adjudicated alike under existing RICO standards.

Epilog:

As we attempt to conclude our work in order to meet the mid-January 2019 submission deadline, Donald J. Trump made his first presidential address to the nation:

> President Donald J. Trump's Address to the Nation on the Crisis at the Border
> January 8, 2019 9:01 P.M. EST
> THE PRESIDENT: My fellow Americans: Tonight, I am speaking to you because there is a growing humanitarian and security crisis at our southern border.
>
> Every day, Customs and Border Patrol agents encounter thousands of illegal immigrants trying to enter our country. We are out of space to hold them, and we have no way to promptly return them back home to their country.
>
> America proudly welcomes millions of lawful immigrants who enrich our society and contribute to our nation. But all Americans are hurt by uncontrolled, illegal migration. It strains public resources and drives down jobs and wages. Among those hardest hit are African Americans and Hispanic Americans.
>
> Our southern border is a pipeline for vast quantities of illegal drugs, including meth, heroin, cocaine, and fentanyl. Every week, 300 of our citizens are killed by heroin alone, 90 percent of which floods

across from our southern border. More Americans will die from drugs this year than were killed in the entire Vietnam War.

In the last two years, ICE officers made 266,000 arrests of aliens with criminal records, including those charged or convicted of 100,000 assaults, 30,000 sex crimes, and 4,000 violent killings. Over the years, thousands of Americans have been brutally killed by those who illegally entered our country, and thousands more lives will be lost if we don't act right now.

This is a humanitarian crisis—a crisis of the heart and a crisis of the soul.

Last month, 20,000 migrant children were illegally brought into the United States—a dramatic increase. These children are used as human pawns by vicious coyotes and ruthless gangs. One in three women are sexually assaulted on the dangerous trek up through Mexico. Women and children are the biggest victims, by far, of our broken system.

This is the tragic reality of illegal immigration on our southern border. This is the cycle of human suffering that I am determined to end.

My administration has presented Congress with a detailed proposal to secure the border and stop the criminal gangs, drug smugglers, and human traffickers. It's a tremendous problem. Our proposal was developed by law enforcement professionals and border agents at the Department of Homeland Security. These are the resources they have requested to properly perform their mission and keep America safe. In fact, safer than ever before.

The proposal from Homeland Security includes cutting-edge technology for detecting drugs, weapons, illegal contraband, and many other things. We have requested more agents, immigration judges, and bed space to process the sharp rise in unlawful migration fueled by our very strong economy. Our plan also contains an urgent request for humanitarian assistance and medical support.

Furthermore, we have asked Congress to close border security loopholes so that illegal immigrant children can be safely and humanely returned back home.

Finally, as part of an overall approach to border security, law enforcement professionals have requested $5.7 billion for a physical barrier. At the request of Democrats, it will be a steel barrier rather than a concrete wall. This barrier is absolutely critical to border security. It's also what our professionals at the border want and need. This is just common sense.

The border wall would very quickly pay for itself. The cost of illegal drugs exceeds $500 billion a year—vastly more than the $5.7 billion we have requested from Congress. The wall will also be paid for, indirectly, by the great new trade deal we have made with Mexico.

Senator Chuck Schumer—who you will be hearing from later tonight—has repeatedly supported a physical barrier in the past, along with many other Democrats. They changed their mind only after I was elected President.

Democrats in Congress have refused to acknowledge the crisis. And they have refused to provide our brave border agents with the tools they desperately need to protect our families and our nation.

The federal government remains shut down for one reason and one reason only: because Democrats will not fund border security.

My administration is doing everything in our power to help those impacted by the situation. But the only solution is for Democrats to pass a spending bill that defends our borders and re-opens the government.

This situation could be solved in a 45-minute meeting. I have invited Congressional leadership to the White House tomorrow to get this done. Hopefully, we can rise above partisan politics in order to support national security.

Some have suggested a barrier is immoral. Then why do wealthy politicians build walls, fences, and gates around their homes? They don't build walls because they hate the people on the outside, but because they love the people on the inside. The only thing that is immoral is the politicians to do nothing and continue to allow more innocent people to be so horribly victimized.

America's heart broke the day after Christmas when a young police officer in California was savagely murdered in cold blood by an illegal alien, who just came across the border. The life of an American hero was stolen by someone who had no right to be in our country.

Day after day, precious lives are cut short by those who have violated our borders. In California, an Air Force veteran was raped, murdered, and beaten to death with a hammer by an illegal alien with a long criminal history. In Georgia, an illegal alien was recently charged with murder for killing, beheading, and dismembering his neighbor. In Maryland, MS-13 gang members who arrived in the United States as unaccompanied minors were arrested and charged last year after viciously stabbing and beating a 16-year-old girl.

Over the last several years, I've met with dozens of families whose loved ones were stolen by illegal immigration. I've held the hands of the weeping mothers and embraced the grief-stricken fathers. So sad. So terrible. I will never forget the pain in their eyes, the tremble in their voices, and the sadness gripping their souls.

How much more American blood must we shed before Congress does its job?

To those who refuse to compromise in the name of border security, I would ask:

Imagine if it was your child, your husband, or your wife whose life was so cruelly shattered and totally broken?

To every member of Congress: Pass a bill that ends this crisis.

To every citizen: Call Congress and tell them to finally, after all of these decades, secure our border.

This is a choice between right and wrong, justice and injustice. This is about whether we fulfill our sacred duty to the American citizens we serve.

> When I took the Oath of Office, I swore to protect our country. And that is what I will always do, so help me God.
> Thank you and goodnight.
> END 9:11 P.M. EST

President Trump's prime-time speech to the nation has hallmarks of fear-mongering by misusing data in order to create a sense of a security emergency and impending crisis which does not exist while, at the same time, demonizing Hispanics, Indians, and Mestizos seeking asylum in the United States which is a right under international law of which America is a co-signee. The Trump administration has deliberately created a self-fulfilling prophecy by orchestrating the "humanitarian crisis" alluded to in the presidential address. This crisis was created by systematically reducing the number of legitimate points of entry as well as limiting the availability of immigration judges needed to hear asylum appeals. These actions caused most potential applicants to attempt other entry points and, by doing so, labeled these individuals as entering illegally, which the administration has deemed a criminal offense. Furthermore, President Trump fails to recognize the legitimacy of those seeking asylum by his administration's attempts to return these people, including children, "back home." The assumption given in the speech is that most, if not all, of those seeking entry into the United States are not eligible or welcomed.

The president also misrepresents marketplace demands, first by stating that these migrants, if allowed to enter the United States, will put a strain on public resources and drive down jobs and wages, especially for other minorities in America (African Americans and Hispanic Americans). This is a weak argument given America's booming economy and the fact that Mexicans and Central Americans have traditionally taken on jobs that are unpopular among U.S. citizens regardless of race or ethnicity. Another market fallacy is the impression that a secure wall will end America's drug dependency. Even if a barrier was erected along the entire 1,933-mile border, it would not, in itself, adequately address the supply issue, let alone the demand for these substances within American society. The greatest fallacy in the president's speech, however, is his attempt to paint the majority of those seeking entry into the United States along the southern border as a dangerous and violent race of people. This is a popular propaganda tactic based on the "confirmation bias"—whereby taking a few unrepresentative examples out of context and attributing these to the entire class of people. By deliberately doing so, President Trump has joined the ranks of other overtly prejudiced American leaders, including Andrew Jackson (1829–1837); James Polk (1845–1849); Franklin Pierce (1853–1857); Andrew Johnson (1865–1869); Ulysses S. Grant (1869–1877); and Woodrow Wilson (1913–1921). Granted, there were other presidents who held strong racial biases, like Dwight D. Eisenhower, but they avoided making bold public proclamations like those presidents who are listed.

NOTES

1. L.A. French, & M. Manzanarez. *NAFTA & Neocolonialism: Comparative Criminal, Human & Social Justice.* Lanham, MD: University Press of America, 2004.
2. T. Dunn & J. Palafox. "Border Militarization and Beyond." *Borderlines,* Vol. 8 (4), April 2000, pp. 1–12.
3. L. Astorga, & D. Shirk. *Drug Trafficking Organizations and Counter-Drug Strategies in the U.S.-Mexican Context.* San Diego, CA: University of California-San Diego, 2010; & E. Munsing, & C. Lamb. *Joint Interagency Task Force South The Best Know, Least Understood Interagency Success,* Washington, DC: National Defense University, Institute for National Strategic Studies, 2011.
4. S. Brackin, J. Cole, W. Hester, C. Pena-Guzman, R. Schroeder, J. Taylor, & M. Young. *U.S. Southwest Border Security: An Operational Approach.* Fort Leavenworth, KS: U.S. Army Command and General Staff College, December 12, 2012, pp. 28–30.
5. L.A. French. *Policing American Indians: A Unique Chapter in American Jurisprudence.* Boca Raton, FL: CRC Press/Taylor & Francis Group, 2016.
6. *WHTI-Western Hemisphere Travel Initiative.* http://www.getyouhome.gov/html/eng_map.html; & *New Passport Requirements for US/Canada Border Crossings.* http://www.viasplace.com/blog-immigration-law.
7. V.E. Tiller (ed.). *Discover Indian Reservations USA.* Denver, CO: Council Publications, 1992, pp. 27–40.
8. Ibid., pp. 123–128.
9. Ibid., pp. 229–241.
10. Ibid., pp. 251–256.
11. Ibid., pp. 157–171.
12. Ibid., pp. 99–105; 325–343.
13. Ibid., pp. 309–313.
14. Ibid., pp. 9–48.
15. Ibid., pp. 49–82.
16. L.A. French. *Policing American Indians: A Unique Chapter in American Jurisprudence.* Boca Raton, FL:CRC Press/Taylor and Francis Group, 2016, pp. 138–141.
17. L. Coser. *The Functions of Social Conflict.* New York, NY: The Free Press, 1956.
18. M. Weber. *The Protestant Ethic and the Spirit of Capitalism* (T. Parsons, trans.), London, England: Allen & Unwin, 1930; J. Dollard. *Caste and Class in a Southern Town.* New Haven, CT: Yale University Press, 1937; & O. Lewis. *Five Families.* New York, NY: New American Library (Mentor Books), 1959.
19. B. Palmer, & S.F. Wessler. "The Costs of the Confederacy," *Smithsonian,* Vol. 49 (#8), 2018, p. 55.
20. Ibid., p. 58.
21. *Hate and Extremism in 2018.* Montgomery, AL: 2018, www.splcenter.org .
22. C. Higgins. "Fully fund the border wall," *The American Legion Magazine.* January 2019, www.legion.org, p. 12.
23. SPLC, "By the Numbers." *Intelligence Report,* Vol. 165 (Fall 2018), p. 11.
24. SPLC. *America the Trumped: 10 Ways the Administration Attacked Civil Rights in Year One.* Montgomery, AL: Southern Poverty Law Center, 2018, pp. 6–27.
25. Public Law 109-367. *An Act To establish operational control over the international land and maritime borders of the United States (Secure Fence Act of 2006).* 120 Stat. 2638-2640; 8 U.S.C.; 1103, 14 U.S.C, 637.
26. R. Miseach. "Borderlands: A visual meditation on the walls and fences that separate the United States and Mexico—and divide public opinion." *National Geographic,* Vol. 232 (#3), September 2017, pp. 128–130.

27. J. Manuel Krogstad & A. Gonzalez-Barrera. *Hispanics split on how to address surge in Central American child migrants.* Pew Research Center, 2014.

28. Pew Research Center. "U.S. unauthorized immigrant population continues to decline," Pew Research Center: Hispanic Trends (info@pewresearch.org), December 21, 2018.

29. T. Monmaney. "Military Intelligence: In a New Smithsonian Poll, Troops and Veterans take aim at Conventional Wisdom," *Smithsonian,* Vol. 49 (#09), January-February 2019, p. 79; & J. Slack, D.E. Martinez, & J. Heyman. "Immigration Authorities Systematically Deny Medical Care for Migrants Who Speak Indigenous Languages," http://cmsny.org/publications/slackmartinezheymand-medical-care-denial/ December 21, 2018.

30. N. Merchant (Associated Press). "New medical checks conducted on migrant children," *Concord Monitor,* December 27, 2018 (concordmonitor.com), p. B4.

31. W. Ring (Associated Press). "Along the back road to hope—Seeking Security: Migrants race to border, flood Canada at remote N.Y. outpost," *Concord Monitor,* August 10, 2017, p. B6: concordmonitor.com.

Chronology of Major Events

1492/3	Christopher Columbus "discovers" the Americas; first to term inhabitants "Indians."
1521	Spain claims the Philippine Islands in the Pacific.
1534–1536	Cartier explores the St. Lawrence River.
1539	De Soto "discovers" Florida for New Spain.
C1540	Horses introduced to the Americas by Spanish explorers.
1562	Edict of Saint-Germain led to rights for Huguenots in France.
C1600	Sheep brought to the Americas by Spanish.
1603	James I united Scotland and England creating Great Britain.
1603–1615	Samuel de Champlain establishes fur trade in New France.
1607	John Smith establishes 1st English settlement, Jamestown, Virginia.
1608	Champlain establishes first permanent French settlement, Quebec City.
1608	Spanish establish Santa Fe, New Mexico.
	Henry Hudson trades alcohol for Indian goods.
1611	Jesuit missionaries arrive in New France.
1613	French introduce policy of scalp bounties to Indians.
1619	First Anglican missionaries arrive in Virginia.
1620	Pilgrims land at Plymouth Bay, Massachusetts from Holland.
1619–1633	Spanish establish missions among Pueblo tribes.
1621	Pilgrims and Wampanoag Indians share "Thanksgiving."
1624	Dutch claim New Amsterdam (Manhattan) & Fort Orange (Albany), NY.
1641	Dutch offer scalp bounties on Indians.
1653–1658	Oliver Cromwell's "Round Head Rebellion" against the Church of England.

1659	Navajos carry out first raid on horseback.
1661	Spanish raid Pueblo tribes, destroying cultural attributes—Kivas & Kachinas.
1670	Hudson Bay Company chartered by Britain.
1682	Rene Cavalier de la Salle claims Mississippi Valley & Gulf of Mexico for France.
1685	King Louis XIV revokes Huguenots' rights in France.
1691	Virginia banishes Anglos who marry Indians, blacks, or those of mixed-ancestry.
1728	Bering explores Alaska.
1755/56	Acadian Expulsion led by "Red Coat" British & "Blue Coat" colonists.
1756–1763	"Seven Years' War" concluded with France losing most of its North American colonial holdings to Britain.
1763	*Treaty of Paris* ceding New France to Great Britain.
	English introduce biological warfare to Americas with smallpox-infected blankets in Pontiac's Rebellion.
1775–1783	Revolutionary War in 13 British colonies; 1776—U.S. Declaration of Independence from Britain.
	Spanish found San Francisco, California.
1778	Cook "discovers" Hawaiian Islands; explores the Bering Strait.
1783	Treaty of Paris ends U.S. Revolutionary War.
1789	George Washington elected 1st President of the United States (1789–1797).
	Federal Judiciary established.
	U.S. Marshals established as 1st federal law enforcement agency.
	French Revolution.
1790	Naturalization Act—prohibited "naturalization" of non-Whites. Indigenous peoples already excluded.
1791	12 Constitutional Amendments (1–10 aka *Bill of Rights*) outlining U.S. system of Due Process.
1792–1795	George Vancouver claims Pacific Coast for England.
1794	Treaty of London, aka "Jay Treaty," allowing free passage for transnational Indian tribes residing on either side of the U.S./British North America (Canada) border.

1801 Thomas Jefferson elected 3rd U.S. President (1801–1809).

1802 French Republic established Napoleon's reign (1802–1814).

President Jefferson doubles the size of the United States with the Louisiana Purchase from France. Treaty ratified by U.S. Senate on October 20, 1803.

1809–1821 Sequoyah creates Cherokee syllabary, creating written native language.

1810 Mexico begins revolts against Spanish rule.

1812–1814 U.S. initiates the War of 1812 with Britain in attempt to gain territory in Canada.

Georgia militia invades Spanish Florida seeking runaway slaves.

1817 James Monroe elected 5th U.S. President (1817–1825).

General Andrew Jackson starts war with Spain over Florida—First Seminole War—resulting in U.S. acquiring Florida in 1819.

1819 The Adams-Onis Treaty ends the Seminole Wars not only ceding Florida to the United States but also establishing the Mexico/United States border at the Sabine River (ratified in 1821).

1820 Mexican Constitution outlaws slavery and enfranchises all adult males regardless of race or social status.

1821 Mexico gains independence from Spain. Republic of Mexico est. September 21, 1821.

Emperor Agustin de Iturbide, 1st ruler of Mexico (1822–1823).

Americans seek land grants (*empresarios*) in northern Mexico (Eastern Interior Provinces). Conditions include converting to Catholicism.

Texas Rangers begin as "rangers" for policing the Austin empresario in Mexico.

1823 Monroe Doctrine: USA proclaims itself as the premier colonial authority in the Americas.

1824 Mexico emperor Agustín de Iturbride's reign is short-lived and replaced with a federalist system, which evolved into a centralized government in 1830.

1826 Fredonian Rebellion: The Edwards brothers lead rebellion among Anglo empresarios and declare independence from

	Mexico, calling the new nation Fredonia. The rebellion ended in 1827 with the rebels escaping back to the United States.
1828	*Cherokee Phoenix* published using Sequoyah's syllabary.
1829	Andrew Jackson elected 7th U.S. President (1819–1837).
1830	U.S. Congress passes Indian Removal Act to allow whites to take Indian lands east of the Mississippi (Indian Territory established in lands acquired under Louisiana Purchase). U.S. Supreme Court challenges law but President Jackson overrides Justice Marshall.
1832	Black Hawk War, Indian uprising in Illinois and Wisconsin.
1833	Antonio López de Santa Anna's first term as president of Mexico.
1835–1842	Second Seminole War led by Osceola.
1836	Texas declares independence, stating opposition to Catholicism and Mexico's antislavery stance.
	Santa Anna's forces defeat rebels at the Alamo (San Antonio).
	U.S. forces defeat Santa Anna's forces at San Jacinto.
	Sam Houston becomes president of the Republic of Texas.
1838	Potawatomi "Trail of Death"—removed from Indiana.
1838–1839	Cherokee Nation forcefully removed to Indian Territory (Oklahoma) in drama termed the "Trail of Tears."
1839	Santa Anna's second term as president of Mexico.
1840	Union Bill established the Province of Canada.
1841	Santa Anna's third term as president of Mexico.
1842	Webster-Ashburton Treaty ended the *Aroostook War,* establishes eastern border between USA & Canada; dividing the Algonquin tribes (Maliseet & Mi'kmaq) between the Maritime Provinces of Canada and the USA state—Maine.
	Union between Upper and Lower (Quebec) Canada.
1843	Russian-Greek Orthodox Church established Indian mission school in Alaska.
1844	Santa Anna again elected president but is replaced by José Joaquin de Herrera.
1845	James Polk elected 11th U.S. President (1845–1849).

	Texas annexed by the United States as a slave state.
1846	Oregon Territory becomes part of U.S. including dominance of Indians.
	United States declares war on Mexico.
	Santa Anna's fourth term as president of Mexico.
	Sam Houston becomes U.S. senator from the state of Texas.
1847	Brigham Young brings the Mormons (LDS) to Salt Lake, Utah.
1848	Treaty of Guadalupe Hidalgo ends Mexican War with United States gaining half of Mexico.
1850	U.S. Compromise of 1850 and Fugitive Slave Act.
1853	Franklin Pierce elected 14th U.S. President (1853–1857).
	Santa Anna returns from exile in Venezuela and assumes presidency of Mexico for fifth time.
	Ostend Manifesto—ill-fated attempt to force Spain to sell Cuba to the United States to be added as a slave state.
	U.S. president Franklin Pierce gets Santa Anna to relinquish more Mexican territory with the Gadsden Purchase.
1855	Third Seminole War in Florida (ends in 1858).
	Santa Anna again exiled; returns in 1874; dies in 1876.
1857	Gradual Civilization Act passed in Upper Canada disenfranchising all Indian and Métis peoples, classifying them as an inferior category than Canadian citizens.
1859	Sam Houston becomes governor of Texas (loses second term; dies in 1863).
1861	Abraham Lincoln elected 16th U.S. President (1861–1865).
	Benito Juárez (1861–1872) becomes first full-blooded Indian president of Mexico.
	Tripartite Convention in London initiates armed intervention in Mexico with forces from Britain, France, and Spain arriving in Veracruz due to the default of 82 million pesos in loans.
	U.S. Civil War begins, ending in 1865.
1862	Cinco de Mayo: General Díaz defeats Napoleon III's forces at Puebla on May 5, 1862—an important anniversary celebrated to the present.

	Spanish and British forces withdraw leaving only French forces.
	Homestead Act opens up Indian lands to White settlers in Kansas and Nebraska.
	Largest mass execution in USA—38 Santee Sioux warriors publically hanged on single platform (December 26).
	U.S. president Lincoln enacts Emancipation Proclamations on September 22, 1862 and January 1, 1863.
1863–1866	Navajo War in New Mexico and Arizona: Navajo prisoners forced on "Long March" to Bosque Redondo.
1864	Colonel Chivington's Colorado Militia kills over 300 Indians in Sand Creek Massacre.
	Archduke Maximilian accepts Mexican crown as European dictator (1864–1867).
1865–1890	USA's longest official war: Indian Campaign (began in 1862 with Santee Sioux).
1865	13th Amendment to U.S. Constitution abolishes slavery.
1866	Twenty tribes from Kansas and Nebraska removed to Indian Territory (Oklahoma).
	Napoleon III withdraws French troops from Mexico.
	Fenian crisis in Canada; raids from the United States.
1867	Maximilian defeated and executed (on orders of General Porfirio Díaz).
	USA purchases Alaska from Russia, adding Inuit, Aleut, Athabaskan, and Tlingit Indians to U.S. indigenous population.
	Sir John Alexander Macdonald, Canadian Prime Minister (1867–1873 1st term).
	British North American Act creating the Dominion of Canada.
1868	14th Amendment to U.S. Constitution—guarantees "Due Process" to all citizens.
1869–1885	Louis Riel & the Red River Rebellion in Manitoba, Canada.
1869	Ulysses S. Grant elected 18th U.S. President (1869–1877).
1870	U.S. Naturalization Act of 1870.
1871	U.S. Congress ends treaty-making with Indian tribes.
1872	Benito Juárez dies.

1873 Colonel Ranald Mackenzie enters Mexico to raid Indian villages.

1874 "Mounties" established as federal police force in Canada, aka Royal Canadian Mounted Police—RCMP.

Indian Act passed in Canada making its indigenous peoples legal wards of the State who are compelled to be imprisoned on set-aside reserve lands.

1875 Page Act—1st restrictive federal immigration law, prohibiting "undesirables"; made immigration a federal, not state, matter.

1877 Rutherford B. Hayes elected 19th U.S. President (1877–1881).

Porfirio Díaz elected president of Mexico and remains either president (six terms overall) or de facto leader until his resignation and exile to Paris in 1911; he dies in 1915.

1878 Posse Comitatus Act (18 U.S.C.: 1385): Act restricted the use of federal troops in the South during Reconstruction era. Currently applies to any domestic situation outside of an immediate crisis. Exempt under Martial Law conditions.

Sir John Alexander Macdonald—Canadian Prime Minister (1878–1891, 2nd term).

1879 Standing Bear wins federal recognition for Indians to file habeas corpus appeals, gaining recognition of American Indians as "persons."

1881 Chester Arthur became 21st U.S. President (1881–1885).

1882 U.S. Chinese Exclusion Act; Repealed by Magnuson Act, December 1943.

U.S. Immigration Act of 1882—expanded on Chinese Exclusion Act by imposing head tax on those entering U.S. as well as restricting criminals, the insane, and the poor.

Mexico and United States sign treaty allowing reciprocal border crossings.

1884 State-funded, church-administrated Indian Residential Schools established in Canada.

1885 Louis Riel hanged for treason in Canada.

1885 U.S. Congress passes Major Crimes Act imposing federal laws throughout Indian Country.

1887	U.S. Congress passes General Allotment Act ending federal treaty protection for Indian Country, opening up reservations to white settlers.
1888	U.S. Scott Act expanded Chinese Exclusion Act prohibiting "reentry" of Chinese leaving U.S. mainly to visit China.
	Mexico and the United States form International Boundary Commission along with extradition provision.
1890	Wounded Knee massacre: U.S. Army guns down unarmed Sioux Indians with early version of a machine gun.
1891	U.S. Immigration Act of 1891 establishes Office of Superintendent of Immigration.
1892	U.S. Geary Act prevents further immigration from China; requires Chinese residents to carry certificates of residence; repealed in 1943 when China became an ally during WWII.
	Indian Wars in U.S. conclude (1862–1892).
1894	"Canadian Agreement" allows U.S. immigration agents to curtail Chinese immigrants at Canadian ports of entry.
1896	*Plessy v. Ferguson,* U.S. Supreme Court decision upheld Jim Crow segregation in the South, hence 2nd-class citizen status for Black Americans.
	Sir Wilfred Laurier becomes Canada's first French Canadian Prime Minister (1896–1911).
1898	Spanish-American War: United States declares war on Spain over Cuba and Puerto Rico.
	United States v. Wong Kim Ark establishes that 14th Amendment of U.S. Constitution grants U.S. citizenship to all children born to alien parents (birth rights citizenship).
1899	Peace treaty signed with Spain with United States acquiring Puerto Rico and Spanish colonial holdings in the Pacific—Philippine Islands, Guam, Mariana, Caroline, and Marshall Islands. Spain relinquishes control over Cuba. United States begins war in Philippines.
1900	Boxer Rebellion; U.S. deploys Marines to China.
1901	Theodore Roosevelt; 26th U.S. President (1901–1909).
	Rebellion in the Philippines ends.
1904	President Theodore Roosevelt issues his Roosevelt Corollary establishing the right of the United States to unilaterally intervene in the Caribbean and Central America

to protect them from foreign interventions. U.S. Marines become the international police force for this policy.

1906 Nationalization Act—required that immigrants needed to know English before becoming nationalized citizens.

1907 Former "Indian Territory" becomes a state now dominated by White settlers.

Medical Inspector, Canadian Department of Indian Affairs reports on poor conditions in the compulsory Church-run Indian residential schools.

"Gentlemen's Agreement" between U.S. and Japan restricting immigration to educators and professionals—no laborers.

1908 Duncan Campbell Scott, notorious Canadian Superintendent of Indian Affairs, suppresses the Medical Inspector's report.

1910 D. Campbell Scott forges his "final solution to the Indian Problem" by contracting churches to run the harsh Indian Residential Schools.

Angel Island, in California Bay Area, opened to process Asian refugees.

1911 Mexican Revolution begins. Ciudad Juarez falls: 20,000 U.S. troops muster along the Mexican/U.S. border.

1913 Woodrow Wilson elected 28th U.S. President (1913–1924).

1914 U.S. troops occupy Veracruz just as the First World War begins in Europe.

Civil war begins in Mexico between Generals Carranza and Obregón fighting Generals Villa and Zapata.

Sir Robert Laird Borden, Canadian Prime Minister (1911–1920).

World War I begins; Canada joins British forces. French Canadians disproportionately drafted—many flee to United States.

1915 Plan de San Diego exposed as an unlikely revolution to regain Mexican territory lost to the United States. It was initiated by a small radical element of Hispanic revolutionaries. Overreaction by the Texas Rangers leads to excessive force and terror among Mexican Americans living in Texas.

Wilson's critique: President Wilson sides with the Carranza forces (Carranzitas) believing they would better protect U.S. oil interests in Mexico.

1916 General Villa attacks U.S. military facility (Camp Furlong) in Columbus, New Mexico.

Zimmermann communiqué exposes German attempts to involve Mexico in World War I.

1917 U.S. joins allies in First World War.

U.S. Immigration Act of February 5, 1917 establishes "Asian Barred Zone" with Mexican laborers exempt due to manpower shortage during World War I.

Mexico establishes a new Revolutionary Constitution restricting presidents to one six-year term and also allowing for a free secular primary education. The constitution has a de facto prohibition of the death penalty for civilian offenses.

The new constitution greatly restricts the role of the Catholic Church in public matters.

Venustiano Carranza, Mexican President (1917–1920).

U.S. begins 11-month Punitive Expedition into Mexico under General John (Black Jack) Pershing without finding General Villa.

U.S. enters World War I with Pershing as commander of U.S. Expeditionary Forces.

1918 World War I ends; Armistice signed November 11, 1918 (U.S. Veterans Day).

1919 D. Campbell Scott abolishes the post of Medical Inspector for Indian Residential Schools in Canada resulting in a marked rate of tuberculosis deaths among the Indian children (some as high as 75%).

18th Amendment to U.S. Constitution—Prohibition of alcohol.

1920 Canada makes it mandatory for every Indian child, seven or older, to be interned at Residential School.

Adolfo de la Huerta, Mexican President (1920).

Álvaro Obregón, Mexican President (1920–1924).

1921 U.S. Quota Law of May 19, 1921 (Emergency Quota Act) designed to stem the mass immigration from southern Europe and Russia.

William Lyon Mackenzie King, Canada's longest-serving Prime Minister (1921–1926; 1926–1930; 1935–1948).

1922 Cable Act (Married Women's Independent Nationality Act) reversed previous rules that stripped a woman of her citizenship when marrying a foreigner—a standard that did not apply to men marrying foreigners.

1924 U.S. Immigration Act of May 26, 1924 (43 Statutes-at-Large 153).

Act of May 28, 1924 (43 Statutes-at-Large 240) establishes U.S. Border Patrol.

U.S. Indian Citizenship Act enfranchises all American Indians and Alaska Natives at the federal level as citizens; Idaho, Maine, Mississippi, New Mexico, and Washington continue to exclude enrolled tribal members from voting until prohibited by the passage of the Indian Civil Rights Act in 1968.

U.S. Immigration Act sets quotas for European immigrants to 2 percent of 1890 cohort.

Plutarco Elias Calles, Mexican President (1924–1928).

1928 Meriam Report findings out regarding deplorable conditions in Indian Country; also declares the Allotment system a failure.

1929 Act of March 4, 1929 articulates deportable classes convicted of felonies.

League of United Latin American Citizens (LULAC) emerges as a political front for Hispanics, notably Mexican Americans.

1930 U.S. Senate investigation discloses kidnapping of Navajo children by government Indian schools.

1931 Act of February 18, 1931 expands deportation for illicit drugs—heroin, opium, or coca leaves, among those of immigrant stock.

1933 Franklin Delano Roosevelt (FDR) elected 32nd U.S. President (1933–1945)—only president to be elected to four consecutive terms.

19th Amendment to U.S. Constitution—repeals Prohibition (18th Amendment).

Canada makes Residential School officials legal guardians of all Indian students at their facility. Parents are compelled to do or face imprisonment.

1934	U.S. Congress passes Indian Reorganization Act & Johnson-O'Malley Act; both pertaining to governmental and educational standards within Indian Country.
1935	Texas Rangers brought under the authority of the Texas Department of Public Services instead of acting as the governor's private police force.
1935	Philippines made a USA Commonwealth territory. Philippine residents restricted from U.S. residency due to national origin quotas. Changed in 1965.
1939	World War II begins in Europe; Canada joins British forces.
1940	Manuel Avila Camacho, Mexican President (1940–1946).
	Act of June 14, 1940 transferred INS from the Department of Labor to the Department of Justice.
	Alien Registration Act of June 28, 1940 requires fingerprinting of all aliens over age 14.
	Nationalization Act—eliminated "English language" requirement of the Nationalization Act of 1906; codified and unified all U.S. laws related to Nationalization.
1941	U.S. enters World War II on side of the Allies. Conflict ends in 1945.
1942	Bracero Agreement established between Mexico and United States allowing Mexican migrants to work as seasonal agriculture laborers. The program ends in 1964.
1941–1945	Philippines occupied by Japan, ousting the United States.
1943	Magnuson Act—repealed the Chinese Exclusion Act of 1882 given that China was fighting on the side of the Allies during WWII.
1945	Harry S. Truman becomes 33rd U.S. President (1945–1953).
	WWII ends.
	"War Brides Act" allows foreign-born wives of U.S. GIs to immigrate.
1946	Philippines gained independence from the USA.
	War Brides Act extended to fiancées of GIs.
	USA, CIA enter secret agreement with Canada to use Indian children as involuntary test subjects for medical, biological warfare, and mind control experiments. This practice continues until the 1970s.

	Luce-Celler Act extended rights to naturalization to newly independent nations—Philippines, India, Pakistan . . . with quota set at 100 people per country.
1947	President Truman integrated the U.S. military.
	Office of Indian Affairs now designated Bureau of Indian Affairs (BIA).
1948	Displaced Persons Act—allowed for an influx of immigrants from war-torn Europe following WWII.
	American G.I. Forum (AGIF) was formed by Hispanic veterans of World War II.
1949	Newfoundland leaves Great Britain, joining the Canadian Confederation.
1950–1953	USA & Canada part of UN forces during Korean War
1951	UN Refugee Convention.
	U.S. involved in Korean Conflict as primary UN force. Conflict ends in 1953. More Hispanics join the AGIF.
	Canadian Indian Act grants indigenous peoples the right to vote while subjecting them to the same laws as other Canadians.
1952	Immigration and Nationality Act (McCarran-Walter Act) upheld the National Origin Quota established in 1924.
	Adolfo Ruiz Cortines, Mexican Prime Minister (1952–1958).
1953	Dwight D. Eisenhower elected 34th U.S. President (1953–1961).
	Refugee Relief Act continued the 1948 initiative to accommodate displaced persons from war-torn nations.
	Termination Resolution (House Concurrent Resolution 108) attempts to end federal protection for certain tribes while Public Law 280 unilaterally gives criminal and civil authority to certain states.
1954	"Operation Wetback" begins under the direction of General Joseph "Jumping Joe" Swing in attempt to entice illegal Mexican workers to return to Mexico.
	Indians in Maine given the right to vote.
1955	Indian Health Service (IHS) created for Indians residing in Indian Country in USA.
1958	United States takes over France's role in Southeast Asia leading to the Vietnam conflict, which extends until 1975.

1959	Cuban Revolution led by Fidel Castro.
1959–1975	USA's long involvement in Vietnam. Canada opposes Vietnam War.
1961	John F. Kennedy (JFK) elected 35th U.S. President (1961–1963).
1963	Lyndon B. Johnson (LBJ) becomes 36th U.S. President (1963–1969).
	Lester B. Pearson, Canadian Prime Minister (1963–1968).
1964–1966	24th Amendment to U.S. Constitution—Civil Rights.
	United States enacts Civil Rights Acts that prohibit discrimination based on race, color, religion, sex, or national origin.
	Gustavo Diaz Ordaz (1964–1970). Mexican President during civil rights, Mexico City student massacre.
1965	Immigration and Nationality Act (Hart-Celler Act)—abolished the National Origin Quota formula.
	Cesar Chavez begins to organize Mexican and Filipino farm workers into the United Farms Workers union.
	Hart-Celler Act designed to stimulate immigration from Asia, the Middle East, and Africa, replacing the quota system with one based on family relations and occupational skills deemed critical by the U.S. Department of Labor.
	U.S. Voting Rights Act ensures equal voting rights ending Jim Crow restrictions.
1966	Cuban Adjustment Act giving permanent resident status to exiles in the U.S. at least one year; effective from January 1, 1959.
1968	Pro-democracy demonstration massacre of student protestors in Mexico City.
	Indian Civil Rights Act passed in United States.
	Pierre Trudeau becomes Prime Minister of Canada (1968–1979; 1980–1984).
1969	Richard M. Nixon elected 37th U.S. President (1969–1974)—1st president to resign.
	MECHA (El Movimiento Estudiantil Chicano de Aztlan) begins at the Chicano Youth Liberation Conference held in Denver.

	American Indian group occupies Alcatraz Prison in San Francisco Bay.
	Canada passes the Official Language Act making both English and French the official languages.
1970	La Raza Unida Party (LRUP) and Bronze/Brown Power movements bring nonwhite Hispanics together as a political force.
	The Racketeer Influenced and Corrupt Organizations Act (RICO) is established in the United States.
1971	U.S. voting age lowered from 21 to 18.
	Canadian Métis Society forms Native Council of Canada representing off-reserve Natives.
1972	U.S. Supreme Court finds death penalty unconstitutional.
1973	Wounded Knee II at Pine Ridge Oglala Indian Reservation.
1975	U.S. Congress passes Indian Self-Determination and Education Assistance Act.
	Wounded Knee II—part 2, FBI agents killed in firefight.
1976	U.S. Supreme Court reinstates death penalty with conditions for its application.
	Canada outlaws the death penalty.
1978	U.S. Congress passes Indian Child Welfare Act.
	American Indian Religious Freedom Act passed.
1980	Refugee Act—Amended the Immigration and Nationality Act of 1952 so as to accommodate the influx of Vietnamese refugees seeking asylum subsequent to the Vietnam War.
1981	Ronald Reagan elected 40th U.S. President (1981–1989).
1982	Canadian Constitution (Charter of Rights) established under PM Trudeau.
1984	Canada's last Indian Residential School closes.
	Brian Mulroney, Canadian Prime Minister (1984–1993), presided over NAFTA negotiations.
1985	National Indian Gaming Association (NIGA) established to regulate Indian gaming.
1988	President Reagan signs the Anti-Drug Abuse Act which includes the Drug Kingpin Act (DKA) allowing the reinstatement of the federal death penalty.

1989	President George H. W. Bush elected 41st U.S. President (1989–1993): establishes the Joint Task Force-6 (JTF-6) as part of the U.S. war on drugs.
	Carlos Salinas de Gortari, Mexican President (1988–1994).
	American Homecoming Act—gave preferential immigration status to Vietnamese children fathered by U.S. servicemen.
1990	Immigration Act of 1990—reformed and enlarged the 1965 standards with marked increases in numbers as well as providing a lottery for underrepresented countries.
1991	Ontario becomes first Canadian province to allow Indians to self-govern.
1993	William (Bill) Jefferson Clinton elected 42nd U.S. President (1993–2001); 2nd president to be impeached but not removed from office.
	Jean Chretien, Canadian Prime Minister (1993–2003).
	Nunavut Act ratified by Canadian Parliament creating new Inuit Territory.
	Reno v. Flores 507 U.S. 292: U.S. Supreme Court Settlement Agreement regarding separating immigrant children from adults; and to place children in "least restrictive" settings if alone.
1994	North American Free Trade Agreement (NAFTA) goes into effect on January 1.
	On the same day, the Zapatista Army of National Liberation (EZLN) declares war on Mexico in protest to NAFTA's opposition to land reform and the ejido system.
	Ernesto Zedillo, Mexican President (1994–2000).
	American Indian Religious Freedom Act amended to accept the use of peyote in tribal ceremonies.
1996	Illegal Immigration Reform and Immigrant Responsibility Act (HRIRA) provided penalties for undocumented persons removed from the U.S.—providing compulsory waiting periods for applications for reentry.
1997	Nicaraguan Adjustment and Central American Relief Act (NACARA)—provided protection from deportation for those who were registered asylum seekers who had resided in the U.S. for at least five years. Also included under this law were asylees from the former Soviet Union.

1998 First Independent Tribunal, the UN-International Human Rights Association of American Minorities (IHRAAM) is convened in Vancouver, Canada, finding the Catholic, United, and Anglican Churches guilty of complicity in Genocide regarding its formal Indian Residential School programs.

1999 NATO forces (including USA & Canadian military) unilaterally attacks Serbia in response to events in Kosovo.

2000 Vicente Fox (2000–2006) becomes first Mexican leader to break the Institutional Revolutionary Party's (PRI) monopoly on the presidency. He was a member of the conservative National Action Party (PAN).

Legal Immigration Family Equity Act aka "LIFE Act."

2001 George W. Bush elected 43rd U.S. President (2001–2009).

Terrorist attacks on United States on September 11 initiate the war on terror, which combined with the existing war on drugs leads to the increased militarization of the U.S./Mexico border.

Real ID Act, unification of states' driving licenses for all domestic travel by public or private transportation.

2006 Secure Fence Act: amends Illegal Immigration Reform and Immigrant Responsibility Act of 1996 . . . to fence the 1,933-mile southern U.S. border.

President George W. Bush initiates Operation Jump Start, allowing border-state governors to deploy the National Guard along their section of the U.S./Mexico border.

Felipe Calderon (2006–2012) succeeds Fox as president of Mexico. He also belongs to the conservative PAN party, and like Fox, has welcomed U.S. aid for the war on drugs.

Stephen Harper, Canadian Prime Minister (2006–2015).

2008 Department of Homeland Security (DHS) and Department of Interior waives 40 laws to speed construction of border fence at southern border.

Canadian Parliament endorsed UN Declaration on the Rights of Indigenous Peoples.

2009 Barack Obama elected 44th U.S. President (2009–2017).

Obama administration begins in the United States. Obama is the first post-Columbian North American leader of black-African descent.

2012	Enrique Pena Nieto, Mexican President (2012–2018).
	Deferred Action for Childhood Arrivals (DACA), allowing some who came to U.S. illegally as children to receive renewable two-year extensions while not providing a path to citizenship.
2015	Justin Trudeau, son of Pierre, becomes Canada's Prime Minister (2015–).
2016	Billionaire Donald Trump becomes Republican Party's Presidential candidate.
	Canada's Supreme Court extends "Indian aboriginal status" to Métis and non-status Indians.
2017	Donald Trump elected 45th U.S. President (2017–).
	Protecting the Nation from Foreign Terrorist Entry into the United States: Executive Orders 13769 & 13780 . . . ban from entry for applicants from mainly Muslim nations.
2018	Andres Manual Lopez Obrado, Mexican President (2018–).

Selected Bibliography

Abourezk, J. American Indian Policy Review Commission, Final Report. Washington, DC: U.S. Government Printing Office. 1977.

Abrams, N., & Beal, S.S. The assimilative crimes act and the special maritime and territorial jurisdiction. Federal Criminal Law. St. Paul, MN: West Publishing, 671–692. 1993.

ACLU. The Constitution of the United States of America. New York, NY.

American Civil Liberties Union (www.aclu.org). 2000.

Acuna, R.F. Occupied America: A History of Chicanos. New York, NY: Pearson Longman. 2007.

Ai Camp, R. Politics in Mexico. New York, NY: Oxford University Press. 1993.

Alba, V. The Mexicans: The Making of a Nation. New York, NY: Praeger. 1967.

Allsup, C. The American G.I. Forum: Origins and Evolution. Monograph 6. Austin, TX: University of Texas Center for Mexican American Studies. 1982.

Altshuler, C.W. Chain of Command: Arizona and the Army, 1856–1875. Tucson, AZ: The Arizona Historical Society. 1981.

Anctil, P. A Franco-American bibliography: New England. Bedford, NH: National Materials Development Center. 1979.

Anderson, F. The War that made America: A short history of the French and Indian War. New York, NY: Viking. 2005.

Aquila, R. The Iroquois restoration: Iroquois diplomacy on the Colonial Frontier, 1701–1754. Lincoln, NE: University of Nebraska Press. 1997.

Arreola, D.D., & Curtis, J.R. The Mexican Border Cities. Tucson, AZ: University of Arizona Press. 1993.

Axelrod, P. The Promise of Schooling: Education in Canada, 1800–1914. Toronto, Canada: University of Toronto Press. 1997.

Baca, K. The changing federal role in Indian Country. National Institute of Justice Journal, April, JR 000247, 8–13. 2001.

Bailey, A.G. The Conflict of European and Eastern Algonkian Cultures, 1504–1700. Toronto, Canada: University of Toronto Press. 1969.

Bailey, J. Governing Mexico: The Statecraft of Crisis Management. New York, NY: St. Martin's Press. 1988.

Bailey, L.R. The Long Walk. Los Angeles, CA: Westernlore Press. 1964.

Ball, L.D. The United States Marshals of New Mexico & Arizona Territories 1846–1912. Albuquerque, NM: University of New Mexico Press. 1978.

Bancroft, H.H. History of Arizona and New Mexico, 1530–1885. Albuquerque, NM: Horn & Wallace, (1889; reprinted, 1962).

Barker, E.C. The Life of Stephen F. Austin. Nashville, TN: Cokesbury Press. 1925.

Barker, E.C. Mexico and Texas, 1821–1835. Dallas, TX: Turner. 1928.

Barker, M.L. Policing in Indian Country. New York, NY: Harrow and Heston, 1998.

Bedford, D.R. Tsali. San Francisco, CA: Indian Historian Press. 1972.

Beeching, J. The Opium Wars in China, 1834–1860. London, England: Harcourt Brace Jovanovich. 1977.

Berthrong, D.J. The Southern Cheyennes. Norman, OK: University of Oklahoma Press. 1963.

Becker, H.S. Outsiders: Studies in the sociology of deviance. New York, NY: The Free Press. 1963.

Bernier, G., & Salee, D. The Shaping of Quebec Politics and Society: Colonialism, Power, and the Transition to Capitalism in the 19th Century. Bristol, PA: Taylor & Francis. 1992.
Berton, P. Flames across the Border, 1813–1814. Markham, Ontario, Canada: Penguin Books. 1988.
Beschloss, M. The Presidents: Every Leader from Washington to Bush. New York, NY: American Heritage/Simon & Schuster, Inc. 2003.
BIA. Indian Law Enforcement History. Washington, DC: U.S. Bureau of Indian Affairs. 1975.
Binkley, W.C. The Expansionist Movement in Texas, 1836–1850. Berkeley, CA: University of California Press. 1925.
Bishop, J.B. Theodore Roosevelt and His Time: Shown in His Own Letters, Vol. 2. New York, NY: Scribner Press. 1920.
Blewett, M.J. The Last Generation: Work and Life in the Textile Mills of Lowell, Massachusetts, 1919–1960. Amherst, MA: University of Massachusetts Press. 1990.
Boatner, M.M., III. Encyclopedia of the American Revolution. Mechanicsburg, PA: Stackpole Books. 1994.
Boot, M. The Savage Wars of Peace: Small wars and the rise of American power. New York, NY: Basic Books. 2002.
Borah, W. New Spain's Century of Depression. Folcroft, PA: Folcroft Press. 1951.
Bourassa, R. Power from the North. Englewood Cliffs, NJ: Prentice-Hall. 1985.
Bourke, J.G. On the Border with Crook. Lincoln, NE: University of Nebraska Press. 1971.
Boyce, G.A. When Navajo had too many sheep. San Francisco, CA: Indian Historian Press. 1978.
Brakel, S.J. American Indian Tribal Courts: The Costs of Separate Justice. Chicago, IL: American Bar Foundation. 1978.
Brebner, J.B. New England outpost: Acadia before the conquest of Canada. New York, NY: Columbia University Political Science Monograph no. 293. 1927.
Brebner, J.B. The Neutral Yankees of Nova Scotia: A Marginal Colony during the Revolutionary Years. New York, NY: Columbia University Press. 1937.
Brenner, A. The Winds that Swept Mexico. Meridian, CT: The Meridian Gravure Company. 1971.
Breton, R., & Savard, P. (eds.). The Quebec and Acadian Diaspora in North America. Toronto, Canada: The Multicultural Society of Ontario. 1982.
Brown, D. The Galvanized Yankees. Lincoln, NE: University of Nebraska Press. 1963/1985.
Brown, J.H. History of Texas from 1685 to 1892. 2 Vols. St. Louis, MO: Daniell. 1893.
Buffington, R.M. Criminal and Citizen in Modern Mexico. Lincoln, NE: University of Nebraska Press. 2000.
Bumsted, J.M. The Peoples of Canada: A Post-Confederation History. Don Mills, Ontario, Canada: Oxford University Press. 1992.
Burrough, B. Public Enemies: America's greatest crime wave and the birth of the FBI, 1933–1934. New York, NY: Penguin books. 2004.
Butler, J. The Huguenots in America: A refugee people in New World Society. Cambridge, MA: Harvard University Press. 1992.
Burt, A.L. The Old Province of Quebec. Toronto, Canada: McClelland and Stewart. 1933.
Butler, S.D. War is a racket. New York, NY: Round Table Press. 1935.
Byrne, W.D.D. History of the Catholic Church in the New England States. Vol. I. Boston, MA: Hurd and Everts. 1899.
Cable, G.W. The Creoles of Louisiana. New York, NY: Charles Scribner's Sons. 1885.
Caffrey, K. The twilight's last gleaming: Britain vs. America, 1812–1815. New York, NY: Stein and Day. 1977.
Calhoon, R.M. The Loyalists in Revolutionary America, 1760–1781. San Diego, CA: Harcourt Brace Jovanovich, Inc. 1973.

Calloway, C.G. The American Revolution in Indian Country: Crisis and Diversity in Native American Communities. New York, NY: Cambridge University Press. 1995.
Camp, R.A. Politics in Mexico. New York, NY: Oxford University Press. 1993.
Campbell, G.G. A History of Nova Scotia. Toronto, Canada: The Ryerson Press. 1948.
Canby, W.C., Jr. Crimes punishable under the Federal Enclaves Act (18 USCA 1152), American Indian Law (2nd Edition). St. Paul, MN: West Publishing. 1988.
Cardoso, L.A. Mexican Emigration to the United States, 1877–1931. Tucson, AZ: University of Arizona Press. 1980.
Careless, J.M.S. Canada: A story of challenges (revised edition). Toronto, Canada: Macmillan of Canada. 1970.
Careless, J.M.S. Colonists and Canadians, 1760–1867. Toronto, Canada: Macmillan of Canada. 1971.
Careless, J.M.S., & Brown, R.C. Part one of the Canadians, 1867–1967. Toronto, Canada: Gage Publishing Limited. 1968.
Charlebois, P. The life of Louis Riel. Toronto, Canada: NC Press. 1975.
Chartier, A. The Franco-Americans of New England: A History. Toronto, Canada: ACA Assurance. 2000.
Cave, A.A. The French and Indian War. Westport, CT: Greenwood Press. 2004.
Cherokee Nation v. Georgia, 30 U.S. (5 Pet.) 1, 1831.
Child, B.J. Boarding School Seasons: American Indian Families. Lincoln, NE: University of Nebraska Press. 2000.
Chodos, R., & Hamovitch, E. Quebec and the American Dream. Toronto, Canada: Between the Lines. 1991.
Civil Rights Act of 1968—Titles II-V11 (Indian Matters), U.S. Statutes at Large, 82:77–81, April 11, 1968.
Clark, M.W. Chief Bowles and the Texas Cherokee. Norman, OK: University of Oklahoma Press. 1971.
Clarkson, S. Canada and the Reagan challenge: Crisis in the Canadian-American relationship. Toronto, Canada: James Lorimer & Company & the Canadian Institute for Economic Policy. 1982.
Clendenen, C.C. The United States and Pancho Villa: A Study of Unconventional Diplomacy. Ithaca, NY: American Historical Association, Cornell University Press. 1961.
Cline, H.F. Mexico Revolution to Evolution: 1940–1960. New York, NY: Oxford University Press. 1963.
Coerver, D.M. & Hall, L.B. Texas and the Mexican Revolution: A Study in State and National Border Policy, 1910–1920. San Antonio, TX: Trinity University Press. 1984.
Coerver, D.M., & Hall, L. B. Tangled Destinies: Latin America and the United States. Albuquerque, NM: University of New Mexico Press. 2000.
Coles, H.L. 1966. The War of 1812. Chicago, IL: University of Chicago Press. 2000.
Coleman, W.D. The Independence Movement in Quebec, 1945–1980. Toronto, Canada: University of Toronto Press. 1984.
Conner, S.V., & Faulk, O.B. North America Divided: The Mexican War, 1846–1848. New York, NY: Oxford University Press. 1971.
Cook, R. (ed.). French-Canadian nationalism: An anthology. Toronto, Canada: Macmillan. 1969.
Coser, L.A. The Functions of Social Conflict. New York, NY: The Free Press. 1956.
Coser, L.A. Continuities in the Study of Social Conflict. New York, NY: The Free Press. 1962.
Cosmas, G.A. An Army for Empire: The United States Army in the Spanish-American War. Columbia, MO: University of Missouri Press. 1971.
Costo, R., & Henry-Costo, J. Indian Treaties: Two centuries of dishonor. San Francisco, CA: Indian Historian Press. 1977.
Costo, R., & Henry-Costo, J. The Missions of California. San Francisco, CA: Indian Historian Press. 1987.

Cothran, D.A. Political Stability and Democracy in Mexico: the "Perfect Dictatorship"? Westport, CT: Praeger Press. 1994.
Coupland, Sir. R. The Quebec Act: A study in statesmanship. Oxford, England: Clarendon Press. 1968.
Craig, R.B. The Bracer Program: Interest Groups and Foreign Policy. Austin, TX: University of Texas Press. 1971.
Cuneo, J.R. Robert Rogers of the Rangers. New York, NY: Oxford University Press. 1959.
Cullather, N. Secret History: The CIA's classified account of its operations in Guatemala, 1952–1954. Palo Alto, CA: Stanford University Press. 1999.
Curtis Act. U.S. Statues at Large, 30, 497–498 (June 28, 1898).
Dallison, J.A. Turning back the Fenians: New Brunswick's last colonial campaign. Fredericton, New Brunswick, Canada: Goose Land Press & The New Brunswick Military Heritage Project. 2006.
Daniel, C. Bitter Harvest: A History of California Farmworkers, 1870–1941. Ithaca, NY: Cornell University Press. 1981.
Darroch, G.A., & Marston, W.G. The social class basis of ethnic residential segregation: The Canadian case. American Journal of Sociology, Vol. 77 (November): pp. 491–510. 1971.
Davis, K.C. God and Country. Smithsonian (October): pp. 86–96. 2010.
De Leon, A. Mexican Americans in Texas: A Brief History. Arlington Heights, IL: Harlan Davidson. 1993.
Demers, N.J. Revolution in Quebec: A past rejected, a future in Doubt. Portsmouth, NH: Peter E. Randall Publishing. 1995.
Desbarats, P. Rene: A Canadian in search of a country. Toronto, Canada: McClelland and Stewart-Bantam Limited. 1977.
Dickerson, J., & Young, B. A short history of Quebec. Montreal, Canada: McGill-Queen's University Press. 2003.
Dillon, R.H. North American Indian Wars. Greenwich, CT: Brompton Books. 1983.
Dion, L. Quebec: The unfinished revolution. Montreal, Canada: McGill-Queen's University Press. 1992.
Dollard, J. Caste and class in a southern town. New Haven, CT: Yale University Press. 1937.
Donaldson, G. Eighteen Men: The Prime Ministers of Canada. Toronto, Canada: Doubleday Canada. 1985.
Ducharme, J. The shadows of the trees: The story of French-Canadians in New England. New York, NY: Harper. 1943.
Dufour, C.L. The Mexican War: A Compact History, 1846–1848. New York, NY: Hawthorn Books. 1968.
Durkheim, E. On the normality of crime. Theories of Society: Foundations of modern sociological theory (Parsons, T., Shils, E., Naegele, K.D., & Pitts, J.R., eds.). New York, NY: The Free Press: 872–875. 1961.
Eastman, C.A. The Soul of the Indian. Boston, MA: Houghton Mifflin Company, 1911.
Eccles, W.J. The Canadian frontier, 1534–1760. Albuquerque, NM: University of New Mexico Press. 1983.
Ellis, J.E. American creation: Triumphs and tragedies at the founding of the Republic. New York, NY: Alfred A. Knopf. 2007.
Elson, H.W. History of the United States of America. New York, NY: The MacMillan Company. 1904.
Elting, J.R. Amateurs, to arms! A military history of the War of 1812. New York, NY: De Capo Press. 1995.
Erikson, K.T. Wayward puritans: A study in the sociology of deviance. New York, NY: John Wiley & Sons. 1966.
Esty, C.C. Greening the GATT: Trade Environment and the Future. Washington, DC: Institute for International Economics. 1994.

Everest, A.S. Moses Hazen and the Canadian Refugees in the American Revolution. Syracuse, NY: Syracuse University Press. 1976.
Ewers, J.C. The Blackfeet. Norman, OK: University of Oklahoma Press, 1958.
Ex Parte Crow Dog, 109 U.S. Reports, 557, 571–72. 1883.
Faragher, J.M. A Great and noble scheme: The tragic story of the expulsion of the French Acadians from their American homeland. New York, NY: W.W. Norton. 2005.
Farris, N. Crown and clergy in colonial Mexico, 1759–1821. London, England: University of London Press. 1968.
Fatemi, K. (editor). The Maquiladora Industry: Economic Solution or Problem? New York, NY: Praeger Press. 1990.
Faulk, O.B. Crimson desert: Indian Wars of the American southwest. New York, NY: Oxford University Press. 1994.
Ferling, J. Almost a miracle: The American victory in the War of Independence. New York, NY: Oxford University Press. 2009.
Fitzmaurice, J. Quebec and Canada: Past, present, future. London, England: Hurst. 1985.
Flanagan, T. Louis "David" Riel: Prophet of the New World. Toronto, Canada: University of Toronto Press. 1979.
Foley, A.B. From French-Canadian to Franco-American. Harvard University: Ph.D. Dissertation. 1940.
Fournier, P. The Meech Lake post-mortem: Is Quebec sovereignty inevitable? Montreal, Canada: McGill-Queen's University Press. 1991.
Fox, R., Aull, C., & Cimino, L. Ethnic nationalism and political mobilization in industrial societies. Interethnic Communication, Ross, E.L. (ed.). Athens, GA: University of Georgia Press: pp. 113–133. 1978.
French, L.A. The Franco American working class family, chapter 14 in Ethnic Families in America: Patterns and Variations. (Mindel, C.H., & Habenstein, R.W. (eds.). New York, NY: Elsevier: pp. 323–346. 1976.
French, L.A. The French Canadian American family, chapter 14 in Ethnic Families in America: Patterns and Variations—2nd Edition. (Mindel, C.H., & Habenstein, R.W. (eds.). New York, NY: Elsevier: pp. 326–349. 1981.
French, L.A. The Winds of Injustice: American Indians and the U.S. Government. New York, NY: Garland Publishing, Inc. 1994.
French, L.A. Counseling American Indians. Lanham. MD: University Press of America. 1997.
French, L.A. Addictions and Native Americans. Westport, CT: Praeger Press. 2000.
French, L.A. Native American Justice. Chicago, IL: Burnham, Inc. 2003.
French, L.A. Legislating Indian Country: Significant Milestones in Transforming Tribalism. New York, NY: Peter Lang. 2007.
French, L.A. Running the Border Gauntlet: The Mexican Migrant Controversy. Santa Barbara, CA: Praeger, ABC-CLIO, LLC. 2010.
French, L.A., & Manzanarez, M. NAFTA & Neocolonialism: Comparative criminal, human, & social justice. Lanham, MD: University Press of America. 2004.
French, L.A., & Manzanarez, M. North American Border Conflicts: Race, Politics, and Ethics. Boca Raton, FL: CRC Press/Taylor & Francis. 2017.
French, L. Policing American Indians: A Unique Chapter in American Jurisprudence. Boca Raton, FL: CRC Press/Taylor & Francis. 2016.
Freud, S. The Future of an illusion. Robson-Scott, W.D., trans.; Strachey, J., ed.). Garden City, NY: Doubleday Anchor. 1964.
Frost, S.B. The History of McGill in relation to the social, economic and cultural aspects of Montreal and Quebec. Montreal, Canada: Commission de' etude sur les universities. 1979.
Frothingham, R., Jr. History of the siege of Boston and of the battles of Lexington, Concord and Bunker Hill. Boston, MA: Charles C. Little & James Brown. 1849.

Fukumi, S. Cocaine Trafficking in Latin America: EU and US Policy Responses. Hampshire, UK: Ashgate Publishing. 2008.
Fullerton, D.H. The dangerous delusion: Quebec's independence obsession, as seen by the former adviser to Rene Levesque and Jean Lesage. Toronto, Canada: McClelland and Stewart. 1978.
Galarza, E. Merchants of Labor: The Mexican Bracero Story. Charlotte, NC: McNally and Loftin. 1964.
Gamboa, E. Mexican Labor and World War II: Braceros in the Pacific Northwest, 1942–1947. Austin, TX: University of Texas Press. 1990.
Gamio, M. Mexican Immigration to the United States. Chicago, IL: University of Chicago Press. 1930.
GAO. Treaty of Guadalupe Hidalgo: Findings and Possible Options Regarding Longstanding Community Land Grant Claims in New Mexico (GAO Report number GAO-04-59. Washington, DC: U.S. Government Printing Office. 2004.
Gara, L. The Presidency of Franklin Pierce. Lawrence, KS: University Press of Kansas. 1991.
Garcia, J.R. Operation Wetback: The Mass Deportation of Mexican Undocumented Workers in 1954. Westport, CT: Greenwood Press. 1980.
Garff, D. Heirs of New France: An ethnic minority in search of security. Tufts University, Fletcher School of Law and Diplomacy: Ph.D. Dissertation. 1970.
Garner, P. Porfirio Diaz. Harlow, England: Pearson Education Limited. 2001.
Gavin, D-B. Ending slavery North and South, Historical New Hampshire, Vol. 64: 67–127. 2010.
General Allotment Act (Dawes Act). U.S. Statutes at Large, 24, 388–391, February 8, 1887.
Getches, D.H., Rosenfelt, D.M., & Wilkinson, C.F. Public Law 280—A Transfer of Jurisdiction in Some States. Case Material on Federal Indian Law. St. Paul, MN: West Publishing. 1979: 467–481.
Getches, D.H., Wilkinson, C.F., & Williams, R.A., Jr. Cases and Materials on Federal Indian Law, 4th Edition. St. Paul, MN: West Publishing. 1998.
Giago, T.A. Children left behind: Dark legacy of Indian mission boarding schools. Santa Fe, NM: Clear Light Publishing, 2006.
Gilman, C.M. The Huguenot Migration in Europe and America: Its cause and effect. Colts Neck, NJ: Arlington Laboratory for Clinical and Historical Research. 1962.
Ginsburg, R. 100 Years of Lynching. New York, NY: Lancer Books. 1962.
Gleijeses, P. Shattered Hope: The Guatemalan Revolution and the United States, 1944–1954. Princeton, NJ: Princeton University Press, 1992.
Goetzman, W.H. Army exploration in the American West, 1803–1863. New Haven, CT: Yale University Press. 1959.
Gomez, L.E. Off-White in an Age of White Supremacy: Mexican Elites and the Rights of Indians and Blacks in Nineteenth-Century New Mexico. Chicano-Latino Law Review, Vol. 25 (Spring): 9–59. 2005.
Gonzalez, M.J. The Mexican Revolution, 1910–1940. Albuquerque, NM: University of New Mexico Press. 2002.
Gordon, W.L. Troubled Canada: The need for new domestic policies. Toronto, Canada: McClelland and Stewart. 1961.
Gordon, M.M. Assimilation in American life: The role of race, religion, and national origin. New York, NY: Oxford University Press. 1964.
Graham, H.D., & Gurr, T.R. 1969. The history of violence in America: A report to the National Commission on the causes and prevention of violence. New York, NY: Bantam Books. 1969.
Grant, A. No end to grief: Indian residential schools in Canada. Winnipeg, Canada: Pemmican. 1995.
Grayson, G. The Politics of Mexican Oil. Pittsburgh, PA: University of Pittsburgh Press. 1980.

Grayson, L.M., & Bliss, M. (eds.). The wretched of Canada. Toronto, Canada: University of Toronto Press. 1971.
Griffith, N.E. From migrant to Acadian: A North American border people, 1604–1755. Montreal, Canada: McGill-Queens University Press. 2005.
Grinnell, G.B. The Fighting Cheyennes. Norman, OK: University of Oklahoma Press, 1956.
Griswold del Castillo, R. The Treaty of Guadalupe Hidalgo: A Legacy of Conflict. Norman, OK: University of Oklahoma Press. 1990.
Grodzins, M. American Betrayal: Politics and the Japanese evacuation. Chicago, IL: University of Chicago Press. 1949.
Guindon, H., Hamilton, R., & McMullan, J.L. Quebec Society: Tradition, modernity, and nationhood. Toronto, Canada: University of Toronto Press. 1988.
Gusfield, J. Symbolic Crusade: Status, politics, and the American Temperance Movement. Chicago, IL: University of Chicago Press. 1963.
Hall, L.B., & Coerver, D.M. Revolution on the Border: The United States and Mexico, 1910–1920. Albuquerque, NM: University of New Mexico Press. 1988.
Hamilton, E.P. The French and Indian Wars: The story of battles and forts in the wilderness. Garden City, NJ: Doubleday. 1962.
Hamilton, J. Canadians in America. Minneapolis, MN: Lerner Publications Company. 2006.
Handler, R. Nationalism and the politics of culture in Quebec. Madison, WI: University of Wisconsin Press. 1988.
Hansen, M.L. The Immigrant in American History. New York, NY: Harper & Row. 1964.
Hanson, R.P. America's First People: Including New Hampshire's First People. Hopkinton, NH: The New Hampshire Antiquarian Society. 1996.
Harring, S.L. Crow Dog's Case: American Indian Sovereignty, Tribal Law, and United States Law in the 19th Century. New York, NY: Cambridge University Press. 1994.
Harris, C.H., III, & Sadler, L.R. The Texas Rangers and the Mexican Revolution: The Bloodiest Decade, 1910–1920. Albuquerque, NM: University of New Mexico Press. 2004.
Henderson, P.V.N. Felix Diaz, the Porfirians, and the Mexican Revolution. Lincoln, NE: University of Nebraska Press. 1981.
Hickey, D.R. The War of 1812. London, England: Thornton. 1990.
Hine, R.V. Bartlett's West: Drawing the Mexican Boundary. New Haven, CT: Yale University Press. 1968.
Holder, P. The hoe and the horse on the plains. Lincoln, NE: University of Nebraska Press. 1970.
Hoffman, A. Unwanted Mexican Americans in the Great Depression: Repatriation Pressures, 1929–1939. Tucson, AZ: University of Arizona Press. 1974.
Horseman, R. The causes of the War of 1812. New York, NY: A.S. Barnes. 1962.
House Concurrent Resolution 108 (Termination), U.S. Statutes at Large, 67, B132, August 1, 1953.
Hoxie, F.E. (ed.). Encyclopedia of North American Indians: Native American History, Culture, and Life from Paleo-Indians to the Present. Boston, MA: Houghton Mifflin Company. 1996.
Hughes, E.C. French Canada in transition. Chicago, IL: University of Chicago Press; Phoenix Books. 1943/1963.
Hurst, J.W. The Villista Prisoners, 1916–1917. Las Cruces, NM: Yucca Tree Press. 2000.
Hyde, G.E. A Sioux Chronicle. Norman, OK: University of Oklahoma Press. 1956.
Immerman, R.H. The CIA in Guatemala: The Foreign Policy of Intervention. Austin, TX: University of Texas Press. 1982.
Indian Citizenship Act, U.S. Statutes at Large, 43:253, June 2, 1924.
Indian Self-Determination and Education Assistance Act. U.S. Statutes at Large, 88: 2203–14, January 4, 1975.
Inglis, B. The Opium War. London, England: Hodder and Stoughton. 1976.

Jackson, H. A Century of Dishonor: A sketch of the United States government's dealings with some of the Indian tribes. Boston, MA: Little, Brown & Company. 1917.
Jahoda, G. The Trail of Tears: The Story of the American Indian Removals, 1813–1855. New York, NY: Wing Books. 1975.
Jennings, F. Empire of fortune: Crowns, colonies and tribes in the Seven Years War in America. New York, NY: Norton. 1990.
Johansen, B., & Maestas, J. Wasi'chu: The continuing Indian Wars. New York, NY: Monthly Review Press. 1979.
Johnson, B.H. Revolution in Texas: How a Forgotten Rebellion and Its Bloody Suppression Turned Mexicans into Americans. New Haven, CT: Yale University Press. 2003.
Johnson, S.L. Guide to American Indian Documents in the Congressional Serial Set: 1817–1899. A Project of the Institute for the Development of Indian Law. New York, NY: Clearwater Publishing Company. 1977.
Josephson, H. The Golden Threads: New England's Mill Girls and Magnates. New York, NY: Russell & Russell. 1949/1967.
Katcher, P.R.N. Encyclopedia of British, provincial, and German army units, 1775–1783. Harrisburg, PA: Stackpole Books. 1973.
Katz, F. The Secret War in Mexico: Europe, the United States, and the Mexican Revolution. Chicago, IL: University of Chicago Press. 1981.
Katz, F. Riots, Rebellion, and Revolution: Rural social conflict in Mexico. Princeton, NJ: Princeton University Press. 1988.
Kaufman, S. The Pig War: The United States, Britain, and the balance of power in the Pacific Northwest, 1846–1872. Lanham, MD: Lexington Books. 2004.
Kilbourn, W. The Firebrand: William Lyon Mackenzie and the rebellion in Upper Canada. Toronto, Canada: Clarke, Irwin. 1956.
Kluckhohn, C., & Leighton, D. The Navajo. Cambridge, MA: Harvard University Press. 1946.
Kneale, A. H. Indian Agent. Caldwell, ID: Caxton Printers. 1950.
Kobler, J. The Rise and Fall of Prohibition. New York, NY: G.P. Putnam's Sons. 1973.
Korda, M. IKE: An American Hero. New York, NY: Harper Perennial. 2008.
Kramer, J.R. The American minority community. New York, NY: Thomas Y. Crowell. 1970.
Kroeber, C.B. Theory and history of revolution. Journal of World History, Vol. 7: pp. 21–40. 1996.
LaFarge, O. Laughing Boy. Boston, MA: Houghton Mifflin Company. 1929.
Lanctot, G. Canada and the American Revolution 1774–1783. (Cameron, M.M., trans.). Toronto, Canada: Clarke, Irwin. 1967.
Langguth, A.J. Patriots: the men who started the American Revolution. New York, NY: Simon & Schuster. 1988.
Leach, D.E. Arms for Empire: A military history of the British colonies in North America, 1607–1763. New York, NY: Macmillan. 1973.
Leckie, W.H. The Buffalo Soldiers: A Narrative of the Negro Cavalry in the West. Norman, OK: University of Oklahoma Press. 1967.
Lee, M. Dictionary of British History. Edinburgh, Scotland: Larousse. 1994.
Leupp, F.E. The Indian and His Problem. New York, NY: Scribner's. 1910.
Lewis, O. Five Families. New York, NY: Basic Books. 1959.
Lieberson, S. Language and ethnic relations in Canada. New York, NY: Wiley. 1979.
Lines, K. British and Canadian Immigration to the United States since 1920. San Francisco, CA: R&E Research Associates. 1978.
Linton, R. The Study of Man. Appleton, WI: Appleton-Century-Croft. 1936.
Lipscomb, A.A. (ed.). The writings of Thomas Jefferson: Monticello Edition, Vol. 10. Washington, DC: The Thomas Jefferson Memorial Association. 1903.
Locke, R.F. The Book of Navajo. (5th ed.). Los Angeles, CA: Mankind Publishing Company. 1992.

Lyon, E.W. Louisiana in French Diplomacy, 1759–1804. Norman, OK: University of Oklahoma Press. 1934.

MacKirdy, K.A., Moir, J.S., & Zoltvany, Y.F. Changing perspectives in Canadian history: Selected problems (Revised Edition). Ontario, Canada: J.M. Dent & Sons. 1971.

Mahon, J.K. The War of 1812. Gainesville, FL: University of Florida Press. 1972.

Mails, T. Dog Soldiers, Bear Men, and Buffalo Women. Englewoods Cliffs, NJ: Prentice-Hall. 1972.

Major Crimes Act (Federal Index Crimes). U.S. Statutes at Large, 23: 385 918 U.S.C.: 1153, 1885.

Malone, H.T. Cherokees of the Old South. Athens, GA: University of Georgia Press. 1956.

Marks, F.W., III, Velvet on Iron: The Diplomacy of Theodore Roosevelt. Lincoln, NE: University of Nebraska Press. 1979.

Matthews, W. Navajo Legends. Boston, MA: Houghton Mifflin. 1897.

Marshall, B., & Johnston, C. France and the Americas: Culture, politics, and history. New York, NY/Oxford, England: ABC-CLIO. 2005.

Martell, J.S. The second expulsion of the Acadians. Dalhouise Review, Vol. 13: pp. 359–371. 1933.

Martinez, O.J. Mexico's Uneven Development: The Geographical and Historical Context of Inequality. New York, NY: Rougledge. 2016.

May, R.E. Manifest Destiny's Underworld: Filibustering in Antebellum America. Chapel Hill, NC: University of North Carolina Press. 2002.

McCartney. L. The Teapot Dome scandal: How big oil bought the Harding White House and tried to steal the country. New York, NY: Random House. 2008.

McDermott, J.D. A Guide to the Indian Wars of the West. Lincoln, NE: University of Nebraska Press. 1998.

McNaught, K.W.K. The Penguin History of Canada. New York, NY: Viking Penguin. 1988.

Meriam, L. The Problem of Indian Administration. Baltimore, MD: Johns Hopkins University Press. 1928.

Merk, F. Slavery and the Annexation of Texas. New York, NY: Knopf. 1972.

Meyer, R.W. History of the Santee Sioux. Lincoln, NE: University of Nebraska Press. 1967.

Meyer, M.C., Sherman, W.L., & Deeds, S.M. The Course of Mexican History. New York, NY: Oxford University Press. 2014.

Mooney, J. The Ghost Dance Religion and the Sioux Outbreak of 1890. Washington, DC: Bureau of American Ethnology. 1896.

Mooney, J. Myths and Sacred Formulas of the Cherokees. Reproduced in 1972 by Charles Elder—Bookseller. Nashville, TN. 1972.

Moir, J.S. Church and State in Canada 1627–1867. Toronto, Canada: McClelland and Stewart. 1967.

Morrison, W.R. The Mounted Police and Canada's northern frontier, 1895–1940. Ph.D. Dissertation in Modern History: Columbia University. 1973.

Murphy, W.F., J.E. Fleming, & S.A. Barber. American Constitutional Interpretations. Westbury, NY: The Foundation Press. 1995.

NAFTA Revisited: Expectations and Realities. The ANNALS of Political and Social Sciences, Vol. 50 (March). 1997.

Navarro, A. The Immigration Crisis: Nativism, Armed Vigilantism, and the Rise of a Countervailing Movement. Lanham, MD: AltaMira Press. 2008.

Neihardt, J. Black Elk Speaks. New York, NY: Pocket Books. 1972.

New Federalism for American Indians. (S.Prt 101–60), 101st Congress, 1st Session, 1989.

Neatby, H. The Quebec Act: Protest and policy. Scarborough, Ontario, Canada: Prentice-Hall of Canada. 1972.

Neatby, H. Quebec: The revolutionary age, 1760–1791. Toronto, Canada: McClelland and Stewart. 1977.

Nish, C. Quebec in the Duplessis Era, 1935–1959. Toronto, Canada: Copp Clark Publishing Company. 1970.
Norrie, K., & Vaillancourt, F. (eds.). The Meech Lake Accord. Canadian Public Policy, XIV Special Supplement (September). 1988.
Nugent, W. Habits of Empire: A History of American Expansion. New York, NY: Alfred A. Knopf. 2008.
O'Brien, J.M. Firsting and Lasting: Writing Indians Out of Existence in New England. Minneapolis, MN: University of Minnesota Press. 2010.
Oehler, C.M. The Great Sioux Uprising. New York, NY: Oxford University Press. 1959.
Ogburn, W.F. Social Change: with respect to cultural and original nature. New York, NY: Dell Publishing Company. 1966.
Paradis, W.H. Upon This Granite: Catholicism in New Hampshire, 1647–1997. Portsmouth, NH: Peter E. Randall Publisher. 1998.
Pareto, V. The Mind and Society (Bongiorno, A., & Livingston, A., trans.). New York, NY: Harcourt, Brace & Company. 1935.
Parker, J.H. Ethnic Identity: The Case of the French-Americans. Lanham, MD: University Press of America. 1983.
Parkman, F. France and England in North America: A series of historical narratives. London, England: Macmillan. 1899, 1906.
Paul, D.N. First Nation History—We were not the savages: Collision between European and Native American Civilizations. (3rd ed.). Halifax, Nova Scotia, Canada: Fernwood Publishing. 2008.
Peckham, H.H. The Colonial Wars, 1689–1762. Chicago, IL: University of Chicago Press. 1964.
Peters, J.D. "Removing the Heathen": Changing motives for Indian Slavery in New Hampshire. Historical New Hampshire, Vol. 58 (3&4): 67–79. 2003.
Poitras, J. Imaginary Line: Life on an Unfinished Border. Fredericton, New Brunswick, Canada: Goose Lane Editions. 2011.
Potter, C.E. The military history of the State of New Hampshire, 1623–1861. Concord, NH: McFarland & Jenks. 1869.
Quinney, R. Critique of Legal Order: Crime Control in Capitalist Society. Boston, MA: Little, Brown and Company. 1974.
Quintal, C. (ed.). The Little Canadas of New England. Worcester, MA: Assumption College French Institute. 1983.
Randall, W.S. Benedict Arnold: Patriot and traitor. New York, NY: Dorset Press. 2001.
Reid, J., et al. The conquest of Acadia, 1710: Imperial, colonial, and Aboriginal constructions. Toronto, Canada: University of Toronto Press. 2004.
Reid, J. Louis Riel and the creation of modern Canada. Albuquerque, NM: University of New Mexico Press. 2008.
Remini, R.V. The Legacy of Andrew Jackson: Essays on Democracy, Indian Removal, and Slavery. Baton Rouge, LA: Louisiana State University Press. 1988.
Reynolds, D.S. Waking Giant: America in the Age of Jackson. New York, NY: HarperCollins Publishers. 2008.
Resnick, P. Toward a Canada-Quebec Union. Montreal, Canada: McGill-Queen's University Press. 1991.
Richardson, J.D. A compilation of the messages and papers of the Presidents, 1789–1897: Published by Authority of Congress, Vol. 5. Washington, DC: U.S. Government Printing Office. 1897.
Rioux, M., & Martin, Y. French-Canadian Society (vol. 1). Toronto, Canada: The Carleton Library/McClelland and Stewart Limited. 1964.
Rivard, P.E. A New Order of Things: How the textile industry transformed New England. Hanover, NH: University Press of New England. 2002.
Rogers, E.S., & Smith, D.B. (eds.). Aboriginal Ontario: Historical perspectives on the First Nations. Toronto, Canada: Dundurn Press, Ltd. 1994.
Ross, J.F. War on the Run: the epic story of Robert Rogers and the conquest of America's first frontier. New York, NY: Bantam Books. 2009.

Ruiz, R.E. Triumphs and Tragedy: A History of the Mexican People. New York, NY: W.W. Norton and Company. 1992.
Ruymbeke, B.V. New Babylon to Eden: The Huguenots and their migration to colonial South Carolina. Columbia, SC: University of South Carolina Press. 2006.
Ryerson, S.B. Unequal Union: Confederation and the roots of conflict in the Canadas, 1815–1873. New York, NY: International Publishers. 1968.
Sadler, L.R. The Texas Rangers and the Mexican Revolution: The Bloodiest Decade, 1910–1920. Albuquerque, NM: University of New Mexico Press. 2004.
Sandos, J. Rebellion in the Borderlands: Anarchism and the Plan of San Diego, 1904–1923. Norman, OK: University of Oklahoma Press. 1992.
Saul, J.R. The Collapse of Globalism: And the reinvention of the World. Toronto, Canada: Viking. 2005.
Schroeder, J.H. Mr. Polk's War: American Opposition and Dissent, 1846–1848. Madison, WI: University of Wisconsin Press. 1973.
Schubert, F.N. Black Valor: Buffalo Soldiers and the Medal of Honor, 1870–1898. Wilmington, DE: Scholarly Resources Inc. 1997.
Schull, J. Rebellion: The rising in French Canada, 1837. Toronto, Canada: Macmillan of Canada. 1971.
Seymour, G.D. Documentary Life of Nathan Hale: Comprising all available official and private documents bearing on the life of a Patriot. Whitefish, MT: Kessinger Publishing. 2006.
Sheehan, B. Seeds of Extinction. New York, NY: W.W. Norton. 1974.
Silbey, J.H. Storm over Texas: Controversy and the Road to Civil War. New York, NY: Oxford University Press. 2005.
Silverstone, S.A. Divided Union: The politics of war in the early American Republic. Ithaca, NY: Cornell University Press. 2004.
Simmel, G. Conflict (K.A. Wolff, trans.). New York, NY: The Free Press. 1955.
Simpson, E.N. The Ejido: Mexico's Way Out. Chapel Hill, NC: University of North Carolina Press. 1937.
Smith, A. An inquiry into the nature and causes of wealth of nations. (2 vol.). London, England: Strahan Cadell. 1776.
Squires, J.D. The Granite State of the United States: A History of New Hampshire from 1623 to the Present. New York, NY: The American Historical Company, Inc. 1956.
Stanaard, D.E. American holocaust: The conquest of the New World. New York, NY: Oxford University Press. 1992.
Stanley, G.F.G. The birth of Western Canada: A history of the Riel Rebellions. Toronto, Canada: University of Toronto Press. 1992.
Stephanson, A. Manifest Destiny. New York, NY: Hill and Wang. 1995.
Szasz. M.C. Education and the American Indian: The Road to Self-Determination since 1928. Albuquerque, NM: University of New Mexico Press, 1976.
Taylor, A. Writing early American history. Philadelphia, PA: University of Pennsylvania Press. 2005.
Taylor, A. The Divided Ground: Indians, Settlers, and the Northern Borderland of the American Revolution. New York, NY: Alfred A. Knopf. 2006.
Taylor, V.H. Memoirs of Pancho Villa. Austin, TX: University of Texas Press. 1965.
Theriault, G.F. The Franco-Americans in a New England Community: An experiment in survival. New York, NY: Arno Press. 1980.
Thornton, R. American Indian holocaust and survival. Norman, OK: University of Oklahoma Press. 1987.
Tilly, C. European Revolutions, 1492–1992. Hoboken, NJ: Blackwell Publishing. 1995.
Tocqueville, A. de. Democracy in America. New York, NY: New American Library. 1835/1956.
Trask, D.F. The War with Spain in 1898. New York, NY: Macmillan. 1981.
Truesdell, L. The Canadian born in the United States. New Haven, CT: Yale University Press. 1943.

Utley, R.M., & Washburn, W.E. Indian Wars. Boston, MA: Houghton Mifflin Company. 1977.
Vallieves, P. White Niggers of America: The precocious autobiography of a "Terrorist." Pinklam, J. (trans.). New York, NY: Monthly Review Press. 1971.
Vandiver, F.E. Black Jack: The Life and Times of John J. Pershing. Vol. 1 & 2. College Station, TX: Texas A&M University Press. 1977.
Van Nuys, F. Americanizing the West: Race, Immigrants, and Citizenship. Lawrence, KS: University of Kansas Press. 2002.
Verney, D.V. Three civilizations, two cultures, one state: Canada's political traditions. Durham, NC: Duke University Press. 1986.
Vicero, R.D. Immigration of French Canadians to New England, 1840–1900. University of Wisconsin: Ph.D. Dissertation. 1968.
Vronsky, P. Ridgeway: The American Fenian Invasion and the 1866 battle that made Canada. Toronto, Canada: Penguin Canada-Allen Lane. 2011.
Wade, M. (ed.). Canadian Dualism: Studies of French-English relations. Toronto, Canada: University of Toronto Press. 1960.
Wagley, C., & Harris, M. Minorities in the New World. New York, NY: Columbia University Press. 1964.
Weber, M. The Protestant Ethic and the spirit of capitalism (Parson, T., trans.). London, England: Allen & Unwin. 1930.
Weber, D.J. (ed.). Foreigners in Their Native Land: Historical Roots of the Mexican Americans. Albuquerque, NM: University of New Mexico Press. 1973.
Whalen, W.J. Minority religions in America. Staten Island, NY: Alba House. 1972.
Wirth, J.D. Smelter Smoke in North America: The Politics of Transborder Pollution. Lawrence, KS: University of Kansas Press. 2000.
Womack, J., Jr. Zapata and the Mexican Revolution. New York, NY: Knopf. 1968.
Woodcock, G. The century that made us: Canada, 1814–1914. Toronto, Canada: Oxford University Press. 1989.
Wright, A.J. United States and Canada: A regional geography (2nd Edition). New York, NY: Appleton-Century—Crofts, Inc. 1956.
Wright, J.L., Jr. Anglo-Spanish rivalry in North America. Athens, GA: University of Georgia Press. 1971.
Wrong, G.M. The rise and fall of New France. Toronto, Canada: Macmillan Company of Canada. 1928.
Yackie, L.W. Federal Courts: Habeas Corpus. New York, NY: Foundation Press. 2003.

Index

Author Biographies

Laurence Armand French was born in New Hampshire but whose grandparents were originally from Canada (Quebec; New Brunswick). He enlisted in the United States Marine Corps when he was 17 and went to college as a disabled veteran. He earned his BA, MA, & PhD in sociology/social psychology from the University of New Hampshire; a second MA from Western New Mexico University; and a second PhD in cultural psychology from the University of Nebraska-Lincoln. He is a licensed clinical psychologist. He is the author of over 300 academic publications including 22 books.

Magdaleno Manzanarez was born in Mexico and "adopted" into a family in northern California's wine country. He received his AA from Santa Rosa Junior College; his BA from the Universidad de las Americans in Puebla, Mexico; his MA from Sonoma State University; and his PhD from Northern Arizona University. He is a tenured professor of political science and history and the first Vice-President for External Affairs at Western New Mexico University. He has published and presented papers nationally and internationally on border issues, notably those relevant to the Americas. He co-authored *NAFTA & Neocolonialism: Comparative Criminal, Human, & Social Justice* with L.A. French (University Press of America, 2004).

www.ingramcontent.com/pod-product-compliance
Lightning Source LLC
Chambersburg PA
CBHW022314280326
41932CB00010B/1098
* 9 7 8 1 4 9 8 5 8 4 0 6 7 *